BULLETINS FROM DALLAS

BULLETINS FROM DALLAS

Reporting the JFK Assassination

BILL SANDERSON

Skyhorse Publishing

Skyhorse Publishing books may be purchased in bulk at special discounts for sales promotion, corporate gifts, fund-raising, or educational purposes. Special editions can also be created to specifications. For details, contact the Special Sales Department, Skyhorse Publishing, 307 West 36th Street, 11th Floor, New York, NY 10018 or info@skyhorsepublishing.com.

Skyhorse® and Skyhorse Publishing® are registered trademarks of Skyhorse Publishing, Inc.®, a Delaware corporation.

Visit our website at www.skyhorsepublishing.com.

10 9 8 7 6 5 4 3 2 1

Library of Congress Cataloging-in-Publication Data is available on file.

Cover design by Rain Saukas
Cover photos from AP Images, UPI, and the Smith family collection

Print ISBN: 978-1-5107-1264-5
Ebook ISBN: 978-1-5107-1265-2

Printed in the United States of America

CONTENTS

Prologue ◆ Man and myth

JACQUELINE KENNEDY—BEAUTIFULLY DRESSED AS ALWAYS, in a beige sweater and trim black slacks that matched her hair—leaned forward on the sofa and asked: "What shall I say? What can I do for you?" Her visitor saw these questions as polite subterfuge. "It was more as if she was asking me for help than anything else," said Theodore H. White, who wrote *The Making of the President 1960*, a book about her husband John F. Kennedy's victorious campaign.

It was November 29, 1963, one week after one of the lowest days in American history—the assassination of President Kennedy, shot dead in an open car in Dallas. The state funeral was over, the world leaders who attended it were back in their capitals, and Lyndon Johnson was settling in at the White House. Jacqueline Kennedy had retreated to the Kennedy family's compound in Hyannisport, Massachusetts. A gaggle of reporters waited outside the compound in the damp chill of the late November evening, hoping for a snippet of news. White, on assignment for *Life* magazine, was the only journalist invited in. Mrs. Kennedy was not merely offering a story. She wanted White to aid her plan to secure her husband's legacy.

Earlier, when Mrs. Kennedy and White spoke on the phone to set up this interview, they discussed what journalists would write about her late husband. Jacqueline Kennedy did not want him remembered by the words of Arthur Krock, the Washington bureau chief of the *New York Times,* or Merriman Smith, the White House reporter for United Press International, or "all those people"—the rest of the political press corps.

From his end of the sofa, White followed up on the ideas they'd discussed earlier. He asked: How did she want people to remember the Kennedy presidency? When White posed this question, it became clear to him that Mrs. Kennedy already "had a series of thoughts of her own, and whether she took off from the springboard I offered, I don't know."

"Do you know what I think of history?" Mrs. Kennedy said. "The more I used to read of history, the more I thought—when something is written down, does that make it history? . . . Jack loved history so. But history to me was just a lot of bitter old men like Merriman Smith." Earlier on the telephone, she and White talked about Smith, Krock, and the Washington press corps in general. But during the interview itself Jacqueline Kennedy named just one journalist: Merriman Smith.

It's not clear why Mrs. Kennedy called Smith bitter and old— for one thing, he was just two years older than her husband. Maybe she was mad that Smith had poked fun at the Kennedys' lifestyle in a book, *The Good New Days*. Maybe she didn't like Smith's aggressive pursuit of stories about President Kennedy's health. Perhaps she was thinking of the time Smith hinted in a newspaper column about the womanizing her husband strove to hide from the public. Her husband had had several favorite reporters—Smith wasn't one of them.

In the terrible days before that interview in Hyannisport, Smith reached a high point in his career. He was the star reporter for United Press International, a wire service with reporters stationed all over the world that churned out hundreds of news articles read by millions of people every day. On November 22, 1963, Smith was in the front seat of a press car about one hundred yards behind John F. Kennedy's limousine as a presidential motorcade steered through Dallas. Kennedy and his wife waved and smiled happily as thousands cheered them in the city's downtown skyscraper canyon.

At 12:30 p.m., as the motorcade rolled through grassy Dealey Plaza on its way out of downtown, Smith heard the three rifle shots fired by Lee Harvey Oswald. He immediately picked up the radiotelephone in front of him—the only mobile phone available to the fifty-eight Washington reporters on Kennedy's trip. Smith dictated his first dispatches about the assassination to UPI's Dallas bureau while an apoplectic competitor from the Associated Press punched him and tried to wrest the phone away.

Smith's first bulletin—"Three shots fired at President Kennedy's motorcade today in downtown Dallas"—clattered across UPI's Teletype machines at 12:34 p.m., just four minutes after Oswald fired his rifle. Smith's dispatch was the first the world heard of Kennedy's assassination. The Associated Press, which competed story-for-story with UPI, didn't move its first report of the shooting until 12:39 p.m. Smith and UPI beat the AP by five minutes—an eternity in the wire services' war of seconds.

At Parkland Hospital, just moments after the shooting, Smith dashed up to the blood-spattered presidential limousine and saw the dying president cradled in his wife's arms. A Secret Service agent he knew told him Kennedy was dead—another bit of exclusive news Smith soon put on the UPI wire. Later, Smith was one of three reporters watching as Kennedy's vice president, Lyndon Johnson, was sworn as the nation's new chief executive aboard Air Force One while it was parked on the Dallas airport tarmac. His AP competitor chose not to go to the airport—giving Smith and UPI yet another win over the competition. Smith accompanied Johnson, Mrs. Kennedy, and the slain president's body on the flight back to Washington, all the while gathering details for the vivid, Pulitzer Prize–winning story he wrote for the next day's morning newspapers.

Smith was one of the most widely read and influential journalists of his time. He earned his readership and influence by closely covering his beat. Smith arrived at the White House in 1941, and over the next twenty-nine years he earned sources among everyone who worked there—presidents, their aides, Secret Service agents, valets, gardeners. No matter who was president, Smith was a White House insider. Franklin Roosevelt died in Warm Springs, Georgia, on the day he was supposed to attend a picnic Smith had organized for him. Harry Truman once took his shirt off to disprove one of Smith's news tips. After Dwight Eisenhower had a heart attack, he was photographed wearing a bathrobe embroidered with the words "Much Better, Thanks." The embroidered message was Smith's doing.

He was fast and accurate. He could juggle several complicated stories in his head at once, and dictate perfect copy for each over the phone—a critical skill for a wire service reporter who competed fiercely to report the story first. He was a character out of *The Front Page,* cranky, warm and funny, five feet ten, mustachioed, with a staccato voice that seemed to come from the side of his mouth. Smith viewed his job as looking "coldly" at the presidency. Though he sometimes expressed opinions in speeches and TV appearances, in print he focused on digging up facts and news his audience wanted to read. His byline appeared regularly on newspaper front pages across the country, and his insider columns about the presidency and White House life were widely read. Some of Smith's colleagues deemed him the greatest wire service reporter of all time.

Those who read Smith's newspaper stories about President Kennedy's assassination weren't the only ones to gain by his hustle and expertise in Dallas. Many people know that Walter Cronkite of CBS was the first to report the assassination on network TV. Few know that Cronkite learned of the shooting from Smith's dispatches. Because Smith was first with news of the shooting and with other assassination details, his reporting was an important source for broadcasters' TV and radio bulletins.

Some reporters—mostly TV types—used their work on the assassination story to build their reputations and careers. "The struggle for identity by some of these TV characters is incredible," UPI's top editor, Earl Johnson, wrote Smith after attending a party at Cronkite's home several weeks after Kennedy's death.[1] Smith had a healthy ego, and he was proud of his Pulitzer Prize. But he also wished he had won it for some other story. His death in 1970—fore-shadowed by personal tragedy, money woes, illness, depression, and a ferocious drinking problem—kept him from participating in the anniversary stories and other Kennedy remembrances that boosted many reporters' careers and reputations. He led the way reporting one of the biggest stories of the twentieth century—and today his competitors own the credit.

Like many people in public life, Jacqueline Kennedy had issues with what was said and written about her and her family in the media. People like Merriman Smith could thwart her plan to set the terms by which her husband would be remembered. If she could help it, President Kennedy's legacy would not be remembered by the writings of journalists like Smith. Her dislike of Smith's work was one reason she launched what's known today as the Camelot myth.

Mrs. Kennedy wanted the world to see her husband's presidency as akin to the legend of King Arthur and the Knights of the Round Table, who convened in a castle called Camelot and sought to rule justly and wisely. Her husband read about the legend when he was a child, and he enjoyed its retelling in a cast album of the 1960 Broadway musical *Camelot*. He played the record over and over again. Sometimes, Mrs. Kennedy played it for him when it was too cold for him to get out of bed. "I want to say this one thing. It's been almost an obsession with me," Mrs. Kennedy told White. "This line from the musical comedy's been almost an obsession with me. . . . It was the song he loved most." The line was in the last cut on the second side of the album: "Don't let it be forgot that for one brief shining moment there was Camelot."

"There'll be other great presidents," Mrs. Kennedy told White. But, she said, "There'll never be Camelot again."

She wanted White to spread the Camelot idea. When White telephoned his story to his editors in New York later that night, Mrs. Kennedy stood nearby to make sure he used the Camelot references. She got her way. The last sentence of White's story said: "For one brief shining moment there was Camelot."

Mrs. Kennedy realized that if she didn't push out the Camelot myth, journalists like Smith would control the narrative by which her husband was remembered. The journalistic digging and questioning Smith undertook was not conducive to the legacy she wanted for her husband. As White put it in his story, she did not want her husband remembered in "dusty and bitter histories."[2] For Jacqueline Kennedy's purposes, the Camelot story was far better than anything Merriman Smith would write.

Jacqueline Kennedy realized Smith had no interest in boosting her husband's Arthurian stature. That was something she could leave to the reporter she had invited into her family's home. "Men are such a combination of bad and good," she told White. "And what is history going to see in this except what Merriman Smith wrote, that bitter man?"[3]

If you asked Smith what he had against the Kennedys, he would have answered: nothing. He just reported the news. He never would have authored any "dusty and bitter histories." The books he did write were full of revealing anecdotes about the White House and its occupants, and were anything but angry and dry. Smith had his blind spots, like every journalist. He was part of the establishment he covered, and sometimes failed to see issues as ordinary Americans saw them. But he looked out for his readers, always. One of the most tragic days in American history—the day John F. Kennedy died—was the day he did his job best.

Chapter 1 • The White House beat

It's OK to call him Smitty. Everyone did, and he wore the name like a press card in the band of a brimmed hat.

Albert Merriman Smith was born on February 10, 1915. As a teenager, he added two years to his age so he could get a job. That's why government records say Smitty was born in 1913. The lie stuck, and even his gravestone is marked with the wrong date. By the official records, Smith arrived in the world more than a year before his parents wed. This bothered his mother, who didn't want anyone to think she bore her only child out of wedlock. She was still fussing about it in 1965, when her son turned fifty. Smith worried about the scandal or investigation that might arise if he tried to set the record straight. "Now, really, Mother. Let's let this one drop," Smith wrote her. "I'm the one who should feel awful. I've reached that age."[4]

Smith grew up in Savannah, Georgia. Journalism was the only career he imagined. "It never occurred to me to do anything else," he said. Smith began working for newspapers as a child. He delivered them, collected classified advertising money, and submitted news items about the Boy Scouts. As editor of *The Blue and White,* the student newspaper at Savannah High School, Smith was suspended for writing an editorial that called the school building a firetrap. He also got in trouble with an English teacher over an essay "about what the Savannah waterfront looked like at dawn, complete with drunk sailors, tawdry women, ships coming to life and in general the start of another day." The teacher advised him that "young writers should stick to subjects with which they were acquainted personally." "I insisted this was true in my case. She was shocked," Smith recounted years later. He explained to her that during the summer, he worked overnight at a Savannah boarding house owned by a relative. The teacher accepted his paper, but excused Smith from reading it aloud in class.[5]

Smith enrolled in Oglethorpe College in Atlanta in 1932, planning to major in English. He worked on Oglethorpe's school paper and wrote press releases for the college's president. He also covered sports for the *Atlanta Georgian,* one of William Randolph Hearst's newspapers. The newspaper business lured him from his studies. In 1934, during his junior year, Smith dropped out of Oglethorpe and took a job writing features for the *Atlanta Journal Sunday Magazine.* The following year, he was hired as managing editor of the *Athens (Ga.) Daily Times.*

In April 1936, Smith covered the aftermath of a tornado that killed 203 people when it destroyed downtown Gainesville, Georgia. President Franklin Roosevelt's train stopped in Gainesville on April 9. "I am happy to see that you are determined to rebuild this city on bigger and better lines than ever before," the president told a crowd. Smith noticed the relative luxury enjoyed by the reporters on Roosevelt's train. He hadn't had a change of clothes in days, and he had to file his copy by climbing a utility pole to a spot where a temporary telephone was installed. He envied the lot of the White House press. "Man, that's the way to cover news!" Smith thought.

Soon, he found his way up. Late in 1936, Smith went to work for the United Press, one of the three big American news services of the day—the others were the International News Service and the Associated Press. He started out as a sportswriter in Miami. When the UP's man in Tallahassee took sick in 1937, Smitty went there to cover the Florida legislature. He spent the following three years assigned to the UP's Atlanta bureau. Smith covered so many calamities in the South that he described himself as the Atlanta bureau's "holocaust man."[6]

Smith married a social worker, Eleanor Doyle Brill, in September 1937. By 1940, the Smiths and their young son, Merriman Jr., had a home in a suburban neighborhood about three and a half miles north of downtown Atlanta.

Smitty climbed rapidly at the UP. In December 1940, he transferred to the Washington bureau. He was twenty-five years old and felt obliged to grow a mustache so he would appear older—Washington was a city for senior reporters. First he covered the Treasury. Then he was assigned to the State Department. He shared those beats with other reporters. The idea was to break him in and figure out where he'd fit best. "UP is putting me through a painful process known as learning the town," he explained to his mother. "New places and new people every day. . . . Last week, met [Treasury Secretary Henry] Morgenthau, [Assistant Attorney General] Thurman Arnold, [FBI Director] J. Edgar Hoover and a lot of other people who eat, drink and smoke like the rest of us."[7]

Sometimes he covered the White House on weekends and holidays. His bosses decided the White House suited him. Smith was assigned to the beat full time in the fall of 1941, and there he stayed for the next twenty-nine years, with only a few interruptions.

His first days at the White House were easy. No newspaper or wire service had more than one reporter on the beat, and usually no more than eight or ten reporters were at the White House at any one time. Most days, Steve Early, Roosevelt's press secretary, finished his briefings by 10:30 a.m. After the reporters filed their stories, they headed for a nearby bar. Presidential press conferences usually consisted of a dozen or so reporters gathered around Roosevelt's desk in the Oval Office. The patrician president had a cordial but adversarial relationship with the White House press. He joked and debated, and bullied the reporters if it suited his interests. If a reporter asked a hostile question, Roosevelt would give an elaborately formal answer that might include a greeting to that reporter's editor. He knew editors often planted such questions. The reporters mostly liked him.[8]

In the White House reporters' caste system, Smith saw himself as a member of an "inner clique" he labeled "the regulars." This exalted group included the three wire service reporters and reporters for newspapers in New York, Chicago, Philadelphia, and Washington. "These are the men whose full-time job is reporting the activities of the President and they are on the job in close proximity to the Chief Executive regardless of whether he is in the White House or in Honolulu," Smith explained. In his view, the regulars' role was to "serve as the eyes of the world, staring coldly at everything he does and telling all about it a few minutes later."[9]

As war clouds gathered, the reporters spent less time at the bar. Within weeks of Smith's arrival, covering the White House turned into an eight- to ten-hour-per-day job.

Smitty was off on Sunday, December 7. He loafed around his house all morning. Early in the afternoon, while he was shaving, his wife knocked on the bathroom door.

"You know what the radio just said?"

"No, what?" Smitty answered.

"It said the Japanese bombed Hawaii."

He dashed from the bathroom to the phone. A UP editor called just as Smith picked up the handset to call his office. "Japs just bombed Pearl Harbor. Get to the White House fast as you can," the editor said.[10]

Smitty grabbed a coat and tie and drove to the White House. Steve Early soon held a briefing giving details of the Pearl Harbor attack, which Smith called in to the UP's Washington bureau. "From then until about midnight there occurred the maddest scramble, the most rapid succession of world-shaking stories in the memory of the oldest old-timer in the newspaper business around Washington," Smith said. Within four hours that day, he handled eight bulletins and four "flashes," which are the highest-priority wire service news. Flashes denote big, big stories, like the death of a statesman or the outbreak of war. "This means to a press association man that the heat was on about as hot as it ever will be. Men spend an entire lifetime in press association work without ever handling one flash story."[11]

Smith spent much of the war traveling with Roosevelt. "Did I marry a man or a traveling salesman!" Eleanor Smith remarked in a letter to her mother-in-law.[12] Frustratingly to Smith, much of the president's travel during those years was secret. Roosevelt left Washington for days or weeks. Usually the only reporters on these trips were Smitty and his wire service colleagues. Often, they wrote nothing. Even the president's weekend trips home to Hyde Park, New York, were off the record. If something newsworthy did happen, the reporters sent out their stories after Roosevelt was back at the White House, if they sent out any copy at all. One five-day cross-country train run was so slow and boring, Smith rode through most of Oklahoma atop the engine cab, "waving to astonished trackwalkers who never before saw a man riding on top of an engine."[13]

"You wire service men are just sitting around like vultures waiting for something to happen to me," Roosevelt said to them once. "Isn't that right?"

Well, not exactly, the reporters replied. "We're here *in case* something happens." Roosevelt called the reporters his "ghouls."[14]

Several times during the war, Smith asked to be reassigned as a combat correspondent. His boss, UP Washington bureau manager Lyle Wilson, rejected all of his requests "on grounds that the White House was an important war front in itself and there I would remain."[15] His itch to be a combat correspondent did not diminish his enjoyment of the White House beat. Smith reveled in the job. He liked being an insider, someone who saw the president every day. As the senior wire service reporter, he had the duty of declaring the end of White House news conferences with the phrase, "Thank you, Mr. President," which was the title of his first book in 1946. The book spent a month on the *New York Times'* best-seller list.

"I wouldn't trade the experience for anything. There is just no other way to get a front seat at the making of history except to be President, and my mother didn't raise me to be one," he wrote.[16]

He also liked the celebrity aspect of his beat. *Thank You, Mr. President* included snippets about White House visits by Spencer Tracy and Frank Sinatra. He also wrote about Bob Hope's comedy routine at the 1944 White House Correspondents' Association dinner. "I sat by the President that night and Hope will never know how much Mr. Roosevelt enjoyed his gentle—and sometimes not so gentle—kidding," Smith wrote.

He shared the excitement of his life with his family. It would be years before women were admitted to the Correspondents' Association dinners. But in 1945, when Smith set up the entertainment as the association's president, he arranged with the Secret Service for his wife, Eleanor, and some of his colleagues' wives to watch the show from a film projection booth at the back of the hall. The entertainment that year included singer/comedians Fanny Brice and Danny Kaye and comedians Jimmy Durante and Danny Thomas. Smitty "sat between the president and the Earl of Athlone [the governor-general of Canada] and maintained the most beautiful poise and dignity in handling the introductions and details of the program you have ever seen," Eleanor Smith wrote her mother-in-law.[17]

Smith gathered details about White House life from everyone from gardeners to Secret Service agents. He wrote about how much Roosevelt enjoyed stamp collecting, his model ship collection, movies, and swimming. In *Thank You, Mr. President*, published the year after Roosevelt died, Smith said Roosevelt's swimming "made up for his inability to walk."[18] Roosevelt's inability to walk went unmentioned in White House reporters' copy when Roosevelt was alive. Rumors of the president's paralysis circulated around the country. The Washington press did not report on his condition, though there were hints: The proceeds of the 1944 Correspondents' dinner went to the National Infantile Paralysis Foundation, "the President's favorite philanthropy." Roosevelt himself brought up his infantile paralysis in a March 1945 address to Congress after his return from the Yalta conference. The *New York Times* transcript quotes him apologizing for delivering the speech while sitting down, and explaining that he must "carry about ten pounds of steel around on the bottom of my legs."[19] Smith believed this was the first time Roosevelt mentioned his paralysis in public.[20] But newspaper summaries of the speech omitted that part of his remarks.

Many reporters doubted Roosevelt would survive his fourth term. The presidency was clearly sapping his energy. Smith noticed that Roosevelt's voice was lower and his hands trembled. But he and other reporters told readers nothing about what they saw.[21]

Smith was at Roosevelt's retreat in Warm Springs, Georgia, on April 12, 1945. That afternoon, he had helped organize a barbecue for the president that was to be held on a Warm Springs mountainside. "The Brunswick stew was bubbling in a huge cook pot, country fiddlers were playing 'The Cat and the Chicken,' and everyone was on his toes for the Chief Executive's arrival," Smith wrote. When Roosevelt didn't show up on time, he called the White House's Warm Springs switchboard to ask where he was. "What's going on?" Smith asked. "Just get down here as fast as you can," the operator said.[22]

Only after Roosevelt's death did Smith write a comprehensive story about the president's maladies. "Did President Roosevelt know he was an ill man and that the time had come to husband his strength?" Smith asked in his first paragraph. "Many of us who saw him often and traveled with him believe he did."[23]

After Roosevelt's death, Smith asked one last time to be reassigned as a war correspondent. Wilson turned him down again, and told Smith: "Get on over to the White House and start learning to know the new boss."[24]

On the morning of President Harry S. Truman's first workday at the White House, Tony Vaccaro, an AP reporter who had covered Truman in the Senate, caused quite a splash among his competitors when the new president gave him a ride to work. Smitty worried that Vaccaro's relationship with Truman assured AP a steady stream of scoops. Vaccaro knew better. He announced to his new colleagues in the White House press room: "Please forget this business about my being close to the President. Every one of you will be, too, before long."[25]

Vaccaro was right. Truman quickly struck up good relationships with Smitty and the other reporters who covered him regularly.

Covering the White House is not as dramatic or dangerous as being a war correspondent or a big-city street reporter. Smith faced his biggest risk of injury when he ran to the telephone to call in a story. When Truman announced Germany's surrender in May 1945, Smith sprinted from the president's office so fast he tripped over a photographer's ladder, bounced several feet in the air, and hit the floor hard enough to dislocate his shoulder. He was hurt, but duty came first. Smitty spent an hour dictating his story to the UP's Washington bureau. When he walked out of his phone booth, he toppled over on the press room sofa. "I could not hold anything in my left hand. I hurt plenty," he said.[26] The White House doctor gave him a shot of morphine, and Smith spent several days in the hospital. His reporter friends sent him a bottle of whiskey, Merriman Jr. drew him a Purple Heart in crayon, and Smitty got a lot of what he called "cheap notoriety."[27]

Smitty sailed with President Truman aboard the USS *Augusta* to the July 1945 postwar Potsdam Conference in Germany. On the way back on August 3, Truman gathered Smith and the other reporters in the *Augusta's* flag cabin and laid out the story of the atomic bomb that was about to be dropped on Japan. "Here was the greatest story since the invention of gunpowder. And what could we do with it? Nothing. Just sit and wait," Smith said. Truman waited too. The president expected to hear the result of the bombing sometime on August 4. "But when we caught him on deck next day, he shrugged his shoulders. No word yet."[28]

Finally, just before noon on August 6, the first news of the successful Hiroshima bomb was radioed to the *Augusta* and to Truman.

Smitty reported what happened next in a story radioed from the warship: "The president himself broke the news of the awesome atomic bomb to officers and men aboard this cruiser during the 'chow' hour. 'We have just dropped a bomb on Japan that is more powerful than 20,000 tons of TNT,' he said. 'The experiment has been an overwhelming success.' The president said the announcement was the happiest he ever made because it meant a quicker end to the war, a saving of American lives. The men cheered."[29]

Once everyone on the ship was briefed and the reporters' copy had been radioed home, it was time for poker. "Out came the cards and chips," Smith wrote years later in an article for *This Week,* a magazine inserted in Sunday newspapers around the country. Smitty suspected Truman went easy on the "comparatively low-salaried reporters. He became quite embarrassed when he won heavily. Consequently, he would stay in utterly impossible hands in an effort to plow his winnings back into the game."[30]

Just about all the reporters drank. Smitty drank more than most. He hinted at his boozy habits in an anecdote in *Thank You, Mr. President.* The book recounted a 1945 item in the *Boston Globe* about his appearance at a news conference. The item included this back-and-forth between Smith and Truman's press secretary:

"Were you up late last night, Merriman?"

"Slightly," Smitty replied.

"Did your wife speak to you this morning?"

"Slightly," said Smith.

This item "caused anguish around our house," Smith said.[31]

Smitty's relationship with Truman was tested during the 1948 presidential campaign. United Press policy required Smith to spend some time covering Truman's challenger, Thomas Dewey. The idea was to make sure writers were not too close to one campaign or another and would be plugged in with whichever side won the election. Like just about everyone in Washington, Smith believed Dewey would win and oust Truman from office. So he had no trouble letting it be known that he was leaving Truman's campaign train "because he wanted to become acquainted with the incoming President," recalled George Tames, a *New York Times* photographer.

"Well, needless to say, the word got down to Harry Truman . . . he felt betrayed."

Even late on election night, Smith remained convinced that Dewey would win. At Dewey headquarters in New York, William Murphy, the national publicity director for the Republicans, warned Smitty of the impending loss. "We're licked," he said.[32] But Smith didn't believe him. At least he wasn't the only journalist to wrongly assess the race. The famous picture showing Truman smiling as he waved the *Chicago Daily Tribune's* unfortunate "DEWEY DEFEATS TRUMAN" headline perfectly conveyed the president's glee at the election results.

Smitty was back at Truman's side days later, like a shamed puppy dog with its tail between its legs. At the time, the White House was being rebuilt, so the Trumans were living across the street in Blair House, the presidential guest quarters. The morning of Smith's return, Tames recounted, Truman headed from Blair House to his office, "walking that brisk military walk," as usual. Smith approached Truman from across the street. "Congratulations, Mr. President," Smith said. "Congratulations! Congratulations?"

"The President continued walking. Merriman was walking crablike, sideways, because the President never even hesitated in his stride." Finally, Truman looked up at Smith and grinned.

"How's Dewey?" Truman asked.

The president never forgot that Smith pegged him a loser. "Neither did Merriman," said Tames. "He tried to make up for it the next four years."[33]

In 1950, Smith nearly had to cover the ultimate White House story—an assassination. Two gun-wielding Puerto Rican nationalists tried to shoot their way into Blair House. A White House police officer was shot—but before he died, he managed to shoot and kill one of the assassins. The other assassin, shot in the chest during a gunfight, survived. "Mr. Truman, awakened by the shots, ran to the open window in his underwear and looked out," Smith reported. "A policeman saw the President at the window and roared: 'Get back!'" Truman was unhurt, and Smith wrote that the next day he "went about his business as usual, taking a morning stroll through downtown Washington and scheduling a full list of visitors at the White House."[34]

Always in the back of Smith's mind was the possibility he would have to report the biggest story of all involving a president—"death or serious injury, from natural causes, accident or assassination. [It] has to be thought about by the men who cover a President because when bodily harm or pain come to a Chief Executive, it is the hottest news an American reporter can possibly handle," he wrote.[35] Smith went through his career "relentlessly alert," said Robert Donovan, a competitor and friend. "What was the most gripping story that could possibly fall into the lap of a White House Correspondent?" Donovan asked. "Anyone who was as romantic about reporting as Smith knew the answer: the assassination of the president."[36]

SIDEBAR · THE SCREENING ROOM

In his second book, *A President Is Many Men*, Smith wrote that during a time of White House crisis in 1946, President Truman took a bit of time off to watch a short movie documentary about the presidency. Truman watched the film in the White House screening room.

The opening scene showed a young mother rolling a baby carriage past the White House. She stopped, gazed at the North Portico, and looked down at her infant son.

"The narrator of the movie intoned, 'Yes, she realizes that her child, like anybody in this great country, can become President!'"

"Mr. Truman, sitting in the dark, chuckled and nudged his wife who was beside him.

"'I'm living proof of *that*,' he said."[37]

The story says a lot about Truman's personality, how he viewed himself, and how he viewed his ascendance upon Franklin Roosevelt's death to a job Smith was convinced he never wanted. But any reporter would want to know: How did Smith know what the president said to the First Lady in a darkened room? The book doesn't say.

CHAPTER 2 ✦ FAME

SMITH WROTE TWO MORE WELL-RECEIVED books, 1948's *A President Is Many Men* and 1955's *Meet Mr. Eisenhower.* He also began appearing on TV, on Sunday Washington interview programs like *Meet the Press* and *Face the Nation,* and on a prime-time current events quiz show called *Who Said That?* He traveled the country giving speeches. And, of course, his stories ran on newspaper front pages everywhere.

Smith's books and newspaper copy are loaded with entertaining stories, anecdotes, and eyewitness observations. They are informative and short on deep thinking. Smith strove to provide information, not commentary. That suited his bosses at the United Press. They marketed their service to newspapers of varying ideologies, and Smith's reports would have less appeal if they were opinionated. His reports were more valuable when they were first with the news and first with exclusive details. As one of the wire service White House "regulars," he observed events and cultivated sources other reporters would never access.

His zeal sometimes angered his competitors. Smith found himself in big trouble in October 1950 with his colleagues and with President Truman. The president traveled to Wake Island, a balmy spit of sand and coral in the middle of the Pacific Ocean, for a meeting with Douglas MacArthur, the five-star general who oversaw American forces in the Pacific region.

The meeting's main topic was the prosecution of the war then under way in Korea, which was nearly completely taken over by North Korean forces in the summer of 1950. Weeks before the meeting, MacArthur commanded the successful invasion of Inchon, which forced the North Koreans to retreat. MacArthur was also a World War II hero, a bigger-than-life figure whose opinion was respected by many Americans. But before the successful Inchon invasion, he angered Truman with a statement to the Veterans of Foreign Wars supporting Chinese nationalist leader Chiang Kai Shek's control of Taiwan. The statement broke a promise by MacArthur not to dabble in policy matters. During the meeting, Truman and his military aides hoped to make sure MacArthur's thinking was in sync with their own.

On the way to Wake, the president and his party stopped in California. There, Smith filed stories reporting that Truman was "unusually taciturn and uncommunicative" and "a picture of concern and preoccupation."[38] The implication was that Truman was nervous about the upcoming meeting. This irritated Truman, who later insisted he was not nervous at all about meeting MacArthur.

The Wake meeting's main news was a communiqué that said Truman and MacArthur had "very complete unanimity of view" on military policy in Korea and Asia.[39] The communiqué didn't tell the full story of the meeting. But it was just about all the information Smith and his colleagues had, and it was front-page news.

The only way the twenty-two reporters on the trip could transmit their stories from Wake was through a single radio Teletype hookup to Honolulu. Smith and his colleagues agreed ahead of time that the wire services—the Associated Press, the United Press, and the International News Service—would collaborate on one story about the communiqué that would be transmitted simultaneously on all three wires. That way, everyone would get the news at the same time.

But Smitty couldn't resist the urge to be first. While the shared communiqué story was still awaiting transmission to the wire services, Smith went to the island's radio shack with his own story and ordered the radio operator to send it to the UP, "in the name of the White House." The gullible radio operator complied.

This subterfuge gave Smith a forty-minute beat over his angry competitors. It was not a breach of any government embargo. But Smith's initiative in getting his story transmitted first broke his pact with his colleagues. It was also a huge victory for the United Press.

Of course, Smith's competitors were furious that he breached their agreement. Back in Washington, he faced their wrath. Carleton Kent of the *Chicago Sun-Times,* the president of the White House Correspondents' Association, was enlisted to tell Smith what his colleagues thought of him. Kent's words were "terse, pithy, unprintable," *Time* magazine reported. "Smith, however, was unabashed, and, his rivals soon were claiming, unreformed." Smith did not apologize publicly. "I was trying to get the communiqué out first in Wake and I did," he said. "I know they are awful mad at me at the White House and in the press room, but there is nothing I can do about it."[40] Smitty liked being ahead of the other reporters. He was a competitor.

Anthony Leviero, a *New York Times* reporter on the trip, made an even more serious charge. When the reporters returned to Honolulu, Leviero sent the *Times* a story predicting that the US military was planning a "knockout blow" in Korea. The story was garbled in transmission, so the *Times* sent it back to him with questions. But Leviero never received that transmission, and his story didn't make the paper. Smith, at the same time, sent out a story of his own that also predicted a "knockout blow" in Korea. Smith's story showed up the next morning in the *New York Herald Tribune,* Leviero's main competition.

The *Times* was furious. It accused Smith of hijacking its message to Leviero that had asked more questions about his copy and then filing a similar story of his own. The charge was plagiarism. If it was true, Smith's career would be over. Smith got out of this scrape simply by denying he had even seen Leviero's story.

Smith also had to face President Truman's anger over the implication that he was nervous about meeting MacArthur. Truman had lots of problems with MacArthur—he fired the general in April 1951. But he felt the Wake Island meeting largely went well. At a news conference Smith skipped, the president told reporters that one news service—he didn't say which one—was less than objective in its coverage. "It's a pity that you columnists and reporters that represent a certain press service can't understand the ideas of two intellectually honest men when they meet," he said.[41]

Truman did not stay mad at Smith. In December 1952, as he was preparing to leave office, he granted Smith an exit interview. Most of the discussion was about policy matters. But Smith extracted a quote from the president that showed his skill at drawing out interview subjects: "Mr. Truman, when asked whether he would need protection after he leaves the White House, snorted and said, 'If any nut tries to shoot me, I'll take the pistol away from him, ram it down his throat and pull the trigger.'" Truman had a reputation for salty language, and you have to figure Smith omitted a few choice words from the quote.[42]

One more story tells of Truman's regard for Smith—and of the power Smith held at the United Press. After Truman left the White House, he and his wife, Bess, returned home to Independence, Missouri, just outside Kansas City. The federal government gave Truman an office in a downtown Kansas City skyscraper. One day in 1953, Smith got a tip: Truman—perhaps having had too much to drink—fell down some steps or slipped on a rug and broke some ribs. Doctors had taped him up so tightly, Smith heard, that the former president had difficulty breathing.

At Smith's behest, Roy McGhee, still a reporter in the UP's Kansas City bureau, went to Truman's office to investigate. "I went in and talked to his secretary and asked if I could see Mr. Truman. She said, 'What about?' I told her. She said, 'Well, sure, Merriman Smith was a friend of his.'"

McGhee entered Truman's private office. "We got a message from Washington that said that Merriman Smith has heard that you broke a couple of ribs and he wanted me to check up on it," he asked the former president.

"No, nothing to it," Truman answered. "I didn't fall down. I'm fine."

"Thank you very much," McGhee said. He went back to the UP bureau and reported what he had learned—that Truman was fine, and that he didn't fall down.

"That's not right," Smitty responded. "My source is absolutely impeccable. I know Truman fell down, and I know a doctor saw him, and I know he broke some ribs. Get back over there and verify this so we can write it."

So McGhee went back to Truman's office. Again, he saw the former president. Again, Truman told him he had no story. "There's nothing to it. I did not fall down," Truman said. "I am not bound up. Nothing's wrong with me at all." McGhee went back to his office and sent a message about his second meeting to Smith at UP's Washington bureau.

Soon he was in trouble with top UP editors in New York. They sent a Teletype to Kansas City: "Merriman Smith says the Kansas City bureau is not following up on his requests, and not doing it properly."

McGhee didn't want to go back to Truman's office. His bureau chief didn't care. Smith's requests had to be obeyed. So back McGhee went to the ex-president's office, grumbling to himself that he'd quit his job before he went a fourth time.

This time, McGhee carried a sheaf of the Teletype messages the Kansas City bureau had received on the matter. "I know this is a burden on you, and I hate like hell to keep bothering you, but I've got to have another comment from you on this," McGhee told Truman.

"I wonder what would please them?" the former president said.

"And with that, Truman took off his shirt and stood there barechested. And there were no bandages," McGhee said.

"I went back to the office and I told the bureau chief what had happened. He couldn't believe it." The bureau chief wrote to Smith:

"Don't bother us anymore. Our man's been over there three times now and there's absolutely nothing to this. Get it from some other sources and print it on your own from your source if you want. We're not verifying a damn word of this. Truman denies it." "Well, that was the end of that!" McGhee said.[43]

Dwight Eisenhower's arrival in the White House in 1953 brought a new twist to Smith's coverage of the beat—a twice-weekly column, "Backstairs at the White House." Usually, "Backstairs" included several gossipy items. A typical 1954 column recounted a surprise birthday party Eisenhower threw for Sherman Adams, his top aide. The same column reported the $150,000 cost of a cabin Eisenhower and his wife, Mamie, used at the Augusta National Golf Club and a couple of paragraphs about the man who did Eisenhower's makeup when he appeared on TV.[44]

The anecdotes gave little insight into Eisenhower's policies—but Smith thought they gave readers a better picture of their president. "I tried to print as much froth about Ike as I could, largely because I thought the public wasn't getting a very close view of him," he said.[45] "Backstairs" was one of the UP's most popular features. It also showed Smith's deep sourcing. "It was impossible to keep him from learning what was happening around the White House," said Jim Hagerty, Eisenhower's press secretary. "He had unlimited contacts with almost everyone who worked there and they trusted his discretion and his protection of his sources."[46]

Eisenhower got along well with the wire service reporters who covered him regularly. He called Smith by his first name—though he usually mispronounced it. "Merriam," he would say. Smith thought Eisenhower was more reserved than Roosevelt and Truman. "He tends to stiffen when he is around reporters, even socially, as though he expects someone to hurl a volley of unpleasant questions at him," Smith wrote.[47]

Smitty added another dimension to his career by breaking in to broadcasting. For a while in the 1950s, he was a regular on an NBC radio program that focused on White House news. Television brought him true fame. He found success as a questioner on Sunday political interview shows like *Meet the Press* and as a regular guest on prime-time game shows. One steady gig was as a panelist on *Who Said That?* The show's host read a quote from a newsmaker. A celebrity panel—two journalists and two entertainers—explained who said the quote, and put it in context. A panelist who answered a question wrongly had to donate $10 to charity. The show got its start on the radio in 1947 and moved to TV in 1948. One researcher says the word *anchorman* was first used not to describe someone who read the news on radio or TV but to describe newsman John Cameron Swayze's role as a permanent *Who Said That?* panelist.[48]

Actress June Lockhart was usually the show's only female panelist—as she put it, the producers felt the show needed a "girl." *Who Said That?* was easy work for Smith and the other journalists on the panel. "They didn't have to do much prep for the show because they were living it every day," said Lockhart. She studied up by collecting three hundred quotes a week from whatever newspapers were available. "I would put them all together and memorize them," she said.

After the broadcasts, everyone went to Toots Shor, a famous midtown Manhattan bar where Smith often stopped when he was in the city. "I would sit there agog while this group of men would talk about what was going to be news the following week," Lockhart recounted.[49] She and Smith became good friends. Over the years that followed, Lockhart sometimes attended White House news briefings with Smith, and Smith stayed at Lockhart's family home when he visited Los Angeles.

A March 1955 "Backstairs" column based on Smith's extensive White House sources gave Hagerty an executive-sized headache. It was about Eisenhower's instruction to the White House staff to get rid of the squirrels that scampered around the White House grounds. "Firm and secret Presidential orders were given one morning to do away with the varmints," Hagerty recounted. The little critters offended Eisenhower by scattering their winter nuts on his putting green.

"This is a warning to all squirrels: Stay away from President Eisenhower's private putting green on the White House lawn or you'll find yourself clapped unceremoniously into a box and shanghaied to some forest miles away from the lush tourist peanuts and other easy pickings around 1600 Pennsylvania Avenue," Smith wrote.[50]

He described extensive efforts by the White House to get rid of the squirrels. An electronics expert suggested scaring the squirrels off with a high-pitched noise. When that didn't work, the Army Signal Corps tried putting together a tape recording of sounds "allegedly offensive to squirrels." That didn't work either. Finally, the gardeners set up a series of box traps around the putting green, which Smith reported were baited with tasty "White House provender." When the squirrels scampered up for a sniff, "plop goes the box," Smith explained. The squirrels captured in the boxes were taken away in a truck.

Eisenhower had to address the matter at a news conference. "You ought to interview the squirrels and find out if anybody is unhappy," he advised the reporters. He said the squirrels enjoy "a freedom I would personally dearly love."[51]

"It made an amusing story," Hagerty said, "except in one very high quarter."

Hagerty was deeply impressed by Smith's skill handling breaking news—not just in writing it, but in dealing with the logistics reporters face getting themselves in place to gather it. Smith called Hagerty at his Washington home "exactly two minutes" after news broke in 1955 of Eisenhower's heart attack at his in-laws' home in Denver. Smith wanted to know if he could fly to Denver with Hagerty on a military transport. Hagerty told Smith to meet him at the airport in an hour. "I didn't have time to call any other news people. I would have taken as many as wanted to go, but no others called," Hagerty said. "[H]is news reflexes automatically told him I would use a government plane to get out there in a hurry—and he was on it."[52]

Smith used whatever sources he could find for his news— which one day got him in a spot of trouble with the Eisenhower administration. Early in 1957, a UP photographer overheard Eisenhower say of his reluctance to run for reelection the year before: "You'll never know how close I came to saying no." The photographer reported the comment to Smith, who used it as a lead item in a "Backstairs" column. The column was transmitted on Monday afternoon for use in Wednesday afternoon newspapers. When the White House complained, the UP's editors killed the item. Nonetheless, some newspapers—including the *St. Louis Post-Dispatch* and the *New York Post*, which was not a UP paper—cited the killed column in stories of their own.

Though the White House strongly denied the story at the time, Smith said he heard later that it was correct.[53] Smith was a smart enough operator to know that sometimes in Washington and in politics, stories that are stoutly denied are in fact true. This knowledge would serve him well in 1958, during an extended exile from the White House beat.

Smith's drinking problem worsened over the years, and sometimes led him to behave like a jerk. When CBS assigned veteran foreign correspondent Robert Pierpoint to cover an Eisenhower motorcade in 1957, Smith, hungover, asked him: "Why did CBS think a punk like you could cover the White House?"[54]

Finally, Smith's bosses got fed up. In March 1958, around the time the beleaguered International News Service merged with the United Press to form United Press International, they yanked Smith out of the White House and had him cover the Commerce Department, the country's recession, and a school desegregation feud in Charlottesville, Virginia. For a while, Smith laid off the sauce. It wasn't easy. "I wanted nothing to do with a living soul for six months, even more," he recalled years later.[55]

Smitty's White House sources still sought him out. On September 10, 1958, Smith got a call from Homer Gruenther, a midlevel Eisenhower aide. Gruenther wanted to talk about the biggest scandal of the day—the relationship between Boston textile manufacturer Bernard Goldfine and Sherman Adams, who was

Eisenhower's chief of staff and a former governor of New Hampshire. The Goldfine scandal remained part of Smith's portfolio during his White House exile. A House committee discovered Adams accepted a vicuna overcoat and an oriental rug from Goldfine, whose business was under investigation by the Federal Trade Commission (FTC). The implication was that in return for the gifts, Adams might have interceded on Goldfine's behalf with the FTC.

None of the investigations resulted in legal action. But there remained a whiff of wrongdoing. Adams was not in the clear. "The story's not over," Gruenther said. Adams at the time was on a fishing vacation in New Brunswick, Canada. Gruenther told Smith: "You'd get a lot of readers with a story saying he'd never even come back, except possibly to clean out his desk."

"So you've decided to can him?" Smith responded.

"If you want to read it that way," Gruenther said. He added: "I wouldn't sit on this very long. . . . The idea could conceivably occur to someone else." The implication was that if Smith didn't write the story, Gruenther would find another reporter who would. "If I were you, I'd sure want to see that story on the wire before 10:30 this morning."[56]

So Smith wrote the story. It began: "An administration official said Wednesday he believed Sherman Adams for all practical purposes was through as Eisenhower's top assistant and that a formal resignation was forthcoming."[57]

Not even Smith's bosses believed it at first. Lyle Wilson, UPI's Washington bureau manager, was in New York that morning with Roy Howard, a semiretired top executive of Scripps Howard, the newspaper company that owned UPI. Howard checked Smith's report with some Eisenhower associates he knew. Wilson called Smith. "Roy says that there's not a word of truth to your story," he said.

Smith told Wilson that Gruenther was his source.

"Good enough for me," said Wilson. "Homer's just doing an errand for somebody."

Adams was back in Washington on September 15, five days after Smith's story ran. It was several days more before Eisenhower and his aides worked out the details of Adams' departure. White House officials denied Smith's story up to the last minute.

By the beginning of October, Smith was back on the White House beat. Eisenhower spotted him in a group of reporters. "Hello, Merriman," he said, according to *Time* magazine. *Time* must have corrected Eisenhower's usual mispronunciation of Smith's name.

"I thought you had been promoted out of here," Eisenhower said.

"I wouldn't say that, Mr. President," Smith answered. "I've been playing in the minor leagues."[58] Smitty always wanted to be in the majors—in the show.

Soon after his return, Smith physically came to Eisenhower's defense. A reporter covering an Eisenhower event in New York muttered ominously that he planned to kill the president. At what seemed like a moment of danger, Smith lunged and grabbed the man around the neck. The reporter, who worked for a New York newspaper, threw Smith to the ground and stomped him in the face. Secret Service agents quickly moved in. Tim Smith recalls that the incident gave his father "a new, better-looking nose." The incident was hushed up. But Eisenhower acknowledged what happened in a personal note to Smith on November 19, saying he was "distressed" over Smith's injury.[59]

Smith now had three children. The eldest was Merriman Jr., who was known to some as Bert, short for his and his father's formal first name, Albert. Smith had another son, Timothy, born in 1948, and a daughter, Allison, born in 1951. Eisenhower was away from Washington a great deal and spent a lot of time at his home in Gettysburg, Pennsylvania. Smitty had to cover these trips, even if nothing happened. Tim Smith recalls that he and his sister often tagged along. Sometimes they got to meet the president. "It was great fun," Tim Smith said.

The Smiths had a vacation place in the Poconos, in eastern Pennsylvania. One day in 1959, Smith told Tim to put on a suit. They were going to New York for the day to appear on *The Tonight Show* with Jack Paar. Smitty was a regular on the show.

Tim Smith was the show's mystery guest. Paar and his sidekick, Hugh Downs, asked a series of questions in an effort to figure out his identity. "I was smart-alecky and evasive in the answers," Tim Smith said. Asked if his father was in the entertainment business, Tim Smith answered: "At times." "It was exciting beyond belief," he recalled. Even better, he said, was comedian Jack E. Leonard's snide comment about his khaki suit. "He said, 'Nice suit, kid. Where are your second lieutenant bars?'"[60]

Smith was a good TV guest "because he was so funny, and he looked like the rumpled news guy," said June Lockhart. Smitty stayed with Lockhart and her family when he covered the 1960 Democratic convention in Los Angeles. Before he arrived, he sent Lockhart a telegram with a list of requests: "Would like air conditioned corner room with pool entrance, kitchen privileges, white convertible and square hammock. But don't go to any trouble, as my butler and maid will handle everything including two dogs. I will need convention tickets all sessions." He signed it, "Irving and all the boys in the band."[61]

"He was just a darling man," Lockhart said.

Even public figures not known to like reporters reciprocated Smitty's humor. One day, while covering Richard Nixon's 1960 presidential campaign, Smith accidentally swung his portable typewriter into Nixon's knee. Smith apologized in a letter. "I'm very sorry and I hope it didn't hurt," Smith wrote. Nixon replied with a handwritten note: "Dear Smitty—I will <u>sue you</u>—but not until after you've voted! RN."[62]

SIDEBAR · THE GOSPEL SINGER

Merriman Smith was a white man of the South. He lived in the time of lynchings and raw racial discrimination, when blacks sat at the back of the bus, drank from separate water fountains, and were denied the vote. Smith did not express his views on racism in his news stories. But he was familiar with the story of black America.

When Smith worked for United Press in Atlanta in 1938, he made front pages across the country with a story about a Christmas celebration held by an elderly group of ex-slaves who planned to "bow their heads and ask salvation for the men who once held them in bondage." Some of the language in the piece is cringe-worthy today. Smith called an individual member of the group a "darky" and wrote that they would pray to "de Lawd." Smith did not intend to demean his subjects. The story was a straight news feature, meant to tell readers about a world of which they probably knew little.[63]

Twenty-one years later, in 1959, Smith arranged for famed black gospel singer Mahalia Jackson to appear at a White House Correspondents' Association dinner honoring President Eisenhower's sixty-ninth birthday. Jackson was an important figure in the civil rights movement and sang at fund-raisers for Martin Luther King's Southern Christian Leadership Conference.

She was nervous about singing for the president that night. "All of my talent has gone to my feet," she joked. She needn't have worried. Eisenhower was a fan—even though she had backed his opponent, Adlai Stevenson, in the 1956 election.

Jackson sang several religious numbers—"He's Got the Whole World in His Hands" was one. She had less religious songs in her repertoire. "Efforts were made to persuade her to sing some of these hotter numbers, but she declined," the *Afro American* newspaper reported. "She said it would not be dignified to do them in the presence of the President."[64]

After the dinner, a member of Jackson's entourage asked Smith if he'd make sure Eisenhower got a copy of her latest album. Smith had a better idea. He told Jackson she should give the album to Eisenhower herself. And he made sure it happened.

Photos of Jackson presenting the album to Eisenhower appeared inside the *Afro American* and on page one of the *New York Age,* another black newspaper.[65] Backstage after the show, Eisenhower talked with Jackson longer than he talked with any of the other performers, the *Afro American* said.

Eisenhower took the cause of civil rights further than his predecessors. He pushed to fully implement Harry Truman's order desegregating the military and successfully sued to desegregate restaurants in the District of Columbia. Smith wrote stories about Eisenhower's decision to send troops to enforce the desegregation of Central High School in Little Rock, Arkansas, and his advocacy of the Civil Rights Act of 1957, the first such legislation to clear Congress since Reconstruction.

There's a good argument that Eisenhower should have done more. But that didn't matter to Jackson at Eisenhower's birthday party. "It is just wonderful that here in America a girl who once worked as a simple washer woman can perform for and be greeted by the President of our country," she said.[66]

CHAPTER 3 ✦ GOOD NEW DAYS

PRESIDENTS CAME AND WENT, BUT Merriman Smith remained a denizen of the White House. He was stationed most days in the press room just off the vestibule at the main entrance of the West Wing. In idle moments Smitty regaled younger colleagues with stories of presidencies past and swapped gossip with everybody. Touring the White House shortly after the 1960 election, president-elect John F. Kennedy introduced him to his wife, Jacqueline, by saying: "I want you to meet Merriman Smith. We inherited him with the White House."[67]

Smith had help covering the Kennedys. Between Kennedy's election and inauguration, Al Spivak joined him full time in the White House press room. Spivak was one of a few International News Service reporters kept on when INS merged with the United Press in 1958. Before Kennedy's election he had covered the White House sporadically.

Smith told his new partner: "Spivak, there will be a lot of presidential travel coming up, and I plan for us to split the trips 50-50, down the middle. I'll take the good ones and you'll get the rest."

"Smitty kept his promise," Spivak said.

Soon Helen Thomas joined Smith and Spivak. "I just started showing up every day," said Thomas, a UP and UPI Washington staffer since the 1940s. She was the first woman reporter assigned to the White House full time. Covering the Kennedys was a seven-day-a-week job, and Smitty and Spivak were not about to turn her away.[68]

Smitty was where he wanted to be. The White House beat was glamorous and important, and keeping ahead of the press pack sated Smith's competitive zeal. "He isn't trying to climb the ladder to an editorship or some other position. To him, being a great reporter is being at the top of the ladder," said Thomas.[69] Smith also had a financial incentive to stay on the beat. Merriman Jr. had just finished college, but his two younger children, Tim and Allison, were enrolled in Washington's elite Sidwell Friends School. The Smiths had a home in Washington and the vacation place in the Poconos. His job helped him obtain book deals and TV appearances that paid living expenses and tuition bills. "I simply could not exist now on my current UPI salary if Ellie were not working and if I were not earning on the outside," he pleaded to his bosses in June 1961 when he asked for a raise.[70] An editing or management job would not have paid Smith much more than what UPI paid him to cover the White House—and would have ended the insider status that let him earn that outside income.

Like every new president, Kennedy changed Smith's routine. Perhaps the biggest change was in the atmosphere in Washington. The handsome, forty-three-year-old president, his beautiful wife, and their young children, Caroline and John Jr., brought an air of excitement and glamour to the White House that was lacking in the Roosevelt, Truman, and Eisenhower administrations. Presidents are always famous, but the Kennedys' celebrity far exceeded their predecessors. They both came from wealthy and socially prominent families, and now they occupied the most famous house in the land. "Hollywood couldn't make a more glamorous couple," said Sid Davis, who covered the White House for the Westinghouse radio network.[71] The Kennedys' glamour forced the reporters to compete more intensely than ever for the kinds of stories that Smith had used for years to fill the "Backstairs" column.

Smith had a theory about Kennedy's election: He believed that after eight years of Eisenhower, the country "needed a spark—it needed inspiration. They [Americans] needed higher targets, higher goals, and Kennedy came in."[72] Kennedy promised his programs would lead the nation to a New Frontier, the label applied to his domestic and foreign platform. Smith believed the young president's ideas appealed to many people.

Another change was Kennedy's decision to put his news conferences on live TV. Kennedy gave sixty-two televised press conferences during his presidency. His first press conference drew sixty million viewers, and he and his staff deemed them an excellent public relations tool.[73] "We couldn't survive without TV," Kennedy said. He thought the TV appearances displayed his intelligence and wit.[74] Smith—one of the most TV-savvy reporters in the White House press room—judged Kennedy a "smooth performer." But the TV press conferences diminished newspapers' and news wires' importance by letting the public see news break in real time. Smitty's breathless telephone bulletins became less important. UPI Washington bureau news editor Julius Frandsen watched the news conferences on TV with a team of reporters. When Kennedy said something newsworthy, Frandsen assigned a reporter to write a story.[75] UPI clients got the news quicker, and Smitty didn't have to risk hurting himself rushing to the phone.

The TV news conferences also added an element of formality in the way questions were presented and answered. There was less casual banter between the president and the press. Smith felt the TV press conferences brought "less interplay between reporter and head of government, and hence less news."[76]

Kennedy and his press secretary, Pierre Salinger, instituted yet another reform—they made the White House an "open beat" by allowing reporters unprecedented access to administration officials, who were freer than before to discuss policy matters. Salinger said he didn't want to "spoon feed" news to reporters at briefings. He thought it was better if reporters were free to dig up stories on their own. "Under the new, competitive system, they either had to go to work or be shown up by their more energetic colleagues," he said.[77]

Many reporters liked this new approach. "The doors opened," said Charles Roberts, who covered the White House for *Newsweek*. Under the Eisenhower administration, information was tightly controlled. Officials needed permission from Eisenhower or his press secretary, Jim Hagerty, to speak to the press. Salinger and Kennedy imposed few such restrictions on his staff. "We had a revolution covering the White House under Kennedy," Roberts said. He believed Kennedy "got a better press because we were kept informed."[78]

Kennedy had some favorite reporters, including Hugh Sidey of *Time* magazine, Sander Vanocur of NBC News, and Charles Bartlett of the *Chattanooga Times*, who had set up Kennedy's first date with Jacqueline. His press operation targeted stories to influential reporters like William Lawrence of the *New York Times* and Ben Bradlee of *Newsweek*, another longtime Kennedy friend. Kennedy's press staff even pitched stories to the Soviet news media, since they knew reporters for the *Izvestia* newspaper and TASS news agency were a good conduit to the Kremlin.[79] Early in his administration, Kennedy himself provided much information that reporters attributed to an anonymous administration source. "He was the biggest leak in the White House," said Roberts.[80]

"He knew many of us," Roberts elaborated. "We were his age, and he had confidence that he could talk to us straightaway and that his confidence would be observed—that if he was talking off the record, it would stay off the record, or that it would not be attributed if he said 'This is for background' or 'Not for attribution.' He knew all the rules. He was in many ways his own press secretary."[81]

Smith observed that there was more interaction between Kennedy's people and the press than in other administrations. "It seems to have become easier to see public officials, and, equally important, to reach them by telephone," he wrote. "Not that they always give the reporter what he's after, but contact can be established."[82] But Smith believed the new policy's practical effect was to allow Kennedy and his staff to play favorites among the reporters "based on personalities and friendships," his son Tim said.

Smith got off to a good start with Salinger. They appeared together on the Jack Paar program days before Kennedy's inauguration.[83] But while he was respected, Smitty had been around the White House for so long, he seemed old school to the Kennedys and those they brought to Washington. Smith was just two years older than the president. But he had covered the White House beat through Kennedy's World War II service and his entire career in Congress. Tim Smith said some Kennedy people described his father derisively as a "hack."[84] Smitty wasn't shut out. But he wasn't a Kennedy intimate, either.

Of course, from time to time some doors were shut to all the journalists. Salinger and Kennedy tried to limit news reporting about the October 1962 Cuban missile crisis, out of fear that disclosing the administration's thinking and tactics—not to mention US nuclear capabilities—would give the Soviet Union an advantage in its effort to install nuclear missiles in Cuba. Arthur Sylvester, a press spokesman at the Defense Department, did Kennedy no favors with a statement that the administration had the right to "manage" the news it released during the crisis. Sylvester spoke a truth: Politicians and governments always try to manage the news they release to the public. They always try to present news—especially bad news—in a way that makes them look as good as possible. But it is a truth government public relations people would best leave unsaid, and many journalists took Sylvester to mean that the government spokespeople had a right in crises to deliberately mislead the public.

Weeks after the Soviets backed down and the crisis had passed, the media was still grumbling about Sylvester's comments. Smith, whose stories about the Cuba crisis ran on front pages across the country, spoke up about the issue in a speech at the national convention of the Society of Professional Journalists. "We don't need to print propaganda," he said.[85]

Kennedy and Salinger devised another end-around of the Washington press corps: regular meetings with newspaper publishers from around the country. Kennedy held twenty-five such meetings during his presidency and intended to hold one for each state. The meetings were friendly, except for one in 1961 involving E. M. Dealey, publisher of the *Dallas Morning News*. Dealey told Kennedy that when it came to dealing with the Soviets, he and his administration were "weak sisters," and that the United States needed a "man on horseback." "Many people in Texas and the Southwest think that you are riding Caroline's tricycle," he said. Dealey was speaking for a far-right-wing branch of Texas Republican politics that didn't reflect the views of the entire state, which in those days was dominated by Democrats. Kennedy had carried Texas in a close vote in 1960.

Kennedy thought it rude that Dealey brought his daughter's name into the debate.[86] Others at the event thought Dealey was simply rude. The publisher of the *Dallas Times Herald*, the *News's* afternoon rival, later sent Kennedy a note assuring him that Dealey spoke only for himself. "I'm sure the people of Dallas must be glad when afternoon comes," Kennedy replied.[87]

Smith covered the biggest news of the Kennedy administration. He traveled with the Kennedys to Europe in June 1961 on a trip that included a state visit with French President Charles De Gaulle in Paris. Jacqueline Kennedy, fluent in French, made a big impression, not just in personal appearances but also in an interview on French TV. Newspapers back home reported she attended a state dinner with her hair in a coiffure that followed fourteenth-century style. Kennedy pretended to be jealous of the attention his wife drew. "I am the person who is accompanying Jacqueline Kennedy to Paris," he quipped.[88]

From Paris, the party went on to Vienna, where Kennedy held a tense summit with Soviet premier Nikita Khrushchev. Smith covered the communiqué and official announcements from the meeting. Khrushchev agreed to a cease-fire between Communist and government forces in the southeast Asian country of Laos, and Kennedy vowed not to yield to Soviet pressure to push the US and other Western countries out of Berlin. Kennedy then flew to London to meet Prime Minister Harold Macmillan. Aside from the official statements, Smith had little to report. But his copy did note that Kennedy and Macmillan met for "three hours and 20 minutes, not including lunch."[89]

Smith took other trips with Kennedy—including his trip to West Berlin in June 1963. "All free men, wherever they may live, are citizens of Berlin and therefore as a free man I take pride in the words: 'Ich bin ein Berliner,'" Kennedy told a crowd of 250,000 West Berliners in one of his most famous speeches. Kennedy's words "brought tremendous roars of approval from the crowd," Smith wrote.[90]

It does not belittle Smith to say many of his stories were no better than those filed by his competitors. On the biggest stories, White House reporters usually end up with pretty much the same information. The Cuban missile crisis, the Berlin speech, and the Vienna summit were never going to be any reporter's exclusive.

But when it came to the everyday drama of White House life, Smith continued to outpace his competitors. His years on the beat gave him sources no other reporter could match. The newcomers in the Kennedy administration could call him a hack, could leak to his competitors, and could go over his head with live TV news conferences. But the Kennedy White House couldn't keep Smith from scoring exclusives about the activities surrounding the wealthy and glamorous first family.

Sid Davis recalled a trip to Palm Beach, Florida, in March 1961 for a Kennedy family vacation. Early on March 31, he and Smitty were alone in the temporary press room that had been set up in a Palm Beach hotel. "Hey, kid," Smitty said. "I'm going downtown to buy a bathing suit." "He was always shopping," Davis said of Smith.

"So we went downtown to Worth Avenue, a very high class shopping center in Palm Beach. We went to a men's store he seemed familiar with. He went to a big table with a bunch of bathing suits on it, 50 or 100 bathing suits in a big pile in the front of the store. 'I wear a 34,' he said. 'See if you can find one you like.'"

The store had a big display window, and Smith saw someone he knew outside. "I'll be right back," Smith said. Davis kept looking through the bathing suits while Smith talked with the man. "Smitty came back in a hurry. He said, 'To hell with the bathing suit. Let's go back to the hotel.'"

Back at the hotel, Davis announced that he was going to take a nap. "It was 2 p.m. or 3 p.m. Smitty said the same thing, 'I'm going to take a break.'"

"I lit a cigar and was lying on the bed. I got a phone call from my boss." Davis's boss asked him: "Don't you know about the plot?" "I said, 'What plot?' 'The plot to kidnap Caroline Kennedy,' he said. 'What the hell are you talking about?' I said. 'For God's sake, I just went shopping with Merriman Smith. There's no plot to kidnap Caroline Kennedy.'

"He read the bulletin to me." Afternoon papers printed that day carried a story under Smith's byline that said: "PALM BEACH, Fla.—Federal, state and local police late today were searching in this area for four Cubans, believed to be agents of the Castro government, for questioning in connection with a plot to kidnap Caroline Kennedy, 3, daughter of the president and his wife."[91]

"I raced down to the pressroom. There was Smitty at his typewriter, typing away. I walked up to him and said, 'You son of a bitch.' He said, 'You didn't think I was going to tell you about it?'" Davis was too new to the beat to recognize the man Smith spoke to outside the men's store. It was U. E. Baughman, the director of the Secret Service, and he was tipping Smith to the story.[92]

Unlike during the Roosevelt administration, the White House reporters did not cover up news of Kennedy's health. Any news about his health was potentially a good political story, since during the 1960 campaign Kennedy had worked hard to dispel rumors of his extensive medical problems. Smith, Spivak, and Thomas teamed up on a lengthy June 1961 piece about Kennedy's back woes.[93] In the following months, Smith and Spivak heard from sources that Kennedy's back problems were getting worse. Smith on October 1 wrote a memo to several of his bosses that said Kennedy was dealing with the problem with daily bed rest and was shying away from physical exertion. "He swims buck naked in the White House pool each day and on some occasions, seems to evidence discomfort or pain getting in and out of the pool," the memo said.

Smith didn't feel he could write the story just then without seeming "persecutory" or without endangering the jobs of his sources.[94] So he bided his time and worked his sources some more.

The result was a story that ran in newspapers on October 20 that said Kennedy was undertaking "a daily program of muscle-building exercises in the small White House gymnasium under supervision of a New York specialist. For from fifteen to thirty minutes each day, the Chief Executive is bending, twisting, stretching and flexing in exercises designed to strengthen his muscles to the point where he can resume out-of-doors exercise without fear of causing another flare-up of chronic back trouble." The story cited "White House sources" as saying Kennedy's regular doctor regarded his "basic health" as "excellent."[95]

The story didn't provide the damaging information Smith hinted at in his memo. Anyone who has ever been a reporter understands what happened: Sometimes, when you seek one story, you end up with another. Sometimes, you can't report everything you know because you simply can't confirm it.

A few months later, Smith's sources and instincts came into play in an incident that brought glee to his editors. While the Kennedy family was visiting Palm Beach in December 1961, a local nightclub owner used the first family's fame to promote his business. John Phelan let it be known to editors at the *Fort Lauderdale News* that Jacqueline Kennedy showed up on a Friday night at his Golden Falcon Lounge and danced the "twist." Editors at the *News* decided Phelan was trying to pull a fast one and killed the story. But somehow, the Associated Press caught wind of Phelan's yarn and put it on the wire. The AP story said Mrs. Kennedy and her entourage, including Secret Service agents, were at the lounge for an hour and a half. "Mrs. Kennedy, wearing black slacks and a blue sweater over her shoulders, danced 'much of the time' she was there," the AP story said.

According to UPI internal memos, the AP moved the story at 8:57 a.m. Eastern time on December 23, a Saturday. That was early enough for the story to be set in type for afternoon papers. More than two and a half hours later—at 11:29 a.m.—AP ordered the story killed. But the kill order came after many afternoon papers were already in print. The bogus story ran on front pages in New York, St. Louis, Los Angeles, and Louisville.

Smitty had heard the same rumor that the AP heard, but quickly determined it was bogus. In fact, Jacqueline Kennedy had spent the evening in Palm Beach with her sister, Lee Radziwill, and her brother-in-law, Polish prince Stanislaus Radziwill. UPI moved a story in which Salinger called AP's account of the night club visit "totally untrue" and "a cheap effort by a night club owner to use the first family for publicity purposes." It was a black eye for the AP, which UPI noted to its employees and customers in a report labeled "confidential."[96] Smitty's handling of the affair made him look golden, again.

The Kennedys didn't make it easy to get personal stories. Jackie Kennedy pushed back hard against the coverage of their family life. "She never came to terms with the reality of living in a goldfish bowl or the intense interest she and her family created by virtue of living in the White House," Thomas wrote.[97]

Her dislike of the spotlight was sometimes fodder for "Backstairs" columns. Just weeks after the Kennedys moved into the White House, Jackie ordered her staff to stop talking to reporters about her redecoration of the family quarters. "She disliked the daily stories about her conferences with art experts, painters and redecorators," Smith reported. "If the lady wants the walls a particular shade, she wants them all done before her color schemes are held up to public appraisal and comment."[98]

Jackie Kennedy particularly disliked handshaking and public appearances. Smith reported in a May 1962 "Backstairs" column that some Democrats grumbled that Jackie needed to take "a more active part in politics." The column reported her shyness before a crowd of two thousand Democratic women who showed up to hear her husband speak on the South Lawn of the White House. Vice President Lyndon Johnson had to nudge her into shaking hands with some in the crowd. "Young lady, c'mon now, they're waiting to see you as much as the President," Johnson told her.[99] "God bless you, Jacqueline!" some of the women shouted. "The First Lady seemed quite embarrassed," Smith wrote.[100] But in a book published years later, Smith said that Jackie was actually pleased that Johnson had encouraged her toward the crowd.

Smith participated in some of the grumbling about Jackie's glamour. One night, Smith appeared on *The Tonight Show* when Groucho Marx was the guest host. Smith remarked that it was undignified for the First Lady to be seen on water skis.

"I'd rather see her on them than Mamie Eisenhower," Marx replied. The line brought a gale of audience laughter.[101]

Some details about the First Family's life were off limits. Salinger and the White House made a very firm rule against reporting the food, toy, or clothing preferences of the Kennedy children. The problem was that people were simply too generous. "Shortly after a story appeared that Caroline liked chocolate, the White House was flooded with everything from Hershey Bars to a six-foot, 190-pound chocolate rabbit from Switzerland," Smith wrote.[102]

The youthful and glamorous atmosphere the Kennedys brought to Washington greatly interested Smith. He wrote a snarky book about how the Kennedys differed from their predecessors. *The Good New Days,* published in 1962, identified those who arrived in Washington after the Kennedy election as "N.P.," or "new people," and those who'd been there before the Kennedys as "O.P.," or "old people."

The Good New Days talked little about policy. But its blind anecdotes about ladder-climbing socialites who boasted of being tossed into swimming pools at wild parties held by the Kennedys and their friends and aides were good fodder for *The Tonight Show* in August 1962, when Merv Griffin was guest hosting. "There are more people who have gone into various Kennedy swimming pools than there are Indian maidens in Lake Minnetonka," Smith said. "Aspiring men in Washington now put on their dinner jackets and jump in the bathtub—and next morning their wives hang the jacket out on the line as a status symbol."[103]

The book discussed the Kennedys' weekends in Virginia horse country—Jackie was an avid equestrian—and the status symbols sought by other Washingtonians of the Kennedy years, such as reserved parking spaces and spots for their children in elite private schools.

Much about Kennedy's personal life went unreported. Just as the press corps overlooked what it knew about Franklin Roosevelt's health, the reporters also overlooked Kennedy's sexual dalliances.

Many had heard the stories. In May 1959, the editors of *Uncensored,* a New York–based scandal magazine, forwarded to the FBI a pair of letters they had received regarding allegations of Kennedy's womanizing. One letter, dated April 29, 1959, was signed by Florence Kater, an acquaintance of a woman with whom Kennedy was supposedly having an affair. Kater, apparently disturbed by the affair—her exact motive is unclear—began following Kennedy around. The letter, which Kater sent to thirty-five journalists, described how she and her husband encountered Kennedy at 3:00 a.m one morning in July 1958 on a Washington street. According to the letter, Kennedy threatened her husband's job as a salesman for a company that did business with the military "if either of you spread any lies about me." The second letter *Uncensored* forwarded to the FBI was a follow-up to the first. It was dated May 27, 1959, and was not signed. This letter was accompanied by a photograph Kater took with the caption: "Here is Senator John F. Kennedy of Massachusetts, hand hiding his face, recently snapped when leaving his girlfriend's house at one o'clock in the morning. She is a 'glamour-type' employee of his." *Uncensored* never used the story. Nor did any of the thirty-five reporters who received the first letter. But a copy of both letters made it into FBI Director J. Edgar Hoover's personal files.[104]

Smith heard some of the evidence himself. During an August 1962 visit to Yosemite National Park in California, Kennedy, Smith, and everyone else in the presidential party stayed at the Ahwahnee Lodge, on the floor of the Yosemite Valley. The hotel's rooms were not air conditioned. Instead, they were fitted with transom windows above their doors, which guests could open if they wanted fresh air. Late that night, Smith walked past Kennedy's room. Seated by the door as always was an Army Signal Corpsman who held the brief-case that carried the codes Kennedy would need to launch nuclear weapons. The Signal Corpsmen were always at Kennedy's side.

The transom over the door to Kennedy's room was open. As Smith passed, he heard a woman's voice through the window: "I don't care if you are the President of the United States. I am not doing that!" Smith soon told the story to his friend June Lockhart. "That transom slammed shut," Lockhart recounted. "Smitty stopped. He made eye contact with the Signal Corps guy and they just shared a little smirk—no conversation. Then he continued on down the hall."[105]

"It is enough to say that the White House press corps and the people working in the White House were very much aware that there were lots of fun and games going on," said Barbara Gamarekian, a Salinger aide who discussed Kennedy's affair with college intern Mimi Alford in a 1964 oral history interview with the John F. Kennedy Library. The interview was sealed until 1984, and was finally reported by historian Robert Dallek in 2003.[106]

Kennedy didn't believe the mainstream press would call him out on his behavior.[107] But Smitty, the most mainstream of all reporters, walked up to the edge of the subject a few months after the Yosemite visit, in a December 1962 "Backstairs" column. The column borrowed from an interview in the *Sunday Times* of London with Jonathan Miller, a British cabaret star who was appearing in Washington. "I think sex is the cement of the New Frontier," Miller told Henry Brandon, the *Sunday Times*'s well-connected Washington correspondent. "A special sort of girl has turned out for it . . . what's interesting is that one attractive president has attracted to him more girls than a president can use."[108]

Smith quoted liberally from the story and wrote that it would be interesting to see whether the piece affected Brandon's relationships in Washington. Brandon was a friend of Jackie's since before she married Kennedy, and he was a regular White House guest. Smith was "clearly hoping to start a little brawl," Brandon wrote in a memoir. "But the president had far too good a sense of humor to react in that way." Kennedy probably saw the story as a help, Brandon said—"Miller's sallies would only add to his sex appeal."[109]

Journalists came even closer to exposing Kennedy's personal life in October 1963, when the *Des Moines Register* dug up a story about Ellen Rometsch, a twenty-five-year-old German woman whom FBI Director J. Edgar Hoover feared was an East German spy. West German investigators said she was not. In any case, Rometsch and her husband were hustled back to West Germany several weeks before the *Register's* story broke. The FBI was reportedly worried about her "friendships in high places." Kennedy biographer Dallek says Rometsch "made repeated visits to the White House, where she attended naked pool parties and had sex with Kennedy."[110] But news stories of the time did not link her to the president.

Spivak heard about Kennedy's dalliances. "One woman told me of having been invited but said she turned him down. Another woman provided me with chapter and verse of episodes involving not her (because she said she was on the scene but with another guy) but other females whom she named to me. And there were some episodes that provided clear circumstantial indications," he said. "But no proof." Even if he had proof, Spivak said, the journalistic conventions of the day would have kept him and any other reporter from getting such a story on the UPI wire. "It just wasn't done, especially if a president was involved," he said.[111]

Other reporters of the era concur that even with proof, the mainstream media would not have exposed Kennedy's affairs. "If I phoned that in to my office and said I wanted to do a story on it, they would have told me I was crazy," said Sid Davis. "There wasn't a legitimate newspaper that would have printed that stuff."[112]

A story about Kennedy's sex life could have come along that the reporters could not ignore. At the same time Kennedy was enjoying his White House dalliances, the Profumo affair was making news in England. John Profumo, minister of war in Prime Minister Harold Macmillan's cabinet, was having an affair with nineteen-year-old Christine Keeler, who was also sleeping with a Soviet naval attaché. It was the height of the Cold War, and Profumo's affair raised fears that Keeler had spread state secrets to the Soviet Union. Profumo lied about the affair to Parliament and had to resign. Macmillan himself quit at the urging of his own government days before the Rometsch story broke. Kennedy followed the Profumo scandal closely.

There were lines Smith and the other reporters covering Kennedy would not cross. Smith wrote what he could reliably learn about the president's health and his sex life—which, in the end, was not much.

That nothing Smith wrote on those topics got him into lasting trouble with Kennedy or his aides speaks to the complexity of relationships between reporters and the people they cover. Reporters might or might not like the people they write about. And newsmakers might or might not like the reporters who cover them. There is always tension between politicians trying to burnish their images and the reporters pursuing stories that might cast politicians in a bad light.

A year after Kennedy's death, Smith wrote that he "felt Kennedy understood me and my (professional) problems; that he never talked down to me, threatened me or attempted flattery. He was a consummate politician . . . but I never got the feeling that Kennedy was lying to me—at least, in private or off-guard conversation."[113] Malcolm Kilduff, Salinger's deputy press secretary, thought highly of Smith, and trusted that when he told Smith something off the record it stayed off the record.[114] Maybe Smith wasn't as close to the president's inner circle as he was during the Truman and Eisenhower administrations, but at least Smith, Kennedy, and Kennedy's aides dealt with each other from positions of mutual respect. Everyone knew the rules.

CHAPTER 4 ✦ TEXAS

THE NIGHT BEFORE HE WAS to leave with President Kennedy on a political trip to Texas, Smitty stewed in his Washington apartment. His family life was in turmoil, he was broke, and he was having trouble at work. His mood was angry and bitter.

Seven months earlier, in April 1963, Smith left his wife, Ellie. Smith long believed she was mentally ill, and what Smith called her "rages and torments" were an issue for the family for years.[115] A succession of psychiatric treatments, including a hospital stay around 1950, was no help. Finally, Smith hit a breaking point. "She shouts in front of the children about my being a drunk, a dope addict, and a keeper of assorted mistresses." Just before the breakup, his mother was considering a visit to the Smiths' house in northwest Washington. "Surely, you don't want to walk into this maelstrom," Smith wrote to her. His mother stayed home.

One of Ellie's allegations was that Smith was having an affair with the proprietor of a restaurant in Middleburg, Virginia, where the Kennedys spent their weekends. "When the mood hits her, she gets on the telephone, denouncing me to friends and deliberately trying to injure me professionally."[116] Ellie even wrote a bitter letter to an elderly member of Smith's family who was on her deathbed. "Let's keep our fight between us and attempt to settle it with a minimum of damage to others," Smith implored his wife after hearing of the letter.[117] She did not back down. "Ellie has undertaken a program of real harassment . . . she calls the office and tells anyone in charge that she and the children 'have no food money,'" Smith told his mother.[118]

The separation worsened his money situation. He was so far behind on his income taxes, the Internal Revenue Service took all of his earnings from *The Good New Days*.[119]

Smith was in this hole even though by the standards of twenty-first-century print or text journalists, he was very well paid. After taxes, he took home $257 per week from his UPI paycheck—$1,028 per month. Adjusted for inflation to 2016 dollars, that's roughly $8,000 per month, or $96,400 per year, after taxes. Before the tax man got his substantial cut, Smitty was making the modern equivalent of a six-figure salary.

And that was just his UPI pay. Smith earned $600 per month, before taxes, to write a column for *Nation's Business,* a monthly magazine published by the US Chamber of Commerce.[120] That works out to about $4,650 per month in 2015 dollars. He also freelanced magazine articles and was paid for lectures he gave around the country. He earned money for TV appearances too, though that income might have been a bit off that year. Smith was a regular on news programs, and that February, he was a panelist on the game show *To Tell the Truth*. But in 1961 Smith stopped appearing on Jack Paar's show because he and his bosses were weary of Paar's denunciations of the news media and of what Smith saw as Paar's "sweeping disregard for fact."[121]

Smith had barely enough cash to live apart from his wife and maintain his family's lifestyle. His two youngest children, Tim and Allison, still attended Sidwell Friends, a costly private school. At least Merriman Jr. was out of college now. Smith fantasized about the day he'd finally be free of tuition bills. "On that distant day when Tim and Allison are through college, I intend to put down my typewriter and walk calmly into the sea like the lemmings of Alaska," he said.[122]

The whole situation was very frustrating. "All I do is work and pay," he complained in a letter to his wife on October 25. He admitted getting behind on some of the family's bills for a "simple" reason: "I didn't have the money," he told Ellie. "God knows, if I had it, I'd pay all bills of any description and thus remove myself from any contentious contact with you. For you to picture me as a profligate skinflint bent on starving you and the children, depriving you of clothes and medical care and in general, persecuting you economically ignores—it tragically ignores the years I labored, and still labor, to provide.

"Think of the countless times I bought beautiful things for you when people were smirking at the inferior nature of my clothes," he went on. "I didn't care then, but to reap the bitter harvest of your twisted wrath now is . . . quite sad."[123]

On top of his day-to-day financial stress, Smith was thousands of dollars behind in his expense reports. In 1963, United Press International was a worldwide operation, with thousands of employees in more than two hundred bureaus around the globe, and an annual budget of $43.5 million—equal to $337 million in 2015 dollars.[124] But despite its global reach, the company seemed to run on a shoestring. UPI employees—"Unipressers"—were always being advised to "downhold" expenses. Unlike the AP, a nonprofit cooperative owned by its customers, UPI's owners expected to have money left over. Smitty was UPI's biggest star, and his bosses wanted to keep him happy. But UPI was also cheap, and its stinginess collided with Smith's inability to keep up with the paperwork he needed to file to be reimbursed for his work-related expenses.

All of it boiled over on November 20, 1963, when UPI Washington bureau news editor Julius Frandsen wrote Smith a "curt note," as Smith put it, denying him an advance on his travel expenses for Kennedy's Texas tour because he was behind on his expenses. The note infuriated Smith. "I've ranged this country from corner to corner on promotional appearances for UPI, at times when I was sick or utterly exhausted; speaking, shaking hands, sitting up all night with clients and staffers, preaching UPI like a religion," he wrote that night in a letter to Frandsen. As Smith read Frandsen's note, he "thought of some of the tanktown airports where I've waited at dawn this past year; the rooms packed with stewed clients; 2 a.m. in a dozen pressrooms doing the overnight after having missed lunch and dinner because we were so woefully understaffed."

Over the years, Smith's bosses at UPI had sent him countless *atta-boy* notes praising his stories. He'd also collected piles of thank-you notes and grateful letters from various UPI managers and customers. That night, all the praise seemed meaningless next to his other problems. In his angry and frustrated state, those notes and letters were just so much garbage. "I picked up the whole mess and threw it down the apartment incinerator because that's where this sort of crap belongs; that is how much it is worth."[125]

This was Smitty's state of mind as he headed with President Kennedy to Texas. He had to go anyhow. Al Spivak was not yet back from a vacation, and Helen Thomas was about to leave on one. There was no one else to pick up the slack. The Associated Press sent two Washington reporters on the trip. UPI sent only Smith.

Kennedy's two-and-a-half-day trip was to include stops in five Texas cities: San Antonio, Houston, Fort Worth, Dallas, and Austin. The visit had two purposes. One was straight-up electoral politics. Kennedy planned to run for reelection in 1964, and he saw winning Texas as essential to his chances. Though the state was dominated by Democrats at the time, its Republican party was growing. Many journalists thought the most likely Republican presidential candidate in 1964, Barry Goldwater, had a good shot at winning the state. The trip was an opportunity for Kennedy to show his flag—to be seen by the public, give speeches about issues concerning Texas voters, and gain some goodwill ahead of the upcoming campaign.

The other purpose of the trip was to heal a feud between warring factions of the Texas Democratic party. On one side were Kennedy's vice president, Lyndon Johnson, and Governor John Connally, political powerhouses who were seen as of the Texas party's moderate to conservative wing. On the other side of the ideological divide was Senator Ralph Yarborough, a liberal Democrat. Robert MacNeil, a reporter for NBC News, was prepped for the trip with an elaborate memo on Texas politics from an NBC producer in Dallas. The dispute between the various party factions "has in the final week preceding Kennedy's visit created a hornet's nest into which he could walk. He will have to delicately control this controversy in his 2½ days here," the memo said.[126]

Much of the feud centered around party money and resources. The party's conservative wing, dominated by Texas businessmen, disliked the idea that a portion of the money it raised at a dinner Connally planned to host for Kennedy in Austin would go to the national party, which they believed sometimes worked against its interests. The party's liberal wing believed the other half of the money, retained by a unit of the Democratic party Connally controlled, would be used against them. Liberals feared the money Connally raised would be used to challenge Yarborough in a party primary in 1964.

The planned three-hour visit to Dallas further complicated the picture. Some of Kennedy's people thought the Dallas stop was a bad idea. The city was a hotbed of radical right-wing politics, stoked by the presence of retired General Edwin Walker, a prominent rightwinger and John Birch Society leader. When Walker was still in the US Army, President Eisenhower admonished him for some of his public statements. Kennedy dismissed him from the US Army in 1961 after he called Eleanor Roosevelt and Harry Truman "pink"—a code word of the time for being sympathetic to communist ideas.

Walker wasn't the only radical in town. During the 1960 presidential campaign, a crowd of Dallas Republicans booed and hissed at Lyndon Johnson and his wife as they headed through the lobby of the Adolphus Hotel to a Democratic rally. The Republicans held signs calling him a "traitor" and a "Texas Turncoat." The state's only Republican congressman, Representative Bruce Alger of Dallas, held a sign calling Johnson a "Judas."[127] And on October 24, 1963, just a month before Kennedy's planned visit, a protester used a protest sign to whack Adlai Stevenson, the former Democratic presidential candidate who was Kennedy's ambassador to the United Nations. Stevenson, who was in Dallas to give a speech, told Kennedy aide Arthur Schlesinger Jr. that he was shocked by the hatred he found there and wondered if it was a good idea for Kennedy to visit the city.[128] Byron Skelton, a Texas member of the Democratic National Committee, was also worried. He forwarded to the White House a statement by Walker calling Kennedy "a liability to the free world." "A man who would make that kind of statement is capable of doing harm to the President," Skelton wrote. "I would feel better if the President's itinerary did not include Dallas." Kenneth O'Donnell, a top Kennedy aide, decided showing the letter to the president would be a waste of time. Kennedy was set on making the trip.[129]

The possibility of mayhem, violent or otherwise, made the trip irresistible to some reporters. If something happened, it would make a great story. Jacqueline Kennedy's decision to go along added to the trip's newsworthiness. Henry Brandon of the *Sunday Times* of London, a longtime friend of Jackie's, originally planned to skip the Texas trip. "But when it was announced that Jackie would be accompanying him and, possibly, even make a campaign speech or two, I was tempted," he said. "Jackie hated politics . . . she loathed crowds, shaking hands and being on display." Even better: Brandon heard from a White House aide "that there had been warnings of possible trouble." He learned later the aide was talking about the Stevenson incident and the Skelton plea. The chance that something might happen clinched Brandon's decision to go.[130] He was the only foreign reporter on the trip.

Air Force One left Andrews Air Force Base at 11:05 a.m. on November 21.[131] Smith, as a wire service representative, was one of four "pool" reporters scheduled to be aboard Kennedy's plane. UPI and its rival the Associated Press were guaranteed spots with the president. Every significant broadcast station and daily newspaper subscribed to one or both of the wires, so having them in the pool assured the news media quick access to the president's activities. Broadcast and newspaper reporters rotated in and out of the other two pool spots. Twenty-two years after his arrival on the White House beat, Smitty was still one of the "ghouls" President Roosevelt had jokingly complained about.

A Pan Am charter carrying the rest of the Washington reporters on the trip left Andrews about an hour ahead of Kennedy's jet. The idea was for the press plane to arrive at each stop before Kennedy's plane, so the reporters could observe the pomp and ceremony of the president's arrival in each city. In all, fifty-eight Washington-based reporters, photographers, and technicians were on the trip. There's never a shortage of people recording a president's activities.

To judge from UPI's copy, not much political healing occurred in the trip's first hours. In Dallas, Kennedy was to speak before 2,400 people at an invitation-only luncheon at the giant hall of the Dallas Trade Mart. UPI ran a story saying that Yarborough's liberal faction of the Democratic party was offended because it believed the invitations were controlled by Dallas's Republican establishment. "From the invitation list so far in Dallas, one would think Nixon won and was coming to Dallas to greet his dedicated workers," an anonymous source grumbled.[132] The Dallas lunch was hosted by the Dallas Citizens Council, a group of corporate CEOs and business leaders.[133] The council's chairman was J. Erik Jonsson, a business-man and Dallas political figure who was Richard Nixon's Texas cam-paign manager in 1960. Connally had put the invitations in the hands of the politically moderate Citizens Council in the hope that it would keep the right-wing elements of Dallas's Republican party away. "On the further basis that the luncheon was to be nonpo-litical, most Kennedy Democrats were uninvited," the NBC memo said.[134] After Dallas Democrats complained, some tickets were even-tually parceled out to Kennedy supporters.[135]

Yarborough and his liberal supporters also took offense at Connally's decision not to invite him to a reception in Austin the evening of the Dallas stop. Yarborough said the snub showed the governor was "terribly uneducated governmentally." It wasn't just that US senators don't like being snubbed by governors; they are not supposed to be snubbed, period. Yarborough urged his supporters "to take no offenses," but confirmed his swipe at Connally by adding: "How could you expect anything else?"[136]

Pointing out that the Texas tour wasn't entirely about the feud, Smith filed a story for afternoon papers on November 21 that said the trip was "alternately labeled 'political' and 'non-political' by the White House."

A "non-political" event might have been Kennedy's speech at Brooks Air Force Base in San Antonio, the first stop of the tour, during which the president said the nation's space program "holds the promise of substantial benefits for those of us who are earthbound."[137] The speech provided the first paragraphs of Smith's November 21 story. After the speech, the president and first lady made an unscheduled visit to a laboratory at the air base where four men were living in an oxygen tank, breathing pure oxygen at a simulated altitude of thirty thousand feet. Kennedy peppered the men with questions via a telephone hookup. Then he asked the scientist leading his tour: "Do you think your work might improve oxygen chambers for, say, premature babies?"[138] A few months earlier, Jackie had delivered a premature son, Patrick, who died after a brief struggle for life. Smith and the other reporters missed this part of Kennedy's tour.

Aside from the big crowds, the speeches, and the controversy over the Yarborough-Connally feud, another storyline was emerging from the trip. Jackie Kennedy, overcoming her dislike of campaigning, was a star. Smith picked up on this when the president and Jackie encountered a big crowd of Air Force personnel and civilian workers as they left the air base's laboratory building. "The President began shaking hands and the First Lady, wearing a white wool bouclé two-piece suit and a soft, black cap-like hat on the back of her loosely flowing hair, moved into the crowd," Smitty wrote in some unpublished copy. He originally wrote that Mrs. Kennedy "plunged" into the crowd. Later, he X-ed out the line with his typewriter.

"She reached over rope barricades in response to cries of 'Jackie, over here!'" Smith wrote.

More workers lined up to watch as the Kennedys motored out of the base on their way back to Air Force One. "Several thousand workers were drawn up in a long line beside the driveway. The president had the car halted as he motioned the workers, most of them civilians, to the site of the car.

"This time Mrs. Kennedy shook hands literally over her husband's shoulder, smiling constantly and murmuring 'Thank you' while he grasped other hands," Smith wrote. "The crowd grew so rapidly that Secret Service agents ordered the car to move on."[139]

At a stop in Houston, Mrs. Kennedy made headlines by delivering a short speech in Spanish to the League of United Latin American Citizens, a Hispanic civic group. The speech was just seventy-three words. "I'm very happy to be in the great state of Texas and I'm especially pleased to be with you, who are part of the great Spanish tradition which has contributed so much to Texas," she said. Her husband and Vice President Johnson stood smiling by her side. The crowd applauded wildly.

Later the Kennedys attended a dinner in honor of Representative Albert Thomas, a Houston congressman. That event got only a brief mention in Smith's copy and little mention by other Washington reporters. After the dinner, Kennedy and his entourage went to the airport and flew to Fort Worth. No events were planned in Fort Worth that evening—the official schedule had the president and Mrs. Kennedy arriving at Carswell Air Force Base at 10:45 p.m. and reaching their hotel in downtown Fort Worth twenty-five minutes later. But a big crowd of people hoping for a glimpse of the president and his glamorous wife showed up to see Air Force One's arrival. "People were asking 'Where's Jackie?'" recalled Charles Roberts, who covered the trip for *Newsweek*. As many people seemed to be yelling for Jackie as for her husband.

She shook hands and chatted with spectators along a rope barricade at the air base. Throngs of people lined the route by which the Kennedys traveled to the Hotel Texas. At the hotel, she and her husband shook even more hands. Mrs. Kennedy was moved enough to issue a statement to the media saying she'd had "a wonderful day. Texas friendliness was everything I'd heard it to be."[140] Asked by a reporter for a Fort Worth paper if she was enjoying her trip, she answered: "Yes, I am, unbelievably."[141]

It was nearly 1:00 a.m. by the time Mrs. Kennedy's Secret Service agent, Clint Hill, got her settled in to the Hotel Texas. "I had a craving for a nice big juicy burger and some fries," Hill said. He and everyone else on the trip were tired and hungry, and Hill hadn't eaten anything since lunch. He ran into Smith in the hotel. "Come on along, Clint. We'll get you fed," Smitty said. Hill and some other agents went with Smith to the Fort Worth Press Club, but found the food was gone. Hill had a scotch and soda and some peanuts. They heard of another open spot that was serving food—but all it had was a fruit punch that Hill found horrible. He went back to his room and went to bed.[142] It was a typical evening on a presidential trip—the kind of evening the agents, Smith, and the other reporters knew well.

The events of the following morning in Fort Worth were such a fine example of the Kennedy charisma at work that they stuck long afterward in the minds of some reporters. Roberts said the enthusiastic reception the Kennedys received from excited crowds in Fort Worth was something he would have remembered about November 22 "even if it hadn't come to the end that it did."[143]

Outside the Hotel Texas, a crowd of twelve thousand gathered in hope of seeing Kennedy deliver a brief speech. Some showed up as early as 3:00 a.m. At around 7:30 a.m., Kennedy looked out a hotel window. "Gosh, look at the crowd!" he cried to his wife. "Just look! Isn't that terrific?"[144]

Fifteen minutes later, Kennedy was on a platform speaking to the group, flanked by Vice President Johnson, Senator Yarborough, and Governor Connally—the feuding Texas Democrats he was aiming to bring together. It was raining lightly—"a chilling drizzle," wrote one reporter—and someone offered Kennedy a coat. "I don't need it. I'm just fine," he said. Kennedy mentioned the unpleasant weather when he began his brief speech: "There are no faint hearts here!" The crowd roared. "Where's Jackie?" someone yelled. The president pointed to the window of her eighth-floor hotel room. "Mrs. Kennedy is organizing herself," he said. "It takes her a little longer, but, of course, she looks better than we do when she does it."[145]

"This crowd was tremendously enthusiastic," Roberts recalled. After the speech, Kennedy stepped down from the platform "and practically disappeared into the crowd."[146] An eight-year-old girl cried because the president passed by without shaking her hand. "Let me touch you: I love you, we all love you," a young woman screamed. After he shook hands all around the perimeter of the crowd, Kennedy worked his way back toward the Hotel Texas. He stopped for a moment to shake hands with a mounted sheriff's deputy. The deputy sat on his horse in the middle of the street wearing a movie-style Western outfit.[147]

As he headed for the hotel's huge ballroom, Kennedy walked past a roped-off area, still shaking hands as he moved along. "They were ecstatic to see him," said Robert MacNeil. "It was like God or Jesus Christ was passing by."[148] MacNeil saw Kennedy wipe one of his hands on a folded white handkerchief. It was stained black with the grime Kennedy had picked up from all his handshaking. The president enjoyed his time with the crowd. "Well, that was very good," he said to Representative Jim Wright, a Texas congressman.

"One woman was hysterical that she couldn't touch Kennedy," MacNeil said. Wright reached out and touched the woman; simultaneously, he touched Kennedy. "She was happy," MacNeil said. "It was as if an electric current had passed through them."

"Things are going much better than I had expected," the president told Henry Brandon as he worked his way toward the hotel ballroom.[149] Brandon thought the rousing reception Kennedy was enjoying in hostile Texas would be an important element of his story that week.

Moments later, in a hotel hallway, Kennedy encountered Senator Yarborough. Though Yarborough, Connally, and Johnson had appeared on the platform with him during his outdoor speech, Yarborough's feud with Connally and Johnson was still alive. Yarborough was still petulant over what he saw as his mistreatment, and Kennedy was fed up. "For Christ's sake cut it out, Ralph," the president snapped.[150] To encourage the appearance of party unity, Kennedy ordered Yarborough to ride in the vice president's car that day. The internecine feud had gotten to the point where such minor points as who rode in which car with whom or who got to sit where on the dais at a party dinner were matters of great importance.

Kennedy's speech inside the Hotel Texas was before a group of two thousand local civic leaders at an event sponsored by the Fort Worth Chamber of Commerce. His main topic was a fighter jet deal awarded to defense contractor General Dynamics, which planned to carry out most of the work at its Fort Worth plant.

MacNeil had Smitty's help making his way into the hotel ballroom. Inside, he saw one empty seat at the head table. "Where's Jackie? Where's Jackie?" said people in the crowd. MacNeil next made his way to the kitchen entrance, and there she was, just out of the crowd's view, wearing a wool suit the color of strawberry ice cream with a matching pillbox hat and white gloves. MacNeil thought she looked "radiant." She was happy, "smirking and laughing," he recalled.

"She was stunningly dressed," said radio reporter Sid Davis. Her suit was "beautiful. It fit her to a 'T.'"[151]

Raymond Buck, the Chamber of Commerce president and the event's master of ceremonies, introduced one by one the local dignitaries seated at the head table: Vice President Johnson, Fort Worth's mayor, several politicians, and officials of the Chamber of Commerce. Finally, he said: "And now is an event that I know you have all been waiting for."[152] And there was Jackie, twenty minutes late. The crowded exploded in wild applause as she headed toward that empty seat next to her husband.

"At the back of the room, the reporters laughed about it and wondered how they could describe so blatant a bit of staging without going too far," MacNeil wrote. He turned to Godfrey McHugh, a US Air Force general and Kennedy military aide, and asked: "How would you describe that entrance?"

"Tactical," McHugh answered.[153] Jackie's entrance was winning Kennedy votes.

Kennedy deployed the same line he'd used in Europe to discuss his wife's appearance. "Two years ago, I introduced myself in Paris by saying that I was the man who had accompanied Mrs. Kennedy to Paris. I'm getting somewhat that same sensation as I travel around Texas. . . . Nobody wonders what Lyndon and I wear." The line brought the house down.

The rest of Kennedy's speech emphasized national defense—red meat for the Texas audience. He pointed out that his administration planned to increase the number of Polaris nuclear submarines and Minuteman missiles. "We're stronger, and with that strength is a determination to not only maintain the peace but also the vital interests of the United States," he said. The speech seemed like a direct response to Dallas publisher E. M. Dealey's crude complaint that Kennedy was a "weak sister."

Upstairs in his hotel room after the speech, Kennedy changed his shirt and tie and then spoke for a few moments with Vice President Johnson and Johnson's sister, Lucia Alexander, a Fort Worth resident. Johnson found that Kennedy was enthused by the crowd that had waited hours in the rain to hear his outdoor speech. Also, Johnson said in an interview years later with Walter Cronkite of CBS News, Kennedy "was stimulated by the leaders of business, labor and political groups and the real power structure of the state that was at this breakfast."

"You can be sure of one thing," Kennedy told Johnson. "We're going to carry two states next year—Massachusetts and Texas. We're going to carry at least two states."

"We're going to carry a lot more than those two," Johnson assured the president.

Johnson said of Kennedy's optimistic words: "It was about as near bragging as I ever heard him."[154]

At the same time, the reporters hurried to file copy. Smith didn't write that morning about Jackie's grand entrance, her strawberry suit, or the other aspects of her appearance. He covered the outdoor speech by emphasizing Kennedy's statement that the United States was about to test a rocket booster powerful enough to, in Smith's words, "put the nation far ahead of Russia in the space race." He covered the indoor speech as being about the new fighter jet, and noted that Kennedy "reminded the businessmen of Fort Worth that Texas—and this city in particular—was getting a major share of the defense dollar." He wrote that Kennedy was "campaigning as though it were election time."[155]

Smitty's copy, aimed at that day's afternoon newspapers, did not cover Mrs. Kennedy's emergence as a top-notch campaigner. He'd tried that angle the night before in his unpublished copy. Maybe his editors were not interested. But some of his colleagues thought that angle was developing into the most interesting news story of the Texas tour.

Brandon considered a lighthearted approach to his *Sunday Times* story. He wrote a draft that portrayed Kennedy's visit as a "guerrilla" incursion into the enemy territory that was Texas. "As his secret weapon and perhaps also with his security in mind he had brought Mrs. Kennedy along," the draft said.[156] MacNeil had a similar idea, though without the battle analogy. As he helped his cameraman collapse their equipment at the Hotel Texas, he said: "If nothing else happens, we have got a story with Jackie."

CHAPTER 5 ✦ THE WIRE CAR

IT TOOK EIGHT MINUTES FOR the journalists to fly from Carswell Air Force Base in Fort Worth to Love Field in Dallas—a flight so quick, Robert MacNeil barely had time to finish the Bloody Mary served him by a Pan Am stewardess. "I was still tipping the glass up and the ice and lemon slice bumped against my nose when we landed," he said.[157] Bloody Marys were a tradition on morning White House press flights. The reporters welcomed them that day—the late-night drinking and partying in Fort Worth had left many in a stupor. MacNeil went to bed at 2:30 a.m. and slept just three and a half hours. Between the Bloody Mary and his insignificant breakfast, he felt light-headed.

At least the Dallas stopover promised the reporters easy duty. The motorcade was essentially a parade, and probably there wouldn't be much to do until Kennedy's speech at the Dallas Trade Mart.

Air Force One landed a few minutes after the press plane, giving everyone a chance to again cover the president and first lady's arrival in a new city. Vice President Johnson greeted the president and Mrs. Kennedy heartily, as if he were welcoming them to Texas for the first time. Of course, Johnson had also greeted the Kennedys the day before in San Antonio, Houston, and Fort Worth. If this pomp and ceremony was interesting at all, it was to the local journalists who glommed on to the tour at each stop.

The crowd at Love Field that morning was bigger and friendlier than anyone had expected. The sun was out, and it was nearly seventy degrees. The sky was so bright, MacNeil's eyes ached. Someone handed Mrs. Kennedy a bouquet of bloodred roses, which MacNeil thought beautifully complemented her strawberry wool suit. The president took his wife by the hand to the airport fence to greet their adoring fans, who wanted to touch them. Charles Roberts of *Newsweek* asked Mrs. Kennedy how she liked campaigning. "It's wonderful. It's wonderful," she said.[158]

Smitty and Associated Press White House reporter Frank Cormier were scheduled to be the wire service reporters in the Dallas press pool. They were to be joined by a broadcast reporter, Bob Clark of ABC News, and a newspaper reporter, Robert Baskin of the *Dallas Morning News*. The pool rode near the front of the motorcade in what White House reporters called the wire car. That day, the wire car was a blue hardtop Chevy equipped with a radiotelephone. AT&T provided the car and phone to the White House press.

Smitty was a competitor. However hungover he was, whatever anger he harbored against his bosses over his expense account, Smith was, as always, poised to battle his colleagues to get the story first and right. Like a prizefighter climbing through the ropes into a boxing ring, Smith that morning took the middle front seat spot next to the wire car's radiotelephone. The driver was on Smith's left. Kennedy's deputy press secretary, Malcolm Kilduff, was on Smith's right.

Cormier, Smith's usual opposite number at the AP, skipped the wire car that morning. In his place was Jack Bell, a veteran AP Washington reporter who specialized in covering the US Senate and national politics. Bell wanted to ride in the wire car so he'd be in a better position to write about the crowds that greeted the Kennedys in Dallas. "He rarely covered the president. This was a big thing for him," said Sid Davis. Cormier preferred the collegiality of the press buses and had no problem giving up his pool spot to Bell. Besides, Bell was more senior.

Sometimes, AP and UPI reporters took turns sitting by the wire car's radiotelephone. It might have been the AP's turn to sit next to the phone that day in Dallas. Bell either didn't know or didn't care. He was not a White House regular like Smitty. He sat in the back, with Clark and Baskin.

If Bell had insisted it was AP's turn to sit by the phone, Smith might have put up a fight. In fact, it didn't matter if the car had a radiotelephone. In motorcades, Smitty demanded choice front-seat spots he believed he needed and deserved as one of the "regulars" in the White House press corps whose job was to always be with the president.

Robert Donovan learned this the hard way in 1947, early in his days as a Washington reporter for the *New York Herald Tribune*. Donovan climbed into the front seat of a limousine that would take some reporters from the White House to a nearby hotel where President Truman was to give a speech. Smith demanded that he move to the back. "The front seat, he gave me to understand, was his by absolute right of something—seniority, I suppose," Donovan said. The fuss escalated to the point where a Secret Service agent politely suggested Donovan move to the back. He did.

Donovan eventually realized Smith had a practical reason for being in front: "He never forgot that by being in the front seat he would be closer to any sudden incident involving the president than the reporters in the rear seat."[159]

Sitting by the phone suited Smith as a gadget freak who liked anything that got his stories out quicker. The radiotelephone, a two-way radio link to the Dallas telephone exchange, would let Smith inform his editors instantly of anything that happened on the motorcade route. His non-wire service competitors didn't care as much about being in constant touch with their offices. Sid Davis, a regular in the wire car's broadcast seat, said Smitty's insistence on sitting next to the radiotelephone was something of a joke to his colleagues, since he was usually the only reporter who wanted to use it.

Smitty, forty-eight years old, and Bell, fifty-nine, were longtime rivals. They stood next to each other at Harry Truman's first presidential news conference in 1945, and they competed with each other to cover New York Governor Thomas Dewey's 1948 presidential campaign. Smith believed Bell tried to undermine him by telling Dewey's staff that he was a secret Truman supporter sent from Washington to do a hatchet job. Smith retaliated by being one of the first reporters to use a wire recorder, a precursor to the tape recorder. Soon his dispatches included long quotes from Dewey campaign events. Bell's bosses at the AP asked why his copy didn't read as well as Smith's.[160]

Smith respected Bell enough to praise him as "a fine, tough, competitive reporter"[161] and an expert questioner on the Sunday TV political shows on which they sometimes appeared together.[162] Bell was an expert on the Senate's arcane machinations, and was on a first-name basis with the capital's top politicians. Al Spivak said that when he and Bell traveled to Germany with Vice President Johnson, Bell called him "Lyndon." Spivak stuck with "Mr. Vice President."[163]

Bell was covering the Texas trip as a political story. Morning papers around the country on November 22 carried his report of Kennedy's first day in Texas. It noted that at one point during the day, Kennedy put his arm around Senator Yarborough. That embrace "made it unlikely" that Johnson or Connally would force Yarborough to face a primary challenge in 1964, "even had they wanted to do so."[164] That kind of political inside baseball was Bell's stock-in-trade.

Bell was not known for covering breaking news. A colleague said it probably had been years since Bell wrote a story the AP labeled on its wire as "urgent." If something happened in the motorcade, there was no doubt who would get the story first. When it came to breaking news, Smitty was a gunfighter. "Jack Bell was a very nice man," said MacNeil. "But he was a rather more passive reporter and less aggressive reporter than Smitty." The array of sources Smith accumulated during his twenty-two years on the White House beat added further to his advantage covering any news that would come up that day.

The motorcade, accompanied on the front, sides, and rear by roaring police motorcycles, was a show by itself. It was designed to give the crowds as clear a view as possible of the president and his entourage.

A pilot car preceded the rest of the motorcade by a quarter-mile. Its occupants, Dallas police officers, were supposed to alert police on the ground that the motorcade was coming, and look for signs of trouble. Next came the lead car, described in the Warren Commission report as a "rolling communications car." It was driven by Dallas Police Chief Jesse Curry, and its passengers included Dallas County Sheriff J. E. Decker and chief Dallas Secret Service agent Forrest Sorrels.

The third car was Kennedy's limousine, a specially built 1961 Lincoln convertible with District of Columbia license plate GG 300. In his copy, Smith called the limo "the famous bubble-top from Washington." It had a clear Plexiglas top that could be removed in good weather. The Secret Service decided at Love Field that the president, First Lady, Governor Connally, and the governor's wife would ride in the open, without the bubble top. Leaving the top off would give the crowds a better view of the president, which was the main point of the motorcade. In any case, the bubble top was not bulletproof.

An American flag was attached to the limo's front right side, and the president's flag was on the front left. The back of the car was designed so Secret Service agents could ride on it like firefighters clinging to the back of a fire truck. Two grab handles were attached to the trunk, above steps in the rear bumper where the agents could stand. But the agents were to avoid riding on the limousine's bumper in Dallas. President Kennedy worried that having agents hanging on to the car's back would distract the crowds from him.

Inside the limo, President Kennedy sat in the right-hand rear seat. His wife was next to him on the left. Governor Connally occupied a jump seat on the right side of the car, in front of the president. His wife occupied a jump seat in front of Mrs. Kennedy. The jump seats faced forward and were positioned about three inches lower than the Kennedys' seats.

Behind the presidential limousine came the Secret Service follow-up car, a custom-built 1955 Cadillac. It carried eight Secret Service agents—two in the front seats, two in the rear seats, and four standing on running boards installed on each side of the car. Clint Hill, Mrs. Kennedy's Secret Service agent, stood on the forward part of the running board on the car's left side. That put him behind the First Lady's position in the presidential limousine. Joining the agents in the car's right and left jump seats were Kennedy aides David Powers and Kenneth O'Donnell.

Two to three car-lengths behind the presidential follow-up car was the Lincoln convertible carrying Vice President Johnson; his wife, Lady Bird Johnson; and Senator Ralph Yarborough. Kennedy succeeded in persuading Yarborough to ride with Johnson in Dallas in a show of party unity. Johnson's car was supposed to maintain some distance from Kennedy's car "so that spectators would normally turn their gaze from the President's automobile by the time the Vice President came into view," the Warren Commission report says.

Next in the procession—directly in front of the wire car—was the vice president's follow-up car, driven by a Dallas cop and carrying three Secret Service agents and Johnson's assistant.

Then came the wire car and cars carrying news photographers and other dignitaries, including the mayor of Dallas and several congressmen. There was a bus for White House staff members and two more buses for the White House press. Tom Wicker, the *New York Times'* White House reporter, was in one of these buses. So was Robert Donovan, who at this point in his career wrote for the *Los Angeles Times*. Also riding on the buses were MacNeil and reporters for the *New York Daily News,* the *New York Herald Tribune,* the *Washington Star,* and the *Washington Post.* The buses also carried writers from papers in Chicago and Philadelphia as well as from smaller cities like Louisville, Newark, Kansas City, and Oklahoma City. In those days lots of newspapers gave readers their own take on national news.

The motorcade headed out of Love Field at about 11:50 a.m., five minutes behind schedule. "It was a balmy, sunny noon as we motored through downtown Dallas behind President Kennedy," Smith wrote in a story that ran in morning newspapers the next day.[165]

The dread some Kennedy associates felt about the Dallas stop was underscored by a full-page ad in that day's *Dallas Morning News* bought by an organization called "The American Fact-Finding Committee." It accused Kennedy of being a Communist sympathizer by asking: "WHY is Latin America turning either anti-American or Communistic?" and "WHY do you say we have built a 'wall of freedom' around Cuba when there is no freedom in Cuba today?" Also ahead of the visit, an anti–United Nations group distributed handbills with Kennedy's picture over the caption "WANTED for TREASON."

The churlish newspaper ad and the handbills did not reflect the mood on the city's streets. Thousands of excited, cheering people lined Dallas's downtown skyscraper canyon hoping for a glimpse of the glamorous president and first lady. "They had a screaming reception," said Donovan. "I can't believe there was ever a point in the life of the Kennedys, in a way, that was as high as that moment in Dallas."[166] Smith called the Dallas UPI bureau to dictate a paragraph about how surprisingly large the crowd was.[167] The enthusiasm matched what the entourage saw during the tour's previous stops. Nellie Connally, "elated by the reception, turned to President Kennedy and said, 'Mr. President, you can't say Dallas doesn't love you.' The president replied, 'That is very obvious.'"[168] All along the route, the Kennedys waved to the adoring crowds.

On its way out of downtown Dallas, the motorcade turned right from Main Street onto North Houston Street, on the eastern side of Dealey Plaza. Next, a short block north, the cars turned sharply left, about 120 degrees, onto Elm Street in front of the Texas School Book Depository, on the plaza's northern side. In the wire car, Smith and Kilduff chatted about how well the trip seemed to be going.[169] Kilduff, misreading the Book Depository's sign, turned to Smith and said: "What the hell is a Book Repository?"[170]

There was a crowd, but it wasn't as thick as downtown—"just a handful of people," recalled Secret Service agent Hill. From his perch on the left side of the follow-up car, Hill scanned the grass on the south side of Elm Street, across from the Book Depository. Kennedy's car was moving at about eleven miles per hour, heading toward an underpass beneath railroad tracks where three roads converged. Once the motorcade cleared this spot, known as the Triple Underpass, it would be a quick ride to the luncheon at the Dallas Trade Mart.

Mrs. Kennedy thought the motorcade had been "hot" and "wild"; the sun was strong in her face. She saw the Triple Underpass up ahead and thought of it as a tunnel. "I thought it would be cool in the tunnel." For a moment, she thought, the sun would not be in her eyes.[171]

Above, at a sixth-floor window in the Book Depository, Lee Harvey Oswald, a Marine-trained marksman, waited until after the presidential limousine passed below. At 12:30 p.m., there was a loud bang, quickly followed by two more.

Oswald fired from behind the president's limousine, above and to its right. His first shot sounded to Mrs. Kennedy like "a motorcycle noise." She heard Governor Connally cry out. "My God, they are going to kill us all," Connally said.[172]

The first shot missed. The second shot traveled through President Kennedy's neck from back to front and continued forward to hit Connally in the right shoulder. Mrs. Kennedy saw a quizzical look on her husband's face. The president raised his left hand to his throat.

Secret Service agent Hill thought he'd heard a firecracker, behind him to his right. He swung his head toward the source of the sound, "and in so doing, my eyes had to cross the Presidential limousine and

I saw President Kennedy grab at himself and lurch forward and to the left."[173] Hill jumped off the follow-up car and sprinted up to the limo.

Then came Oswald's third shot. "The bullet hits its mark, piercing the back of President Kennedy's head, just above and behind his right ear," Hill wrote. "In the same instant, a vile eruption of blood, brain matter, and bone fragments spew out, showering over Mrs. Kennedy, across the trunk, and onto me."[174]

The First Lady saw a flesh-colored piece of her husband's skull torn off—a "perfectly clean piece detaching itself from his head." Then, she said, "he slumped on my lap, his blood and brains were in my lap."[175] "Oh my God, they have shot my husband," she said, cradling him. "I love you, Jack."[176]

The shots came as the wire car passed the front of the Book Depository. It was below Oswald's perch, a few hundred feet behind the presidential limousine. The reporters weren't sure what the first sound was. "There was a loud bang as though a giant firecracker had exploded in the caverns between the tall buildings we were just leaving behind us," wrote Bell. Then they heard the next two shots. Smith was a gun enthusiast—he owned several guns and sometimes visited the Secret Service pistol range. "[T]he second and third blasts were unmistakable. Gunfire," he wrote.

Spectators dived for cover. Some shielded their children.

The journalist with the closest view of the assassination was James Altgens, a Dallas-based AP photographer. Altgens had waited near the Book Depository all morning in hope of snapping a dramatic picture of Kennedy's motorcade as it emerged from Main Street's skyscraper canyon into Dealey Plaza's wide-open space. He was in front of the car to its left when the first bullet was fired. The car continued rolling, and Altgens was just fifteen feet from Kennedy when Oswald fired the second shot. When the third bullet hit the president, "fragments of his head fell right at my feet," Altgens remembered. "That was some heck of an explosion when it hit his head."[177] He was so shocked, he momentarily stopped taking pictures.

The wire car stopped. "Everybody in our car began shouting at the driver to pull up closer to the president's car," Smith wrote. "But at this moment, we saw the big bubble-top and a motorcycle escort roar away at high speed."

Mrs. Kennedy climbed up from the back seat and reached out for something on the limo's trunk—it was part of her husband's brain. Hill tried to grab the handle on the left side of the trunk as he mounted its rear step. "My foot slips off the step, back to the pavement, but somehow I manage to hang on to the handhold. . . . Somehow—I honestly don't know how—I lunge forward, my foot finds the step, and I pull my body onto the car."

Hill pushed Mrs. Kennedy back into the car—he worried she might fall out—and positioned his body to shield her "from whatever shots might still be coming." Mrs. Kennedy was in shock. "Jack, oh, Jack. What have they done?" Then she said, "I have his brains in my hands."[178] She tried to keep her husband's head down as the limousine sped to the hospital.

"I knew he was dead," she said later.[179]

The reporters in the wire car saw none of this, and later gave readers varying accounts of the shooting's immediate aftermath. "I looked ahead at the President's car but could not see him or his companion, Gov. John B. Connally of Texas. . . . I thought I saw a flash of pink which would have been Mrs. Jacqueline Kennedy," Smith wrote. Bell thought he saw someone in the presidential limo's front seat stand up for a moment. "He seemed to have a telephone in hand as he waved to a police cruiser ahead to go on," he said.[180] Kilduff saw a Secret Service agent raise his rifle.

"We screamed at our driver, 'Get going, get going,'" Smith wrote. "We careened around the Johnson car and its escort"—he didn't say how jittery Secret Service agents and cops reacted to this dodgy maneuver—"and set out down the highway, barely able to keep in sight of the president's car and the accompanying Secret Service follow-up car."

On the first press bus, MacNeil and the other reporters heard clearly the blasts from Oswald's rifle. "We all said, 'What was that?' There was enough time for us to say 'shot,' and then there were two more shots close together," he recalled. MacNeil asked the bus driver to let him out. "He closed the door and drove on under the underpass, and I was out there," MacNeil said. "The crowd was making the most incredible screaming noise . . . it was like all kinds of choirs out of tune and harsh, screaming, screaming."

He saw some Dallas cops running up the grassy knoll, a short slope on the right side of Elm Street, between the Book Depository and the Triple Underpass. "I thought, 'Well, they are chasing the guy who fired the gun in protest or something.'" It was hard for MacNeil to imagine Kennedy was shot. "So I ran with them up the hill." The grassy knoll slopes up to a fence, level with the railroad tracks atop the underpass. "We got to the top of the hill and a bunch of us crowded up against the fence, and a policeman went over the fence, and I went over too," MacNeil said.

But no one was there.

On their own, many feet from a telephone, MacNeil and Altgens had a problem. They had news to report, but no way to get it out.

Smith had the advantage of his seat by the wire car's radiotelephone. He picked up the handset and called the Dallas UPI bureau. "Bulletin precede!" he shouted. By shouting "bulletin precede," Smith informed the bureau that he had news that would supersede the other Kennedy stories he had filed so far that day.

Then, Smith yelled: "Three shots were fired at the motorcade!"[181]

"What? I can't hear you," answered Wilborn Hampton, a novice reporter who'd picked up the phone in the UPI office. Static afflicted radiotelephones, so at first no one in the wire car was surprised Smith had difficulty dictating his dispatch. "Smitty was repeating," said Bob Clark. "He was trying to get one sentence off."[182]

"There was a great deal of interference on the circuit," Smith recounted later. He blamed police radio traffic and interference from nearby buildings.[183] But Hampton had no problems with the connection. "I heard Smitty perfectly. He was screaming at the top of his lungs," he said.[184]

Hampton's typewriter was loaded with several sheets of paper separated by carbon paper, a very thin paper coated with dry ink. The carbon paper would produce multiple copies of whatever he typed onto the top sheet.

He typed out Smith's sentence—he thought his fingers fumbled as he took down the words. Then he handed the typed copy to Jim Tolbert, a Teletype operator. Tolbert prepared to transmit the bulletin by retyping it on a machine that converted the words into a long strip of punch paper tape. As Tolbert typed, Hampton handed the phone to Jack Fallon, UPI's Southwest division director. Fallon was sitting at another Teletype machine, typing out a message to UPI's Austin bureau about coverage plans for Kennedy's visit there later in the day. Today, one would do the same thing via a mobile phone text message.

"Jack, this is Smitty on the phone," Hampton said.

"Yeah, what is it? What does he want?" Fallon sounded as if he didn't want to be bothered.

"He says three shots were fired at the motorcade."

"What!" Fallon yelled. "Give me that!" Fallon grabbed the phone, and Hampton showed him a carbon copy of the dispatch he had just written.

Fallon quickly read the two lines. "Send it!" he yelled to Tolbert.

At the time, UPI's A-wire—seen by clients across the country— was under the control of its Chicago bureau, which was transmitting an account of a murder trial in Minneapolis. Tolbert took over the A-wire by pressing a "break" lever on his Teletype terminal that stopped the Minneapolis story midsentence. The A-wire's break lever was like the emergency brake cord on a train. It was only for the most urgent news.

Then, Tolbert fed the coded punch paper tape into the Teletype terminal. The machine converted the code into a bulletin that was printed out on hundreds of UPI Teletype machines across the country. The bulletin said:

> PRECEDE KENNEDY
>
> DALLAS, OV. #22 (UPI) – THREE SHOTS FIRED AT
> PRESIDENT KENNEDY'S MOTORCADE TODAY
> IN DOWNTOWN DALLAS. JT1234PCS..[185]

Everything was capital letters on the wire services in those days. The typos in the dateline didn't stop anyone from understanding the news. The last bit of the dispatch included Tolbert's initials and the time it was sent, 12:34 p.m. Central Standard Time—four minutes after Oswald fired his three shots.

Tolbert also pushed a button that rang a bell five times on UPI A-wire machines, signaling to newsrooms that they were receiving a bulletin.

After the bulletin ran, the Chicago bureau tried to resume sending the murder trial story. Editors at UPI's New York headquarters immediately interceded. They stopped the Chicago transmission, and sent out this terse message in wire-ese: "BUOS . . . UPHOLD DA IT YRS NX." Translation: "All bureaus, hold your copy—Dallas, the A-wire is yours. New York." Next, the Atlanta bureau tried to correct a story. It only managed to transmit "CORRECTE" before New York jumped in again: "BUOS UPHOLD—NX."

On AP machines, there was nothing—because back in the wire car, Smith was hogging the radiotelephone. He scrunched down under the dashboard. "Repeat my bulletin back to me!" Smith shouted into the handset. The other reporters in the car thought the yelling was a ruse. They heard clearly voices on the other end of the line.[186]

Jack Bell wanted his turn on the phone. As the wire car raced to the hospital at sixty miles per hour, the AP man tried to grab it from Smith. "Give me the goddamn phone!" Bell yelled. He swung his fists into Smith's back. Kilduff later told a reporter that he probably took more of Bell's punches than Smith did.[187] Bell realized Smith was beating him on a big story. "Smith is driving an ax through his [Bell's] skull by getting anything off from the wire car," recalled Clark. "Jack got pretty upset."[188]

But Smith and Fallon, who was now taking his dictation in the Dallas bureau, had good reason to keep talking. They needed to sort out what was going on. They did not know if Oswald's bullets hit anyone. It was hard for them to even think that Kennedy had been hit, let alone mortally wounded.

It didn't help that neither man knew much about Dallas. Smith only knew the city as a visitor, and Fallon was a New Yorker who had lived there for only two years. In the wire car, Smith yelled to Baskin in the backseat: "Where did that happen? Where did that happen?" Baskin, shocked, couldn't get the words out.[189] The driver told him the shooting happened at the Triple Underpass. In a short follow-up bulletin, Smith and Fallon reported that the shooting happened near the Dallas sheriff's office, "JUST EAST OF AN UNDERPASS LEADING TOWARD THE TRADE MART." A Dallas native might have written that Kennedy was shot in Dealey Plaza. The out-of-town reporters took the fact that the motorcade was still headed in the direction of the Trade Mart luncheon as evidence that perhaps nothing had happened. Smith and Fallon didn't understand that the Trade Mart was along the same highway as Parkland Hospital.

And Smith said he continued to have problems speaking over the radiotelephone. "I had to repeat every phrase of the two paragraphs—and only two paragraphs—several times," Smith claimed. "On a story of this magnitude, I was not about to let it go until I knew the office had it all. I told them to read it back fast. They did. Several words had been misunderstood or were missing and I filled in the blanks."[190]

While UPI was ahead on the story, it needed more reporting. In the Dallas bureau, UPI reporters called area radio stations seeking more details. Radio stations in the 1960s competed to break live news. But all the radio news editors knew about the gunshots was what they saw on their UPI Teletype machines. Not even the Dallas police press office could confirm what had happened.

Hampton had an idea. "The one person who would know would be the Dallas police dispatcher," he decided. So Hampton called the main Dallas police phone number and said in the most authoritive voice a twenty-three-year-old could muster: "Give me dispatch."

Someone answered: "Dispatch."

"This is Bill Hampton, UPI. What can you tell me about the shots at the presidential motorcade?"

"I just spoke with the motorcycle escort officer," the dispatcher said. "The president has been hit. Governor Connally has been hit. There is blood on the back of the car, and they are on their way to Parkland Hospital."

Hampton, stunned, paused for three or four seconds, trying to think of a follow-up question. "I've got to clear this line," the dispatcher said as he hung up.

Fallon, still on the phone with Smith, was preparing an update that said it didn't appear anyone in the motorcade was hurt.

"Jack, police say he's been hit!" Hampton screamed.

Fallon didn't hear him. But Don Smith, another staffer in the office, did hear. "Jack, listen to Bill," he said.

Fallon looked up at the rookie, displeased. "What is it?" he asked.

"The police say Kennedy has been hit!" Hampton replied.

"What police?" It was a wise question. As a smart wire service journalist, Fallon needed to know the source of Hampton's information.

"The dispatcher. The dispatcher said he's been hit, and they are on their way to Parkland."

"Smitty says they're going to the Trade Mart," said Fallon.

"It's the same way," Hampton replied. "It's a couple more exits past the Trade Mart. It's the same way."

Fallon paused to listen to Smith on the telephone. Then he announced: "Smitty said they are passing the Trade Mart."[191]

Now everyone in the wire car knew for sure something was wrong. "Where are we going?" someone asked the driver. "It looks like we are going to Parkland Hospital," he answered.[192] The reporters talked about what might have happened. Was the president hit? Or the First Lady? Or Governor Connally? It's unclear if Smith relayed what the police dispatcher had told his colleagues in the Dallas bureau.

Still, there was nothing on the AP wire.

Kennedy's open-top limousine pulled into Parkland Hospital at about 12:36 p.m., six minutes after the shooting.[193] The wire car was just behind it. Finally, Smith relinquished the phone. Bell immediately called the AP's Dallas bureau. "This is Jack Bell," he said into the handset. The line went dead, but Bell kept talking. He shouted that three shots had been fired at Kennedy's motorcade. When he realized no one could hear him, he tried to get an operator. But the phone was still dead.[194]

While Bell tried to call the AP bureau, Smith, Kilduff, and the others jumped out of the car and dashed up to the limousine, which was parked headfirst in the emergency room ambulance bay. It was a scene of blood-soaked horror. "The president was face-down on the back seat. Mrs. Kennedy made a cradle of her arms around the President's head and bent over him as if she were whispering to him," Smith wrote.

"Governor Connally was on his back on the floor of the car, his head and shoulders resting on the arm of his wife, Nellie, who kept shaking her head and shaking with dry sobs. Blood oozed from the front of the governor's suit.

"I could not see the president's wound. But I could see blood spattered around the interior of the rear seat and a dark stain spreading down the right side of the president's dark gray suit."

Smith turned to Secret Service agent Hill, with whom he'd socialized the night before. "How badly was he hit, Clint?" he asked.

"He's dead, Smitty," Hill replied.

The hospital gurneys hadn't even arrived yet.

Smith ran into the hospital's emergency entrance. Inside he saw a clerk, shuffling forms in an enclosure much like a bank teller's cage. On a shelf behind the clerk was a telephone.

"How do you get outside?" Smith asked. "The president has been shot and this is an emergency call."

"Dial nine," said the startled clerk as he pushed the phone to Smith.[195] Smith tried twice before he got through to the Dallas UPI bureau with a fresh dispatch.

Fallon wanted to send this news as a flash, the designation reserved for the very biggest stories. Flashes were usually transmitted so quickly that Teletype operators would not bother typing them first onto punch paper tape. Instead, the operators transmitted flashes by sitting down at Teletype terminals and typing the news directly onto the wire.

Tolbert was seated at the Dallas bureau Teletype terminal that then controlled the UPI A-wire. Fallon dictated to Tolbert: "Kennedy seriously wounded—"

Bill Payette, the UPI Southwest Division vice president, overheard Fallon's dictation. He ordered a revision: The flash was to use the word "perhaps." So in those seconds, Tolbert typed this slightly awkward dispatch directly onto the A-wire: [196]

KENNEDY SERIOUSLY WOUNDED

PERHAPS SERIOUSLY

PERHAPS FATALLY BY ASSASSINS BULLET

JT1239PCS

The flash moved at 12:39 p.m. Nine minutes had passed since the rifle shots in Dealey Plaza, and Smitty had already sent several brief dispatches that put UPI ahead on the story. His competitors at the AP were just getting started.

CHAPTER 6 ✦ PUNCHERS

BOB JOHNSON, THE ASSOCIATED PRESS bureau chief in Dallas, thought the day was going well. At 12:20 p.m., the AP updated its report on Kennedy's trip with a description of the warm reception the president and first lady received at Love Field. "There was considerable female squealing over the President and lusty male shouts of 'Hey Jackie!'" the copy said.

It looked like there would be no repeat of the Adlai Stevenson incident of several weeks before. "I guess we'll get through this one without any trouble," Johnson thought. If he got out of work on time that evening, he planned to attend a Dallas Opera performance of Verdi's *Un ballo in maschera,* which is about the assassination of the king of Sweden. Johnson got up from his desk. It seemed like a safe time to take a break. The AP bureau was in the Dallas Times Herald Building, next to the newsroom. The *Times Herald* newsroom had a water fountain, and Johnson went for a drink.

On his way back to the bureau, he saw a cluster of people gathered around the *Times Herald* city desk, listening to a police radio. Felix McKnight, the newspaper's executive editor, called out to Johnson. "Bob, we hear the president may have been shot. But we haven't confirmed it," McKnight said. [197]

Johnson ran back to his desk. Ron Thompson, the AP bureau's night editor, was working a day shift to help with the Kennedy coverage. "Bob, Jack Bell just tried to phone in. But he was cut off,"

Thompson said. It was now around 12:36 p.m., about the time the wire car arrived at Parkland Hospital. It was six minutes after the shooting, and two minutes after UPI moved Smith's first bulletin.

Johnson went to a typewriter and loaded it with a "book"—several sheets of paper, separated by carbon paper. "BULLETIN," he typed. Then, "DALLAS, NOV. 22 (AP) – ." Then he waited. He figured Bell would call again.

Instead, he got a call from James Altgens.

After witnessing the assassination at Dealey Plaza, Altgens sprinted back to the AP photo staff's office a few blocks away at the *Dallas Morning News*'s downtown building. Though AP's Dallas writers and editors were based at the *Times Herald*'s building, the photo staff was based at the *News*. Altgens had good luck on the way—he crossed all the streets in sync with the traffic lights. He even found an elevator car waiting for him in the newspaper lobby. Seconds counted.

Once he arrived at the third-floor photo office, Altgens picked up a phone that gave him a direct line to the AP news office at the *Times Herald*, a mile away. Johnson answered. "Bob, the president has been shot!" Altgens shouted.

"Ike, how do you know?" Johnson asked, calling Altgens by his nickname. It was not an idle question. It was basic wire service journalism. Like his counterparts at UPI, Johnson needed to know the origin of Altgens' information.

"I saw it," Altgens answered. "There was blood on his head. Jackie jumped up and grabbed him and cried, 'Oh no!' The motorcade raced onto the freeway."

"Ike, you saw that?" It was big news, and Johnson had to be sure. He explained later: "If I'm going to say the president has been shot, I'm going to be damned sure I'm right."[198]

"Yes," Altgens answered. "I was shooting pictures and then I saw it."[199]

Johnson's questioning of Altgens was in keeping with AP values. An article about the assassination coverage in *The AP World*, an employee magazine, includes a footnote on why Johnson was right to vet the information he got from the photographer, a Dallas bureau veteran: "[A]n error at that time could have destroyed men's careers, brought permanent embarrassment to The Associated Press and caused great damage to members." At the AP, a nonprofit cooperative, "members" are clients—the newspapers and broadcasters that use the service. [200]

Now Johnson had to get the story on the wire. "Bulletin!" he yelled out to his staff. He typed out a dispatch, which Thompson pulled from his typewriter and handed to Teletype operator Julia Saunders. At 12:39 p.m.—nine minutes after Oswald fired—AP finally transmitted its first report of the shooting. Per Johnson's order, it was labeled a bulletin.

> DALLAS, NOV. 22 (AP) – PRESIDENT KENNEDY
> WAS SHOT TODAY JUST AS HIS MOTORCADE
> LEFT DOWNTOWN DALLAS. MRS. KENNEDY
> JUMPED UP AND GRABBED MR. KENNEDY. SHE
> CRIED 'OH NO!' THE MOTORCADE SPED ON.

This vividly written bulletin had the advantage of coming from an eyewitness account. Usually, wire service bulletins are one sentence—UPI's bulletin "THREE SHOTS FIRED AT PRESIDENT KENNEDY'S MOTORCADE IN DOWNTOWN DALLAS" is typical. Johnson's bulletin ran to four sentences. He knew it was unusually long and detailed. "But I said, 'I'm going to tell everything—I'm going to make this a complete little story because . . . I want people to believe that I know what I'm doing. And so that's why I had those four sentences in it," he explained later.[201]

But the AP bulletin was late. It cleared the Dallas bureau five minutes behind Smitty's first bulletin. It lacked a crucial detail that the assassin fired three shots. Also, the AP bulletin moved at the same minute UPI moved Smitty's report from Parkland Hospital that Kennedy had been shot "perhaps seriously, perhaps fatally" as a higher-priority, ten-bell flash. That flash signaled newspapers and broadcasters that the shooting was a monumental story.

There was another glitch. The AP Dallas bureau's initial report immediately ran into a transmission bottleneck.

At 12:39 p.m. Central time, the AP's A-wire was on a split, which meant that different parts of the country were getting different A-wire copy. News copy was moving to afternoon newspapers in the western United States. Newsrooms in the east were getting a budget of stories planned for the next morning's editions. The A-wire split was "a normal situation at this time of day to adjust for the three-hour time differential between the east and west coasts," the AP explained in an employee newsletter.[202]

The split was managed by the AP's Kansas City bureau, which to the A-wire was like the neck of an hourglass. The dispatch Altgens reported and Johnson wrote and sent from Dallas got stuck in Kansas City until someone there could transmit it to newspapers and broadcasters in New York, Washington, and other eastern points. It took until the next minute—12:40 p.m. Central time—for the Kansas City bureau to relay the Dallas bulletin to the East Coast.

That meant East Coast newsrooms got the AP's bulletin six minutes after Smith's first UPI report on the shooting, and about one minute after Smith's "perhaps seriously, perhaps fatally" top-priority flash. By then, the UPI report was already on the radio, and New York and Washington TV newsrooms were already starting live coverage. In the wire service war of seconds, AP was starting far behind on one of the century's most momentous stories.

Such a time lag on such a big story is hard to imagine in the Internet age. Reporters with mobile phones can now send dispatches directly from a news scene via text or Twitter, without any editors getting in the way. A reporter with a laptop computer can cover a live event as it happens and put the story before thousands of readers without ever getting up from his chair. If the assassination happened today, Smith and Bell would each have their own mobile phones and wouldn't have had to fight for a single phone line.

Smitty's skill and preparedness and the smooth work of his colleagues in the Dallas bureau kept UPI ahead on the story. But Bell's problems in the wire car were just the beginning of the AP's woes that afternoon. In the following hours, Bell and the AP bungled the assassination story at every turn.

At the hospital emergency room bay, Bell quickly gave up on the wire car's radiotelephone. He got out of the backseat and ran toward the presidential limousine, a moment behind the other reporters. Bell arrived at the car just after the hospital attendants. Kennedy was still sprawled out in back. "His natty business suit seemed hardly rumpled. But there was blood on the floor," Bell wrote. Mrs. Kennedy was weeping, trying to hold up her husband's head as Secret Service agents tried to lead her away. "Is he dead?" Bell asked an agent he did not identify by name. "I don't know, but I don't think so," the agent answered. [203]

That differed from the certain answer Smith got from Clint Hill.

Now Bell had to find a phone. By the time he reached the emergency room, Smith had already seized the prime spot. The cashier's cage was next to the emergency room entrance, giving Smith a good view of all the comings and goings. Clark from ABC News had the next-best phone, in a blood bank office. Bell ended up with a phone about seventy-five feet beyond Smith's location. He finally got a call through to the AP's Dallas bureau. "Flash—President Kennedy shot," he said. [204] He was late. The bureau already knew this from Altgens' report.

Meanwhile, Smitty was on a roll, dictating a steady stream of updates to UPI's Dallas bureau. Shortly after UPI transmitted Smith's cautious and awkwardly worded "perhaps seriously perhaps fatally" dispatch, Smith and his editors began the story over, with a new first paragraph, or lead, that freshly summarized the news. It moved at 12:41 p.m., eleven minutes after the shooting:

DALLAS, NOV. 22 (UPI) – PRESIDENT KENNEDY
AND GOV. JOHN B. CONNALLY OF TEXAS WERE
CUTDOWN BY AN ASSASSIN'S BULLETS AS THEY

> TOURED DOWNTOWN DALLAS IN AN OPEN
> AUTOMOBILE TODAY. MORE JT 1241 PCS

Smith quickly followed up with an additional bit of copy—an "add," in wire service lingo—that described what he saw in the president's limousine. It moved on the wire at 12:44 p.m.:

> THE PRESIDENT, HIS LIMP BODY CRADLED
> IN THE ARMS OF HIS WIFE, WAS RUSHED TO
> PARKLAND HOSPITAL. THE GOVERNOR ALSO
> WAS TAKEN TO PARKLAND.
> CLINT HILL, A SECRET SERVICE AGENT
> ASSIGNED TO MRS. KENNEDY, SAID, "HE'S
> DEAD," AS THE PRESIDENT WAS LIFTED FROM
> THE REAR OF A WHITE HOUSE TOURING
> CAR, THE FAMOUS 'BUBBLETOP' FROM
> WASHINGTON. HE WAS RUSHED TO AN
> EMERGENCY ROOM IN THE HOSPITAL.
> OTHER WHITE HOUSE OFFICIALS WERE IN
> DOUBT AS THE CORRIDORS OF THE HOSPITAL
> ERUPTED IN PANDEMONIUM.

Just fourteen minutes after the shooting, Smith quoted Secret Service agent Clint Hill by name saying President Kennedy had died. At the same time, he reported that White House officials were "in doubt" about the president's condition. This hedged Hill's quote—after all, doctors were still treating the president. And by reporting that White House officials were "in doubt," Smith got across the idea that information was fluid. But Clint Hill's brief statement was the public's first solid information that the president may have been killed.

Hill was highly regarded in the Kennedys' circle, and his "He's dead" quote carried great weight with its members. Some time after the assassination, the Secret Service agent said, he heard how his quote was received by John Kenneth Galbraith, the economist and Kennedy confidant who was the US ambassador to India. Galbraith was having lunch in New York when he heard a broadcast report that included Hill's quote. "If Clint Hill said that, it's true," Galbraith said. [205]

When it comes to the media, Secret Service agents are not supposed to be seen or heard. It's remarkable today, in an age where so many government sources are anonymous, that Hill would speak so candidly with a reporter amid the worst crisis Secret Service agents could face. Hill said he had no qualms about answering Smith's question about Kennedy's condition. His superiors had no qualms about it either—Hill was never reprimanded for giving Smith the "He's dead" quote. "Nobody ever said anything to me about it, ever," he recalled.

At about the same time UPI advanced the story with Hill's statement, the AP's Dallas staff was mangling Jack Bell's first reports from Parkland Hospital. In one AP dispatch, the name of Kenneth O'Donnell, a Kennedy aide, came out "KENNETH 0'; $ 9,, 3))/;" "HE LAY" ran as "HE LAAAAAAAAAAA," and "BLOODSTAINED" appeared as "BLOOD STAINEZAAC RBMTHING." The AP also reported, "BELL SAID KENNEDY WAS TRANSFERRED TO AN AMBULANCE," even though Bell had seen Kennedy in the back of his limousine in the emergency room's ambulance bay.

The AP's garbled assassination dispatches did not carry sign-off times, but they clearly moved between 12:41 p.m. and 12:49 p.m., which is the next sign-off time seen on AP's A-wire copy.[206] Though the dispatches were quickly corrected, they still cost the AP valuable minutes.

The garbles were the fault of AP's Dallas Teletype operators. The mid-twentieth-century news distribution system was prone to this kind of human error.

By 1963, Teletype technology had been around for nearly fifty years—the AP began using the machines in 1914.[207] Teletypes were slow by modern standards. The noisy machines—essentially remote-controlled typewriters—clattered out only fifty to sixty words a minute. But they were solidly built, and could run for days without maintenance if they were properly lubricated and supplied with the rolls of paper on which they printed copy. Many machines stayed in service for decades. They were linked by telephone lines that were similarly reliable.

When reporters, editors, Teletype operators, and Teletypes worked in concert, AP and UPI spread news with remarkable speed. But the system had more human elements than a Twitter account, or a website's content management system. It takes only one person to publish something to the Internet. It took many hands to move wire service copy in the 1960s—reporters in the field, editors and writers in offices, and Teletype operators who actually put copy on the wire. If one link in the system failed—if Smith or Bell could not find a telephone, or if their bureaus blundered while transmitting their copy—then the whole system failed.

Teletype operators, known in wire service lingo as *punchers,* were a critical link in the operation. They converted typewritten copy from editors into the punch paper tape that produced printed copy on Teletype machines. If the paper tape was mistyped at the source—as apparently happened at the AP's Dallas bureau on November 22—then the copy would arrive garbled on thousands of Teletype machines across the globe.

Garbled copy was just one possible problem with the system. A series of incidents on UPI's broadcast wire on November 22 showed what else could go wrong.

In Chicago, UPI had a staff dedicated to rewriting national and international news for local radio and TV clients. Its job was to convert A-wire copy written for newspapers into short, punchy stories easily read aloud by radio and TV newscasters.

The broadcast wire required a separate subscription from UPI clients and ran on a separate circuit from the newspaper wire. It was designed so that small-town radio and TV stations could get by with copy from just one Teletype printer. National news from the UPI A-wire was rewritten in Chicago into simple sentences that could be easily read by broadcasters. This rewritten copy was then transmitted on the broadcast wire.

For twenty minutes of every hour, the Chicago bureau stopped transmitting national and international news. That's when local news was sent over regional broadcast circuits. The regional circuits existed because most news that came from someplace like UPI's bureau in Des Moines would only interest UPI clients in Iowa. So for those twenty minutes, the Des Moines bureau operated the Iowa broadcast wire, churning out copy about car accidents, state politics, local crime, and other Iowa news. When this time was up, control of the wire reverted back to UPI's national broadcast desk in Chicago.

At 12:30 p.m. on November 22—just as Lee Harvey Oswald fired his three bullets—UPI Chicago bureau broadcast puncher Henry Renwald hit a series of switches that gave control of the broadcast wire to the local circuits in each state. Four minutes later, Bill Roberts, a broadcast writer, ripped Smith's first dispatch off the A-wire. "Hey—look at this," he yelled to his colleagues.[208]

Suddenly the Chicago bureau had a momentous story to send to UPI's broadcast clients across the country. But it couldn't do so while all the regional circuits were clattering out local news. This was a severe problem for Renwald. He was forced to transmit a direct, desperate plea to his colleagues in local UPI bureaus. "GET OFF GET OFF GET OFF," he typed on the broadcast wire. This was the only way he could signal them to stop feeding paper tape into their Teletype terminals to clear the wire for the Kennedy story.

Five minutes later, the broadcast wire still wasn't clear. "STAY OFF ALL OF YOU STAY OFF AND KEEP OFF GET OFF," Renwald typed. The local news kept moving. "WILL U PLEASE STAY OFF THIS WIRE TILL WE GIVE THE GA [go-ahead]???? STAY OFF STAY OFF," he begged.

The problems continued for an hour. And then, at 1:35 p.m., human emotion became a problem for Chicago broadcast puncher Alice Guenther. An editor, John Pelletreau, turned to her and said: "Alice, type 'Flash President dead.'" She froze. "Oh, my God," she said. A supervisor lifted her out of her chair, sat her on the floor, and typed the flash himself.[209]

UPI's main wire—the A-wire—worked far more smoothly that day. UPI transmitted to its newspaper clients a series of short, clean dispatches from Smith that added detail to the assassination story. In these dispatches—"adds"—Smith reported what he saw at Dealey Plaza: Secret Service agents "quickly unlimbered their automatic rifles. . . . They drew their pistols, but the damage was done. . . . Dallas motorcycle officers escorting the President quickly leaped from their bikes and raced up a grassy hill."[210]

At 12:51 p.m., just twenty-one minutes after the shooting, UPI moved a final add that, tacked on to Smith's 12:41 p.m. "cutdown by an assassin's bullets" lead and several subsequent adds, made a coherent, publishable story. It was enough copy for East Coast afternoon papers then on deadline to put on their presses. This copy finished moving just as AP was recovering from its series of mangled dispatches.

UPI moved several more adds in the next seven minutes. They were more disjointed than the earlier copy. But they would have been useful to big-city papers with rewrite staffs who could weave the information in them into a coherent story.

At 12:58 p.m., the Dallas bureau moved this advisory—the misspelling is in the original:

> THE KNNEDY STORY, DALLAS, MAY BE SIGNED
> BY
> MERRIMAN SMITH
> UPI WHITE HOUSE REPORTER
>   JT1258PCS[211]

Smith's byline appeared on the story in afternoon newspapers that just then were going to press. It also appeared in some morning papers' extras, including one put out by the *Washington Post*.

During the half hour after Oswald fired his three shots, UPI provided both the first reports of the assassination and the first usable newspaper copy. The AP, under the same pressure, fell apart. It moved the news later than its competition, and much of its copy was unreadable and unusable without rewriting. In the news business, being first with clearly written copy is better than being garbled and last.

SIDEBAR • THE DARKROOM

One thing went notably right for the AP that day. James Altgens was supposed to have spent November 22 in the office as a photo editor. But like many Dallas journalists, he wanted to get in on the coverage of the Kennedy visit and asked to be stationed at Dealey Plaza. Altgens' editor gave the assignment reluctantly—it had seemed more important to have him in the office.[212]

After his sprint from Dealey Plaza back to the AP's photo office and his hurried phone call to Johnson, Altgens was shaking so much he couldn't handle his film. "I don't know what I've got. I don't know what I've got," he told colleague Harold Waters. "I was shooting when I heard something pop."

"Get back here, and let's develop the stuff, and let's see," Waters said.

"I can't unload the camera . . . I'm not steady," Altgens said. He was so upset, he could not load his film onto the reel from which it would be suspended in developing solution. Putting film onto the reels was a routine task photographers could do in the dark—in fact, they had to do it in the dark so the film would not be ruined by exposure to light.

So Waters took Altgens' film and developed it. He got several good images, including one showing the front of Kennedy's limousine just after it passed the Book Depository. It was taken just as Oswald fired the first bullet and shows two Secret Service agents looking backward toward the Book Depository, which they believed was the source of the rifle blast.

Another image Altgens shot a few seconds later shows the limousine speeding off, with Secret Service agent Hill clinging to its rear as Jackie Kennedy reaches to grab some of her husband's splattered brain matter from atop the trunk.

Altgens' pictures of the shooting and the scene were the only ones available that first day. They were transmitted on the AP's picture network at about 12:57 p.m., less than a half hour after the shooting and seventeen minutes after the first AP dispatch about the shooting reached East Coast newspapers.

"Man, you've got a Pulitzer Prize here, Ike," Waters said. [213]

Chapter 7 • Parkland

At Dealey Plaza, everyone's ears were ringing from the rifle shots, traffic was jammed, and frightened bystanders and cops ran around trying to figure out what to do. Robert MacNeil was done running alongside the police officers who thought there was a gunman near the railroad overpass west of the Book Depository. Now he needed a telephone. He ran past the front of the Book Depository building to its main entrance, near the building's eastern side. As he headed in to the building, a young man in shirtsleeves came out. MacNeil asked the man where he could find a phone. "He pointed inside to an open space where another man was talking on a phone situated near a pillar and said, 'Better ask him.'"[214]

Months later, author William Manchester determined that the man MacNeil met just outside the building was Lee Harvey Oswald, then making his escape. Oswald told police he encountered a blond man as he left the Book Depository who he thought was a Secret Service agent. MacNeil's hair was blond at the time. "It's conceivable," the reporter says of Manchester's story.

Inside, the man talking on the phone at the pillar pointed MacNeil toward an office. There, he found another phone and called NBC in New York.

Every reporter can relate to what happened next. Whoever answered the phone in the NBC newsroom said, "Wait just a minute," and put the handset down without listening to what MacNeil had to say. MacNeil thought an NBC employee named David Lent had answered the phone. "I screamed down the phone for thirty seconds—'David, David, David.'" He had a big story. Why wouldn't anyone in the newsroom listen to him? Finally another NBC employee, Jim Holden, picked up the handset. "I said, 'MacNeil in Dallas, someone has shot at the President.'" Holden connected the phone to a tape recorder, and MacNeil delivered a short bulletin saying that shots were fired in downtown Dallas, but it was unclear whether they were aimed at Kennedy.

Then he headed out of the building. He saw an eight-year-old boy walk up to a police officer and say: "Mister, I seen a man with a gun up in that window." A man corroborated the boy's statement. A woman spotted MacNeil's press pass. "Was he hit? Was he hit?" she asked. MacNeil answered: "No, I'm sure he wasn't."

"Then it dawned on me that what I thought so impossible could have happened," MacNeil said. "I rushed over to the policeman, who was listening to his motorcycle radio. 'Was he hit?' 'Yes. They're taking him to Parkland Hospital.' I was in a frenzy. The President was hit. I was separated from the story. I had to get to the hospital."

MacNeil ran to Elm Street, which runs next to the Depository building and is the street on which Kennedy and Connally were shot. It was jammed with traffic. But halfway across Dealey Plaza, on Main Street, cars moved freely. MacNeil ran to Main Street and ran in front of the first car that came by. The driver stopped, and MacNeil jumped in the passenger seat. "This is a terrible emergency. I'll give you five dollars if you take me to Parkland Hospital," he said.

"OK," the driver said. The shooting had been reported on local radio. "I heard something about that a couple of minutes ago," the driver said. Traffic was jammed. "I kept urging him on, telling him to go any speed and take the risks," MacNeil recounted. "I would pay for any fines. Besides, what could the police care at the moment?"

On the way, MacNeil had the man stop at a gas station so he could call in another bulletin quoting the motorcycle police officer saying Kennedy had been hit. He got more sorry news from NBC's New York news desk: The bulletin he filed from the Book Depository was the first his editors had heard about the shooting, and he had informed them before they saw any AP or UPI dispatches. But it took five minutes for the bulletin to get on the radio. NBC's newsroom bureaucracy was not as efficient as UPI. "I ran out of the gas station and into the car, kicking over a watering can as I ducked between two gas pumps," MacNeil said. "I forced the man to drive faster." A few minutes later, he arrived at Parkland. MacNeil paid the driver five dollars and ran toward the emergency entrance.[215]

Like MacNeil, *Newsweek* reporter Charles Roberts recalled that he was aboard the first of the two press buses by the Book Depository when everyone heard Oswald's shots. He saw police officers, guns drawn, running up the grassy knoll toward the railroad tracks, thinking they would find a gunman. "Everybody started screaming different advice to the bus driver: 'Open the door.' 'No, close the door.' 'Let's go.' 'Let's go, damn it.'" Someone asked that the bus be stopped so he could get out, Roberts said. So the driver stopped the bus and opened the door. "A few of us jumped out onto the pavement but didn't get far from the bus," Roberts said. Unlike MacNeil, the other reporters didn't run off. "From long experience with motorcades, you know that they start up suddenly, and if sixty people get out of a bus and the motorcade starts up, they simply can't get back in." Roberts said the bus "stopped almost under the windows of the School Book Depository."[216]

Julian O. Read, Governor Connally's press secretary, also recalls being aboard the first press bus. More than fifty years later, he could not recall if Roberts, MacNeil, or anyone else got out. But Read, seated in front and, as a government press secretary, assuming he was in charge of the bus, advised the driver to head to the Dallas Trade Mart as planned. "I thought it was better to go there," he said.[217] None of the reporters complained. Besides, they'd been promised they could reach their offices from the Trade Mart. "There will be adequate Western Union [telegraph] and telephone facilities at every stop," their official schedule said. Their witness to the may-hem by the Book Depository was useless unless they could get the news to their editors.

So the first and second press buses, after clearing the traffic by the Triple Underpass just west of the Book Depository, lumbered the two and a half miles to the Trade Mart and pulled up at its front entrance as planned, as if nothing had happened. Of course, everyone knew something had happened, maybe something horrible. But unlike MacNeil, and unlike Smitty and the reporters in the wire car, they were not sure what. "The first thing we wanted to do was look for the President's car, and we didn't find it," said *Los Angeles Times* reporter Robert Donovan. "But even then it didn't raise any positive proof in my mind, because there were a number of entrances to the Trade Mart and it seemed as though the driver was confused getting us up there. So the mere fact that the President wasn't there, his car wasn't there, the ordinary White House cars, didn't in itself mean too much."[218]

Inside the Trade Mart, the reporters—excited, nervous, and fear-ful—encountered a surreal scene of calm. There sat 2,400 people, upstanding citizens of Dallas, waiting for the president's appearance. "The waiters were bringing out filet mignon to an utterly unsuspect-ing audience," Donovan said. Everyone was eating lunch as if noth-ing had happened. As far as they knew, nothing had. They had no idea Kennedy would never arrive, and knew nothing of the violence that had unfolded at Dealey Plaza. They hadn't heard the news. For a last few moments, all was normal in their world.

It seemed weird to the reporters—"kind of an otherworldly scene," Roberts recounted. Water gushed in the Trade Mart's dec-orative fountain and soft music played over the sound system. The noise of multiple conversations filled the room—"tittering," said Read. "What an eerie feeling it was."[219]

"Where's the president?" the reporters demanded of anyone they thought might know. No one at the Trade Mart had any idea. "They looked up at us like we were men from Mars or nuts of some kind," Roberts said.[220] But word of the gunshots quickly got around as the

reporters spread through the hall, like travelers arriving from a bat-
tlefield where the outcome was still uncertain. "It was the only rumor
that I had ever *seen*; it was moving across that crowd like wind over a
wheat field," said Tom Wicker of the *New York Times.* "A man eating
a grapefruit seized my arm as I passed. 'Has the President been shot?'
he asked. 'I don't think so,' I said. 'But something happened.'"[221]

Read went up to the podium and told the luncheon's chairman,
J. Erik Jonsson. "He just stared down at me for a minute like he
couldn't believe all of this."[222]

Roberts decided there was no story at the Trade Mart. "The
President wasn't going to be there, and I suspected nobody was
going to be there who knew any more than we did," he recounted.
He ran to the parking lot and found a motorcycle policeman listen-
ing to his radio. "The President has been shot," the policeman said.
"They're taking him to Parkland Hospital."

Roberts found a second cop, a sergeant, a few feet away. He
told the officer: "I've got to get to Parkland Hospital, fast." The sergeant walked out to the highway in front of the Trade Mart and
flagged down a car driven by a woman with her teenage daughter as
a passenger. "And this sergeant said, 'You take this man to Parkland
Hospital. And take him there fast.' And she did."[223]

Westinghouse radio reporter Sid Davis found a phone and called
his office. By now, Westinghouse staffers had seen Smith's first UPI
reports, but they had not yet seen his report that Kennedy might
have been killed. "Do a piece as fast as you can," Davis's boss said.
So Davis dictated a bulletin, and then ran outside to the street next
to the Trade Mart. "I flashed my typewriter in the air," he said. "I
got a guy in a white Cadillac to stop. He said, 'Are you a reporter?'
He had heard on the radio that the president had been shot." The
man agreed to take Davis to Parkland. "At that point, traffic was
blocked," Davis said. "We had to weave in and out of stuff. But this
guy was damn good. He got me to Parkland pretty fast."

Inside the press room on the fourth floor of the Trade Mart,
Marianne Means, a reporter for Hearst News Service, hung up a

phone, ran to a group of reporters, and said: "The President's been shot. He's at Parkland Hospital." Everyone ran downstairs to the press buses. An official-looking man grabbed Wicker's arm. "No running in here," he said. The reporters ran anyhow. Douglas Kiker of the *New York Herald Tribune* ran head-on into a waiter carrying a plate of potatoes, sending both the waiter and potatoes flying. Kiker ran on, unhurt. Wicker got on a bus that soon took him and other reporters to Parkland, a short distance away.[224]

Roberts was among the first reporters to make it from the Trade Mart to the hospital. He saw Secret Service men swabbing the blood from the back seat of Kennedy's big Lincoln. "You can't look," one of the agents said. They also put up the car's fabric top. "Why now?" Roberts asked one of the agents. He admitted later that it was a rude question and that he had forgotten "for a bitter moment that every President since McKinley had ridden in open cars."[225] Sid Davis arrived at about the same time as Roberts. "Don't even look. . . . It's too horrible," he was advised by Hugh Sidey, a writer for *Time* magazine.

Nearby stood Senator Yarborough. Having been in Johnson's limousine, he'd witnessed the shooting and had arrived at the hospital just after President Kennedy and Governor Connally. "Gentlemen, it is a deed of horror," he said.[226] "He was talking in an old Southern style," said Roberts.[227] By now several reporters had gathered outside the hospital emergency room entrance. "I counted three shots," Yarborough said over and over. "They carried him in. The President is hurt bad." When Roberts asked Yarborough where Kennedy was hit, he said, "I can't tell you," at the same time he unconsciously held his hand to the right side of his head. Roberts surmised that was where the bullet hit Kennedy.[228]

Some reporters managed to get inside the hospital and grabbed telephones wherever they could get them. "Telephones were at a premium in the hospital and I clung to mine for dear life," Smith said. Bert Shipp, a Dallas TV reporter, pestered Smith for a chance to use his phone. "He told me he was going to show me a new trick with that phone if I didn't leave him alone," Shipp said.[229]

Smith was not about to give up his line to the Dallas bureau, through which he was spreading what he knew to the world. He needn't have worried—his White House friends looked out for him.

Arthur W. Bales, chief warrant officer of the White House Communications Agency, soon arrived at Parkland with several Dallas cops. He evicted several reporters from their emergency room phones. Then he placed a call from each phone to the White House switchboard in Washington and to temporary White House switchboards in Dallas and Fort Worth. A police officer stood by each phone to make sure it stayed available to White House staff. In a memo recounting the day's events, Bales wrote that he "seized all but one line (leaving Merriman Smith on the one most remote from the Emergency Rooms)."[230]

For a time, there was little for the reporters to do but mill around the hospital and ask questions of whomever they could find. Bell soon finished dictating his early dispatches. He handed his phone to a hospital employee who agreed to hold the line open to his bureau while he roamed the emergency room area seeking more news.

At the same time, Wilborn Hampton—relieved of his duties taking telephone dictation at the UPI bureau—arrived at Parkland. He drove as fast as he could, but by the time he arrived at the hospital, there was no place to park. "So I pulled up on a median and just left my car there," he recalled.

The rookie reporter ran across the hospital's front lawn and then around to its rear, where the emergency room entrance was located. There he saw a crowd that included Secret Service agents, hospital employees in white coats, and reporters. The back door of Kennedy's limousine was open, and Hampton saw Jackie's bouquet of red roses strewn on the back seat, as well as some spattered blood.[231]

Hampton's orders were to find Smitty and "do whatever legwork he needed me to do. Although I'd talked to him twice and had just gotten off the phone with him a few minutes earlier, I didn't know what he looked like. I had never seen him."[232]

Hampton went up to one of the reporters and asked: "Have you seen Merriman Smith?"

"Haven't seen him," the reporter answered. His words struck Hampton as having "no friendliness at all."

"Look, I'm Bill Hampton, UPI. I need to find Smitty. Can you point him out to me?"

"You're a reporter," the man answered. "You find him."

Taken aback, Hampton looked at the man's press credential. "It was Jack Bell, obviously just smarting from the fact Smitty wouldn't give him the telephone. . . . He wasn't about to help UPI any further."[233]

Read persuaded a motorist to drive him from the Trade Mart to Parkland. "I was very worried about Governor Connally and Mrs. Connally," he said. He entered the hospital through "an end door which was unguarded—I remember how weird I thought that was. I found a nurse and asked her to take me to Mrs. Connally, and she did very quickly."

The governor's wife stood in a dark hallway outside Trauma Room 2 in the hospital's emergency department. "Trauma Room 1 was across the hall. Right in front of it was Jackie Kennedy," said Read. "Two women, all alone, praying for the fate of their husbands."[234]

"I want to be in there when he dies," Mrs. Kennedy told Dr. George Burkley, a US Navy doctor who accompanied Kennedy on all his trips. Dr. Burkley forced his way in to the operating room. "It's her prerogative," he told the doctors inside. One wanted her to leave. "It's my husband, his blood, his brains are all over me," Mrs. Kennedy answered. She stayed.[235]

Among those who had heard the first news bulletins were Father Oscar Huber and Father James Thompson, two Catholic priests whose parish included Parkland Hospital. They set out for the hospital even before the Secret Service called. At 12:57 p.m., twenty-seven minutes after the shooting, Huber was whisked to the hospital's emergency room. "That means the last rites," said a cop standing near Roberts. "Now I felt a chill," the *Newsweek* reporter said.

There was nothing Parkland's doctors could do. They tried, but it was not long before they realized what Secret Service agent Hill knew outside the emergency room entrance, before the hospital gurneys arrived. The president was mortally wounded. Father Huber administered the last rites: *"Per istam sanctam Unctionem, indulgeat tibi Dominus quidquid deliquisti. Amen."*—"Through this holy anointing, may God forgive you whatever sins you have committed. Amen." As Father Huber worked, Jacqueline Kennedy held her husband's hand.[236]

Soon Father Thompson arrived—he was late because he was parking the parish car. He and Huber led the Catholics in the room in reciting the Lord's Prayer and the Prayers for the Dying and for the Departed Soul. Blood stained the anointment oil they dabbed on President Kennedy's forehead. The doctors set Kennedy's time of death at 1:00 p.m.

At that moment, back at the Trade Mart, Jonsson finally announced the news to the crowd. He didn't know much. "There has been a mishap," he said. Read had told him what had happened at Dealey Plaza, but the chairman didn't share all he had heard. Something happened, he told the crowd, but he wasn't sure exactly what. He said he expected President Kennedy would be late.

Seven minutes later, at 1:07 p.m., Jonsson returned to the podium. "I'm not sure that I can say what I have to say. . . . It is true. Our President and Governor Connally have been shot. We don't know how seriously. Reports are scanty." "After the oppressive first wave of silent shock, people began leaving the hall," the *Dallas Times Herald* reported. "Not another bite was taken. Rows of steaks lay untouched."[237]

At the hospital, Kennedy's staff worried about what might happen next. Maybe the shooting was part of some conspiracy—Russians? Cubans? Dallas right-wingers? Whatever was going on,

Dallas did not seem safe. The president was dead or dying, and they were discussing what would happen next. "At 1:00 it was obvious that it was very bad," said Jack Brooks, a Texas congressman traveling with the Kennedys. He, Mrs. Johnson, and two others went to Trauma Room 1, where they saw Jackie. She was standing in the middle of the hallway outside the trauma room door, Brooks said. Mrs. Johnson hugged her with both arms. Brooks hugged her too.

At 1:10 p.m., Secret Service agent Emory Roberts told Vice President Johnson it would be best if he returned to Washington immediately. Ten minutes later, after checking with colleagues in a hospital corridor, Roberts told Johnson that Kennedy was dead. Kenneth O'Donnell, a Kennedy aide, spoke to Johnson two minutes after that. "He's gone," O'Donnell said.[238]

Soon Father Huber and Father Thompson made their way out of the hospital. An agent stepped in front of Huber and said: "Father, you don't know anything about this."[239] But there was no escaping the reporters, who had seen them enter the hospital and would not let them leave before they answered questions.

UPI reported the purpose of the priests' visit to the hospital in a terse dispatch at 1:23 p.m. It said: "A FATHER HUBER, OF HOLY TRINITY CHURCH IN DALLAS, ADMINISTERED THE LAST SACRAMENT OF THE CHURCH TO THE PRESIDENT." This report came from Smith. How Smith got the words from Huber is unclear. He was standing near the emergency room entrance, and it seems likely the priests passed him on their way outside.

Father Huber's statement was more evidence that Kennedy was dead. Smith and his editors were still reluctant to report the president's death as fact, since they had no official announcement from the White House. So they simply reported what Huber said. This is typical of the wire services' cautious, just-the-facts approach to many stories.

The priests encountered other reporters outside the emergency room. Jerry terHorst, a reporter for the *Detroit News,* waved Sid Davis over. "Is he dead?" asked Hugh Sidey of *Time* magazine. "He's dead, all right," said Huber. He told the reporters how to spell his name.

Davis pondered what to do with this news. He felt that a priest's word that the president was dead was solid information—especially since Huber gave his name; he was not a confidential source. But like Smith and his editors, he preferred to wait for an official announcement. Davis and his editor in Washington agreed to hold off reporting Huber's statement and wait for the word from the White House.[240]

AP was more explicit about the priests' activities. In a 1:27 p.m. dispatch, it reported that the priests delivered the last rites—four minutes after UPI's similar dispatch. Five minutes later, it moved a second dispatch that said, "TWO PRIESTS WHO WERE WITH KENNEDY SAY HE IS DEAD OF BULLET WOUNDS." That was a secondhand report, based on reporting by Val Imm, the society editor of the *Dallas Times Herald,* who was at the hospital. She and Bob Ford, a Dallas AP editor, had found adjacent telephones and agreed to pool their information. When Imm called in the information to her paper, she told Ford: "I'm going to yell so you can hear me."[241]

Smith wrote in his story for morning papers of November 23 that after passing along the news about Father Huber, he clung to his phone "for dear life. I was afraid to stray from the wicket [the emergency room cashier's cage] lest I lose contact with the outside world."

Lyndon Johnson, his wife, his staff, and his Secret Service agents left the hospital via the emergency room doors. MacNeil and Robert Pierpoint of CBS News, who'd clung to telephones in the emergency room area as some of the other reporters dispersed, ran to Johnson's group. "Mr. Vice President, is the President dead?" the reporters asked. Johnson did not answer. "He just bulled me out of the way," MacNeil said. Johnson appeared "white as death," MacNeil recalled. "He just looked at us aghast, as though he was going to be attacked, although he knew us perfectly well."

After Johnson was gone, Malcolm Kilduff, the White House spokesman on the trip, appeared. He grabbed Pierpoint and MacNeil and said, "Come on, we are going to hold a press conference." Smith gave up his phone at the cashier's cage and joined Kilduff, MacNeil, Pierpoint, and several other reporters as they dashed to a nurses' classroom. To get there from the emergency room bay, the reporters had to run around the outside of the hospital building. MacNeil and Pierpoint pestered Kilduff: "Mac, Mac, for God's sake, is he dead? Are you going to tell us? Is he dead?" Kilduff said nothing.[242]

Meanwhile, Hampton set himself up with a pay phone in Parkland Hospital's lobby, aided by his knowledge of the 1960s-era telephone system. In those days, a phone connection could only be broken by the party making the call. If you called someone, and the person on the other end of the line hung up, the connection would stay alive until you hung up too. So Hampton called the UPI Dallas bureau and gave the pay phone's number to coworker Don Smith. He hung up, and Don Smith called him back right away. Now the connection would not break until Don Smith hung up. That gave UPI a dedicated line to the hospital. "As long as Don didn't hang up, that phone belonged to UPI and we could use it the rest of the day," Hampton explained. "And no amount of dimes or quarters would ever connect somebody to anyone else. It was UPI's line."[243]

Then Hampton ran to the nurses' classroom, where he finally had his first in-person encounter with Smitty, his famous colleague. "He talked out of the side of his mouth and wore a rumpled suit. He looked like he came right out of central casting for a foreign correspondent or journalist," Hampton recalled.

Smith was agitated. He was reporting a big, big story, and he'd seen the president's blood and brains spattered across the presidential limousine. He knew the bad news that was to be delivered at the press conference—it was the only news possible. Besides, a staffer at the hospital had told him that any other patient in Kennedy's condition simply would have been declared dead on arrival.[244]

"This will be it—the announcement," he said.[245]

A TV cameraman bumped him from behind. "Smitty turned around. He was absolutely furious," said Hampton. "At this time, he was absolutely certain the President was dead and he was very upset. He grabbed the cameraman by the lapels and said, 'Move that thing back. We've got to get this.'"[246]

By 1:33 p.m.—not even an hour after Smitty's dispatch broke the news of the shooting—more than 90 percent of Americans already knew of the assassination. At that moment, Kilduff, cigarette in hand, stood before the reporters in the classroom.

"Quiet! Quiet!" some of the journalists yelled. The room was jammed full. It was the first time Kilduff had ever given a press conference on a presidential trip. His hands trembled. He put them on the table in front of him and leaned forward slightly. He didn't recognize most of the reporters in the room, even though he knew many well. As he spoke, the people in front of him were just a sea of faces.[247]

"President John F. Kennedy—"

"Hold it!" yelled a photographer.

"President John F. Kennedy died at approximately one o'clock Central Standard Time today here in Dallas.

"I have no other details," Kilduff said.

Now there was a mad dash to the telephones. For once, Smitty didn't get to a phone before one of his colleagues. He tried a phone in a nearby office but couldn't get through—the hospital switchboard was overwhelmed.

Hampton sprinted to his pay phone in the hospital lobby. "There was a man sort of staring at it, with a dime in his hand," Hampton said. "I just said, 'That's my phone,' and I grabbed it." Not that it would have done the dime-wielding man any good. When Hampton picked up the handset, Don Smith was ready on the other end of the line. "I said, 'Don, my God he's dead. He's really dead.' And I could hardly believe it."

Don Smith asked the question a wire service journalist would ask: Who said the president was dead?

"Oh—Kilduff," Hampton answered. "'The White House guy, Kilduff.' And I gave him the exact quotes."

In the background, Hampton heard Jack Fallon shout across the UPI newsroom: "FLASH PRESIDENT KENNEDY DEAD."[248] UPI's flash moved at 1:35 p.m., two minutes after Kilduff's statement. For the second time that day, Hampton had helped keep UPI ahead on the story.

It was another two minutes—1:37 p.m.—before the AP reported the official news: "FLASH DALLAS – PRESIDENT KENNEDY DIED AT 1 P.M. (CST)."

One thing that might have delayed the AP: Jack Bell missed Kilduff's news conference. A Washington-based AP photographer, Hank Burroughs, didn't see any AP reporters at Kilduff's announcement. So he shot a quick picture of Kilduff and then headed to find a telephone. He ran from the nurses' classroom and down a corridor, "and there was Jack Bell. He was on the phone, and I came in and said, 'It's the official announcement of the death of the President.' And he handed me the phone and said, 'Dictate it to the office.'"[249]

Bell just couldn't keep up with Smitty.

CHAPTER 8 ✦ NEWSROOMS

BELLS CLANGED ON WIRE SERVICE machines across the country. Five bells rang for the bulletins, including Smith's first report of the shooting at 12:34 p.m.—1:34 p.m. Eastern time—and the AP's initial dispatch sent five minutes later. Ten bells rang for the flashes— including Smith's "Kennedy seriously wounded—perhaps seriously perhaps fatally" report at 12:39 p.m. Dallas time—1:39 p.m. Eastern. The clattering Teletypes were noisy enough. The clanging bells, meant to alert editors to a big story, made them even noisier.

At CBS News in New York, Walter Cronkite sat in shirtsleeves at the horseshoe-shaped editors' desk in the network newsroom, reading the day's news. When five bells rang on the United Press International A-wire, Ed Bliss, a veteran CBS news editor—he worked for years with Edward R. Murrow—read Smith's dispatch. "They say shots rang out in Dallas as the president's motorcade was going through the city," Bliss shouted.

"Oh my God—stay on that," Cronkite responded. He was from Texas himself and had thought about going on Kennedy's trip— "clearly it would have been a great deal of fun." He was aware that Kennedy might encounter trouble, and he had heard about the full-page ad in that day's *Dallas Morning News* accusing Kennedy of being a Communist appeaser. The ad made him think of how rude his fellow Texans could be. But Cronkite didn't expect anything as serious as gunfire.[250]

UPI soon moved Smitty's ten-bell seriously-perhaps-fatally flash. Cronkite shouted to the newsroom: "Kennedy's been shot! Let's get on the air!"[251]

Newspaper and broadcast newsrooms around the country learned of the mayhem even before some reporters in Dallas were fully aware of what was going on. The first nationally broadcast bulletin interrupted a music show on the ABC radio network at about 1:36 p.m. Eastern time—the announcer merely read Smith's first bulletin. Editors at the *New York Times* became aware of the news at about 1:40 p.m.[252] Tom Pettit, an NBC newsman based in Los Angeles, broadcast the news to the network's West Coast stations soon after the first UPI bulletin. But at the time, NBC was off the air on the East Coast and didn't get the news out to its affiliates there until 1:45 p.m. Eastern.[253]

Cronkite was on the air at eight seconds past 1:40 p.m. Eastern time—ten minutes after the shooting, and one minute after UPI's seriously-perhaps-fatally flash. He interrupted a live broadcast of the soap opera *As the World Turns*. "In Dallas, Texas, three shots were fired at President Kennedy's motorcade in downtown Dallas. . . . United Press says that the wounds for President Kennedy perhaps could be fatal," Cronkite said from an off-camera "announce booth." At the end, Cronkite also read James Altgens' reporting for the AP, which would have appeared on the Teletype just as he got to the booth: "Mrs. Kennedy shouts, 'Oh no.'"[254]

Cronkite was in such a hurry that viewers could hear the booth's door shut behind him as he began speaking. They heard Cronkite's voice but did not see his face. Instead, they saw a slide that said "CBS NEWS BULLETIN." Cronkite spoke from off-camera because TV studio cameras in the early 1960s needed about twenty minutes to warm up, and CBS did not have a camera ready when the assassination news broke.

Soon after Cronkite finished the first bulletin, the network went to a commercial and a station break. He was back three minutes later, at 1:43 p.m., with another voice-only update, also spoken behind a "bulletin" slide. This time, Cronkite used the "He's dead" quote Smith got from Clint Hill, and noted again that reporters in the wire car heard three bursts of gunfire.

Next came another ninety-six seconds of *As the World Turns,* followed by fifty-two seconds of commercials. That was the last CBS viewers saw of non-news programming for the next four days. The *As the World Turns* cast kept playing their roles, unaware that most of their live broadcast that day did not make the air. They didn't know until the show was over that Kennedy had been shot.

At fifty-two seconds past 1:47 p.m., Cronkite was on the air again with more details from eyewitnesses, still talking from behind the "bulletin" slide.[255] He mentioned the Adlai Stevenson incident of several weeks before and noted that Dallas was a hotbed of "rightist" opposition to Kennedy policies. He also reported on a man and woman huddled on the "grassy knoll" next to the Book Depository, and wondered whether they were involved in the shooting. Both those reports proved irrelevant upon Lee Harvey Oswald's arrest.

Finally, at 2:00 p.m., a studio camera was warmed up in the newsroom, and Cronkite sat before it. CBS soon switched to a live report from the Dallas Trade Mart; later Cronkite held up a photograph of Kennedy's limousine taken before the shooting. "If you can zoom in with that camera, we can get a closer look," Cronkite told his cameraman.

It was quaint compared to the flashy, computer-driven video graphics used in TV news today. In 1963, it would have taken too much time for CBS to set up a proper graphic. In any case, Cronkite was not as graphically savvy as modern TV journalists and saw a conflict between pictures or graphics and words. "I was always fighting for more time on air to describe the news. . . . There was always this battle between pictorial and the news copy itself."[256] He didn't always see how words and pictures could work together.

By 2:00 p.m., the word was out, over radio and TV. Several miles away from the CBS newsroom, at Aqueduct Racetrack in Queens, 24,280 people had shown up to watch the horses and place their bets. Their world was turned upside down just before the fifth race, a half hour after Oswald fired the three shots. "We ask your prayers," said track announcer Fred Capossela as he told the crowd of the assassination. The announcement was late: everyone at Aqueduct already knew. They'd heard the news on portable radios, or from other track-goers. "There was no mass reaction because there was nobody in the crowd who hadn't heard," the *New York Herald Tribune* reported.

"How can people get so crazy?" asked a busboy in the track clubhouse.

"Could it be the Cosa Nostra?" asked a jockey.

Jackie Robinson, the baseball player, was in the track's box seats. "Where the hell are we heading?" he asked a reporter.

"That guy had everything in the world," an elevator operator said of the slain president. "And he gave his life." [257]

Motorists pulled over in Midtown Manhattan to hear the news on their car radios, and pedestrians leaned in through open car windows to listen. "Something was happening in New York City that rarely happens: People were talking to each other," said journalist Ike Pappas, who got the news from a distraught woman as he emerged from a Greenwich Village subway station.[258] Pollsters found that half an hour after the assassination, 70 percent of American adults knew about it. Ninety-four percent of Americans knew within ninety minutes. About 39 percent of Americans first heard from radio or TV, and 55 percent heard from other people.[259]

Meanwhile, the big New York papers scrambled reporters. "The first decisions made by the editors were not philosophical. They were logistic. We had to get more men to the scene—and fast," said Harrison Salisbury, the national editor of the *New York Times*.[260] At 2:00 p.m., while Kennedy was still in the Parkland emergency room, four reporters—Salisbury called them "*Times* men"—had been contacted around the country and ordered to Dallas. Five more "*Times* men" were ordered to Dallas in the minutes that followed. The *Times* put "at least thirty-two" New York–based reporters on the story, along with twenty Washington-based reporters. Reporters in its London, Moscow, Paris, Rome, Bonn, Tokyo, and Hong Kong bureaus were assigned to pursue different angles related to Kennedy's death. When it emerged that Oswald had lived in the Soviet Union and had protested US policy toward Cuba, "instructions were sent to correspondents in Moscow and other Communist countries to watch reactions closely and report them promptly."[261] On top of all that, covering the story required half of the *Times'* New York editing staff.

Maurice ("Mickey") Carroll, a *New York Herald Tribune* reporter, was walking to work when he heard about the assassination from radios in cars stopped along Broadway. Almost as soon as he arrived in the newsroom, Carroll's boss, *Herald Tribune* metropolitan editor Buddy Weiss, ordered him to catch a plane to Dallas. Weiss gave Carroll a wad of cash—there were no ATMs in those days—which he was to share with Jimmy Breslin and Bob Bird, the other two *Herald Tribune* reporters sent from New York to Texas. The *Herald Tribune* was always outgunned by the *Times*.

At 2:22 p.m. Eastern time, CBS radio aired a report attributed to reporter Dan Rather that Kennedy was dead. Rather, who had once covered the police beat in Houston, dug up the information with Eddie Barker, a reporter for Dallas TV station WRLD. "We had talked to the hospital. We talked to the doctor. We talked to the priest. We had the head of the hospital board. . . . I had worked the police beat in Houston for a long time. If you have a doctor, two priests, the head of the hospital board telling you the man is dead, what you have is a dead man. I did not have any trepidation about it."

CBS radio editors also had no trepidation about it—they reported flat-out that Kennedy was dead. "I was taken aback a little bit when, suddenly, they played the Star Spangled Banner and announced on the radio the president is dead and quoted me saying so," Rather said. [262] On TV, Cronkite was more careful. He told viewers what Rather had learned, and he reported what the priests told reporters at the hospital. But he cautioned that the news was not official.

Finally, at 2:38 p.m. Eastern time, Cronkite delivered the news. "From Dallas, Texas, the flash, apparently official. President Kennedy died at 1 p.m. Central Standard Time, two o'clock Eastern Standard Time, some thirty-eight minutes ago." Cronkite took off his glasses as he checked the time on the newsroom clock. He paused for a beat before he went back to reading more reports about the assassination.

Around 6:30 that evening, Cronkite took a break from the anchor desk. He wanted to talk to his wife. "I hadn't talked to a non-professional all day, and I didn't know how much she knew," he said. "She was not a daytime television viewer, and she could very well have been home and not even known much about it."

When he got to his office, he had calls lighting up six phone lines. He waited until one of the lights on his phone went dark, indicating that the line was free. Then he pushed the line's button and picked up the phone's handset.

But Cronkite wasn't fast enough. At the moment he picked up the handset, another call arrived on the line. When he put the handset to his ear, he found himself talking to a cranky viewer, a woman with what he thought was a fake English accent. She gave an address on Manhattan's ritzy Park Avenue. "I want to complain to somebody at CBS News," the woman said. "I want to complain about your having that Walter Cronkite on the camera at a time like this, crying his crocodile tears when everybody knows he hated John Kennedy."

"Madam, you are speaking to Walter Cronkite. And you, madam, are a damned idiot." He slammed down the phone. [263]

Chapter 9 ✦ Love Field

A HEARSE FROM THE ONEAL Funeral Home backed up to the emergency room bay at Parkland Hospital, and journalists helped unload an eight hundred-pound solid bronze casket from its rear door.[264] After the casket was rolled into the hospital, Charles Roberts of *Newsweek* and Hugh Sidey, his competitor at *Time* magazine, talked to a man sitting in the hearse's front seat. Roberts and Sidey didn't have to file copy right away, so they had time for more reporting. They lucked out with this interview subject, who turned out to be Vernon Oneal, the funeral home's proprietor.

"They expect me to take this body out to the airport and put it aboard a plane," Oneal told the reporters. "And I can't take the body out to the airport because I don't have a certificate or a permit."[265] Roberts didn't realize it, but he and Sidey had stumbled upon a clue to one of the strangest episodes surrounding Kennedy's death.

In 1963, no federal law covered the assassination of a president. Whoever killed Kennedy would be prosecuted under Texas homicide statutes. Texas law required an autopsy in all homicide cases. Everyone in Kennedy's entourage—including his Secret Service agents—was eager to leave Dallas. They planned to take the president's body with them back to Washington. But Dr. Earl Rose, the Dallas County medical examiner, insisted that the dead president's body could not be moved without his permission. Rose, who was based at Parkland Hospital, didn't plan to give that permission until he had conducted a full autopsy.

Roy Kellerman, the chief Secret Service agent on the scene, confronted Rose. "My friend, this is the body of the President of the United States, and we are going to take it back to Washington," Kellerman said.

"No, that's not the way things are," said Rose, wagging his finger. "When there's a homicide, we must have an autopsy."

"He is the President. He is going with us."

"The body stays," said Rose.[266]

Kenneth O'Donnell, a Kennedy aide, asked Rose if he could make an exception for the president.

"It's just another homicide case as far as I'm concerned," Rose answered.

"Go fuck yourself," O'Donnell yelled. "We're leaving!"[267]

Some of Rose's fellow Texans refused to back him. Dr. Charles Baxter, the chief of Parkland's emergency rooms, officially authorized the removal of Kennedy's body.[268] But the man who really decided the matter was not at the hospital. Rose and Justice of the Peace Theron Ward, who had been summoned to Parkland, consulted by telephone with Henry Wade, the Dallas County District Attorney. In separate phone calls, Wade told Rose and Ward he would not insist the autopsy be performed in Texas. He also got a promise from the White House staff that the doctors who performed Kennedy's autopsy in Washington would testify at any trial. Though releasing Kennedy's body without an autopsy violated Texas law, it didn't seem like a big deal to the district attorney; the punishment was a $100 fine. He didn't want to bother prosecuting such a case. Wade also didn't think the controversy would matter one way or another at a murder trial. He advised Ward to tell the White House doctor: "Take him on back."[269]

The news media at Parkland was totally unaware of this controversy. Not even Governor Connally, then undergoing surgery, learned of the fuss until ten months later, when author William Manchester told him about it.[270]

Roberts went back in to the hospital by climbing through a window and found himself in a room off an emergency room corridor. "I stepped into that corridor just minutes before they brought the President's body out in the bronze casket," he said. Kennedy's coffin rolled right past him. "Mrs. Kennedy was walking on the right side of it. . . . A policeman pinned me up against the wall as they passed by. She was walking with her left hand on the casket and a completely glazed look on her face, obviously in shock.

"It was deathly still in that corridor as this casket was wheeled out," Roberts said. "I had a feeling that if somebody had literally fired a pistol in front of her face that she would just have blinked. It seemed that she was absolutely out of this world."[271] He'd spoken to the First Lady when she and her husband shook hands with the crowd at Love Field just three hours before. Now, Roberts said, "if she saw me at all, there was no glimmer of recognition. . . . Her eyes seemed glazed. She was undoubtedly in shock."[272]

Tom Wicker of the *New York Times* saw the coffin as it was taken to the hearse. "A number of White House staff people, stunned, silent, stumbling along as if dazed, walked with it," Wicker wrote. "Mrs. Kennedy walked by the coffin, her hand on it, her head down, her hat gone, her dress and stockings spattered." She had refused a nurse's offer to help clean the blood from her outfit—"I want the world to see what Dallas has done to my husband," Mrs. Kennedy said.[273]

Wicker watched as she got into the hearse with the casket that held her husband. "That was just about the only eyewitness matter that I got with my own eyes that entire afternoon," he wrote later.[274]

No reporter saw as much that day as Smitty.

After Smith called in his report of Kilduff's official announcement of Kennedy's death, he returned to the nurses' classroom. There, doctors who treated Kennedy and Connally were preparing to answer reporters' questions. Julian Read, the governor's aide, was ready to provide the reporters some details from Mrs. Connally about what had happened in Kennedy's limousine. Smith thought it was going to be "a very interesting news conference."[275]

But the focus of the story was changing. Smitty's job was to cover the president. And the new president was eager to leave Dallas.

Jiggs Fauver, a White House transportation aide, pulled Smith aside. He had instructions from Malcolm Kilduff, the press secretary on the trip. "He wants you downstairs, and he wants you right now," Fauver said. Kilduff was putting together a press pool to accompany President Johnson and the White House entourage back to Washington on Air Force One. Smitty knew right away that he had to go along. "You always follow the football," Smith said, referring to the suitcase containing nuclear launch codes that a US Army Signal Corpsman always carried next to the president.[276]

Next, Fauver sought out Jack Bell, who the White House figured would represent the Associated Press in the pool. He found Bell at a nurses' station, typing out an eyewitness account of what happened in Kennedy's motorcade.

Bell did not grasp the urgency of the situation. He turned down Fauver's request.

Fauver also needed a broadcaster for the pool. He grabbed Sid Davis, who was on a telephone broadcasting his report of Kennedy's death. "We need a pool," the aide said. "For what?" asked Davis. "I can't tell you," Fauver said. But Davis knew it'd be best if he went along.

Fauver led Davis down a hallway, where they passed the nurses' station where Bell was working. "Jack Bell was in there typing," Davis said. "He was sweating. He was single minded, pounding that typewriter and perspiring."

For a second time, Fauver asked Bell to come along. "Jack, I'm not going to tell you again. You have to come with me."

"I'll catch up with you," said Bell.

"You can't catch up with me," Fauver replied. "We're going in a police car. You either come now, or you are going to be left behind."

"I stood there waiting while Fauver and Jack Bell argued," Davis said.

"We left him behind."[277]

Merriman Smith (standing at left, in vest) and colleagues in Warm Springs after FDR's death [Smith family collection]

Smitty gets soaked crossing the equator on the USS *Missouri* [United States Navy/ Harry S. Truman Presidential Library

Smith with President Harry S. Truman in Independence
[Smith family collection]

Who Said That panel with Smith [Smith family collection]

Smith, Kennedy, British Prime Minister Harold MacMillan, unknown man with glasses at White House Correspondents Association dinner [White House photo by Abbie Rowe, collection of John F. Kennedy Presidential Library and Museum]

JFK in Houston on November 21, 1963, with Smith and Secret Service agent Clint Hill to his left [White House photo by Cecil R. Stoughton, collection of John F. Library Presidential Library and Museum]

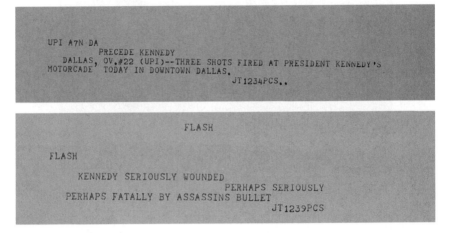

```
UPI A7N DA
        PRECEDE KENNEDY
    DALLAS, OV.#22 (UPI)--THREE SHOTS FIRED AT PRESIDENT KENNEDY'S
MOTORCADE' TODAY IN DOWNTOWN DALLAS.
                                JT1234PCS..
```

```
                        FLASH


FLASH

    KENNEDY SERIOUSLY WOUNDED
                        PERHAPS SERIOUSLY
    PERHAPS FATALLY BY ASSASSINS BULLET
                        JT1239PCS
```

Some of UPI's first dispatches about President Kennedy's assassination
[Texas State Library and Archives Commission]

```
    FLASH
        PRESIDENT KENNEDY DEAD
                        JT135PCS
```

UPI flashes Kennedy's death [Texas State Library and Archives
Commission]

Smith was one of twenty-seven people present when LBJ was sworn in on Air Force One [White House photo by Cecil R. Stoughton, collection of John F. Kennedy Presidential Library and Museum]

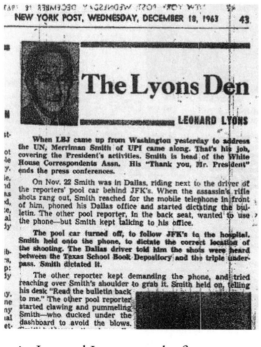

The Lyons Den

LEONARD LYONS

When LBJ came up from Washington yesterday to address the UN, Merriman Smith of UPI came along. That's his job, covering the President's activities. Smith is head of the White House Correspondents Assn. His "Thank you, Mr. President" ends the press conferences.

On Nov. 22 Smith was in Dallas, riding next to the driver of the reporters' pool car behind JFK's. When the assassin's rifle shots rang out, Smith reached for the mobile telephone in front of him, phoned his Dallas office and started dictating the bulletin. The other pool reporter, in the back seat, wanted to use the phone—but Smith kept talking to his office.

The pool car turned off, to follow JFK's to the hospital. Smith held onto the phone, to dictate the correct location of the shooting. The Dallas driver told him the shots were heard between the Texas School Book Depository and the triple underpass. Smith dictated it.

The other reporter kept demanding the phone, and tried reaching over Smith's shoulder to grab it. Smith held on, telling his desk "Read the bulletin back to me." The other pool reporter started clawing and pummeling Smith—who ducked under the dashboard to avoid the blows.

Gossip columnist Leonard Lyons was the first to recount what happened between Smith and Bell in the wire car [*New York Post*]

Captain Albert Smith at Vung Tau orphanage in Vietnam [Smith family collection]

Smith and LBJ enjoy a light moment with reporters on Air Force One [Smith family collection]

Smitty and LBJ and LBJ's ranch [United Press International]

Smitty shakes hands with LBJ after winning Pulitzer [United Press International]

Smith at his typewriter in San Clemente [Smith family collection]

Bell didn't know it, but his refusal to go along cost him his only chance at recovering from the humiliating defeat Smitty handed him in the wire car. "The White House was not his beat," Davis said. Because they knew the ways of the White House, Smith and Davis knew reflexively that they had to go with Fauver. Bell, who was not a White House regular, did not.

The White House needed a print reporter to complete the pool. Outside the hospital emergency room, another White House aide, Wayne Hawks, enlisted Robert Roth of the *Philadelphia Bulletin* to join Smith and Davis. But Roberts remembered that in the original plan for the trip, he was scheduled to be in the pool on the presidential party's journey to Austin later in the day. "Partly out of hunch, instinct, I don't know what, I decided that I ought to make that trip to the airport," said Roberts.

"Wait a minute," Roberts told Hawks. "I was to have been the pooler on the next leg. Wherever the President goes, although he's not going to Austin, I'm going to go."

So Roberts took the print reporter spot in the pool. He, Davis, and Smith piled into an unmarked Dallas police car for the ride to Love Field, about two and a half miles away. They asked the driver to hurry. "We were starting perhaps as much as six, eight or ten minutes after they had removed President Kennedy's body. And so we had to go like hell to get there," Roberts said. "For all we knew they were going to put that casket aboard a plane and fly out immediately."

Davis, who hadn't had time to tell his editors of his plans, asked the officer driving the car if he would relay a message to his office. "We're maintaining radio silence," the cop answered. "We don't know if there are any more shooters."

The officer was also under orders not to use his siren or lights. The police, fearful of another shooter or some other mayhem, didn't want to draw attention to the airport. It seemed to Roberts that the car got up to 80 mph at some points. "We went through red lights and crossed median strips. . . . He wasn't even using his horn much," Roberts said.

Kennedy's casket was loaded on Air Force One at 2:18 p.m. A few minutes later, the pool reporters' car stopped about two hundred yards from the plane. "Kilduff spotted us and motioned us to hurry," Smith wrote in his story recounting the day's events. "We trotted to him and he said the plane could take two pool men to Washington; that Johnson was about to take the oath of office aboard the plane and would take off immediately thereafter."

Smitty saw some phone booths and asked Kilduff if he had time to call his editors. "For God's sake, hurry," Kilduff said.

Smith tried to call the UPI Dallas bureau, but got a busy signal. He couldn't get through to Washington—all of that city's phone circuits were jammed. Finally he got through to UPI headquarters in New York and reported that Johnson was about to take the oath of office.

Kilduff came out of the plane and motioned to Smith. Smith slammed down the phone and ran to the plane's stairs. Sarah Hughes, a federal judge in Dallas, had just arrived and was about to administer the oath to Johnson. "All they were waiting for was the press," said Roberts. "The President, I learned later, had insisted on some press witnesses to his swearing-in."

The reporters climbed up the plane's forward ramp and pushed back to the stateroom in its midsection, which functioned as the president's airborne office.

Suddenly, Smith looked down at his right hand. "My God, I've lost my typewriter," he said.

"As a reflex, I looked at my right hand to see if I had my typewriter, and I did," said Roberts. "But if anybody had asked me then, 'Do you have your typewriter?' without looking, I wouldn't have known."

Davis overheard Kilduff tell President Johnson: "We've got everybody here but AP." Jack Bell could have been there.[278]

The reporters counted twenty-seven people crowded into the stateroom. The window shades were drawn. It was sweltering—the plane's air conditioning was off. Some of the stunned members of Kennedy's staff wept softly. Smith stood behind Johnson to his left, in a far corner of the tiny room. Roberts stood behind Evelyn Lincoln, President Kennedy's secretary. She was standing right behind the new President.

Johnson said to two Kennedy aides: "Do you want to ask Mrs. Kennedy if she would like to stand with us?" He waited until Mrs. Kennedy was at his side, and at 2:38 p.m., he took the oath of office. Judge Hughes could barely be heard above the whine of the jet engines as she read the words to Johnson: "I do solemnly swear that I will faithfully execute the office of the President of the United States . . ." White House photographer Cecil Stoughton, who took pictures of Johnson taking the oath, made sure the bloodstains on Mrs. Kennedy's outfit did not show up in his photos.

When it was done, Lady Bird Johnson turned to Mrs. Kennedy and said: "The whole nation mourns your husband." The reporters thought Mrs. Kennedy could barely control her emotions. But they observed that she remained composed throughout.

"Johnson went over and kissed Mrs. Johnson, and then he kissed Mrs. Kennedy," Davis said. The reporters fussed about this detail. "Chuck Roberts . . . said he embraced Mrs. Kennedy. We had a little argument about that afterwards, whether it was kissed or embraced," Davis said. Smitty said Johnson kissed Mrs. Kennedy, so that's what the reporters wrote.[279]

"She was not bewildered," said Davis. "She just stood there, wide-eyed, unblinking, noticeably grieving." Other women in the room cried. "The sobs got louder and you could see the mascara streaming down their cheeks." Everyone was sad. "Their hero was gone. These people had worked so hard to get him elected and were so excited to be in the White House with him."[280]

"Let's get airborne," President Johnson said.

The reporters quickly checked over their notes so they could agree on the details of a pool report to be delivered to their

colleagues. Kilduff said just two reporters could accompany Johnson
to Washington. Smith, as dean of the White House press corps and
a wire reporter, would be one. He suggested Davis and Roberts toss
a coin for the last seat on the plane.

"I'm not flipping," Davis said. "I'm getting off." He would
deliver the pool report to the rest of the reporters in Dallas. Besides,
he said, "Chuck is with *Newsweek*. He needs the feature material.
They don't go to press until tomorrow. He could use the time, and I
can get off. I need to get off."[281]

Davis was nervous about delivering the pool report. Providing
the other reporters with information about the swearing-in was a
big responsibility, and he didn't want to botch it. "I was not a great
reporter, and I was not a great note taker—and I was afraid I might
leave something out," he said. "I knew this was the biggest story
I would ever cover in my entire life. I knew my reputation as a
reporter in Washington would die if I really screwed this one up,
and I was scared to death that I'd miss something."[282]

Davis left the plane with Judge Hughes. "As I went down the
stairs, she started to tell me that Kennedy appointed her to the
bench . . . and that Lyndon Johnson was a friend of hers. And then
she started to cry.

"And then, there's this voice from the hatch as I'm going down
the stairs. This voice, raspy voice, of Merriman Smith."

"Kid!" Smitty yelled to Davis. He wanted to clarify something:
Johnson took the oath at 2:39 p.m., not at 2:38 p.m. as the reporters
had agreed.

"OK, Smitty," Davis yelled back.

Across the tarmac, Davis saw three pay phones. They were tempt-
ing. He could call his editors and quickly go on the air with a very
nice scoop—the first report of President Johnson's oath of office.
His other choice was to follow the rules and wait for the rest of the
press to show up and hear his report. That meant everyone would
get the same news at the same time. It also meant Davis would be
later than his competitors getting the story on the air, since he could

not run for a phone until the other reporters were satisfied with his report.

"It's the moment of truth. Do I use the telephone to call my office, or do I wait for the reporters?" he asked himself.

"Well, I waited for the reporters." [283]

He didn't wait long. Wicker of the *New York Times* was on a press bus that drove up just as Air Force One was airborne. The Boeing jet took off for Washington at 2:47 p.m., about nine minutes after Johnson took the oath.

Davis stood on the trunk of a shiny white car parked near the press bus, and the reporters gathered around him. Once he said Johnson had been sworn in, the TV and radio reporters all sprinted for telephones. "That's all they wanted," Davis said.

The newspaper reporters stayed behind and asked more questions. Davis described "the blood streaked on Mrs. Kennedy's dress, on her legs, the blood congealed on her wrists. The sadness of it all."

Wicker asked: "How long did it take for the oath to be given?"

"Twenty-eight seconds," Davis answered. Wicker seemed impressed with that bit of detail.

"I gave the time of the ceremony as 2:38 p.m., which was the time in my notepad." That differed from the Smith's belief that the oath took place at 2:39 p.m.

Wicker "asked me more questions than I had answers for. Naturally, they wanted great detail. . . . Wicker kept me there for about twenty minutes, asking me every detail." It was a grilling, but Wicker was pleased with what he got. He called the pool report "magnificent," and said it "gave a picture that so far as I know was complete, accurate and has not been added to."[284] For months afterward, Davis recalled, Wicker referred to him as "the pooler's pooler." Davis didn't miss anything, didn't overlook anything, and his reputation as a reporter was intact.

Elsewhere in Dallas, news was breaking. At 1:15 p.m., fifteen minutes after the Parkland doctors declared Kennedy dead, Dallas police officer J. D. Tippit stopped Lee Harvey Oswald on the street because he resembled a man described as Kennedy's shooter. Oswald shot Tippit three times in the chest. While a witness reported the shooting over the radio in the policeman's patrol car, Oswald fled. He was arrested about six-tenths of a mile away, in a movie theater in Dallas's Oak Cliff neighborhood.

Oswald's arrest was soon on the wires—but it was a story for other reporters. The White House reporters had enough to do already. "We better go write. There'll be phones in the terminal," Wicker suggested to his principal competitor, Douglas Kiker of the *New York Herald Tribune*.

The terminal was a half mile from where Davis had given the pool report. Wicker and Kiker had to cut thorough a baggage-handling room to reach the passenger area. Wicker found a phone and called the *Times'* dictation room in New York.

"Hello, I've got some dictation for you on the, uh, Kennedy story."

"Yeah. Where are you, Tom?"

"I'm in Dallas."

"OK, boy now take it easy," said the dictation taker.

"This is Dallas, November 22. I don't have too much, this is to get you started. Dallas, November 22. President—"

Wicker choked up. He is heard weeping on the recording. Some reporters who admitted being overtaken by their emotions said it was days before they broke down or wept over the assassination. But Wicker felt it right away.

He quickly composed himself and went on: "President John F. Kennedy was shot and killed here today, period. The President suffered a massive gunshot wound in the brain and was pronounced dead at 1:00 p.m. Central Standard Time, period, paragraph."[285]

"Every so often, just as on that dictation, why, the emotion of the thing would come over you," Wicker said years later. "But most of the time you just had to keep working as a professional."[286]

Next, he went to the mezzanine at the airport terminal, where he found writing desks for travelers. Wicker wrote two pages, ran off and to find a phone, and dictated. He repeated the process for the next two hours.

He advised his desk to add in to his story information from AP or UPI on Oswald's arrest. "There was no time left to chase down the Dallas police and find out those details on my own," he said.[287]

Wicker wrote while Smith's copy was already in print in hundreds of afternoon newspapers across the country. Smith got a page-one byline in some editions of the *New York World Telegram and Sun*, an afternoon paper. He also got a front-page byline on the lead story of the *Washington Post's* extra on the assassination. The *Post* used Smith's story even though it had its own reporter on the Dallas trip. So did other newspapers with White House reporters in Dallas. Smith had seen everything, and he had access to information the other print reporters lacked.

And Smitty was still at work. Aboard Air Force One, he and Roberts tracked the doings of the new president and everyone else aboard. When the jet reached cruising altitude, Mrs. Kennedy went to the rear compartment and sat by her husband's casket. "There she remained throughout the flight," Smith reported.

Smith and Roberts were seated at a table. Because Smitty had lost his portable typewriter, Evelyn Lincoln provided him with a big electric typewriter that she had used to type President Kennedy's speeches. It took Smith a few minutes to learn how to work it.

A radio transmission from Air Force One offers more evidence of Jack Bell's misstep in failing to heed Jiggs Fauver's request to join the press pool. At about 3:13 p.m.—twenty-six minutes after the jet left Love Field—Malcolm Kilduff radioed ahead to Washington to instruct White House staff about arrangements for a statement Johnson wanted to give to the press when the plane landed. "We lost Bell somewhere along the line. We don't have AP aboard," Kilduff reported.[288]

Soon President Johnson approached Smith and Roberts. "I'm going to make a short statement in a few minutes and give you copies of it," he said. "Then when I get on the ground, I'll do it over again."

The statement said: "This is a sad time for all people. We have suffered a loss that cannot be weighed. For me it is a deep personal tragedy. I know the world shares the sorrow that Mrs. Kennedy and her family bear. I will do my best. That is all I can do. I ask for your help—and God's." He issued the statement at 3:40 p.m., fifty-three minutes after the plane left Dallas.[289]

Johnson spoke to the reporters twice during the flight. "This was the first time in my twenty-odd years as a reporter that I felt like saying to the President of the United States: 'I know you want to talk, but I've got a long story to write,'" Roberts said.[290] His pool report noted that four Kennedy aides joined Mrs. Kennedy in her vigil next to her husband's casket. His report also offered some idea of the horror in the presidential limousine. "Both Mrs. Kennedy's legs were stained and her dress was spattered with blood. Secret Service agents reported that she threw herself over his body when he slumped down in the rear seat," he wrote. Both Roberts and Smith reported Johnson's phone call to Rose Kennedy, the late president's mother. "I wish to God that there was something I could do. I just wanted you to know that."[291]

At 5:59 p.m. Eastern time—a bit more than two hours after leaving Dallas—Air Force One arrived at Andrews Air Force Base in Maryland. Smith recounted: "I thanked the stewards for rigging up the typewriter for me, pulled on my raincoat and started down the forward ramp. Roberts and I stood under a wing and watched the casket being lowered from the rear of the plane and borne by a complement of armed forces body bearers into a waiting hearse. We watched Mrs. Kennedy and the president's brother, Attorney General Robert F. Kennedy, climb into the hearse beside the coffin."[292]

Al Spivak and Helen Thomas were waiting at the airport. Smith handed them the copy he'd written on Evelyn Lincoln's typewriter and asked them to call it in to the UPI Washington bureau. "Smitty had to hop on a helicopter that was taking the press pool to the White House," Spivak said.[293]

Smith could dictate perfect copy off the top of his head. But much of his copy that day was, by necessity, written by rewriters and editors in UPI bureaus in Dallas and Washington. The bureaus were getting information from many sources. The rewriters and editors had to sort the information into stories that their newspaper clients could use with little or no further editing.

But Smith was not done writing. Before the night was out he was back in UPI's Washington bureau in the National Press Building, where he wrote a 2,800-word account of what he saw in Dallas and on Air Force One, aimed at the next day's morning newspapers. The editors didn't change any of it. They didn't even have to fix Smith's punctuation. Bill Umstead, the bureau's overnight editor, only had to mark the beginning of Smith's paragraphs. "You've got to know when to leave it alone," Umstead said.[294]

Smith's story ended with a scene aboard the helicopter that carried Smith, Roberts, and several presidential aides from Andrews Air Force Base back to the White House.

"In the compartment next to ours in one of the large chairs beside a window sat Theodore C. Sorensen, one of Kennedy's closest associates with the title of special counsel to the president. He had not gone to Texas with his chief but had come to the air base for his return," Smith wrote.

"Sorensen sat wilted in the large chair, crying softly. The dignity of his deep grief seemed to sum up all of the tragedy and sadness of the previous six hours."[295]

It was another scene of the day unwitnessed by any AP reporter. Sorensen's tears were not news. But it was the kind of detail in which Smith specialized during his career as a White House reporter. It was a bit of information that conveyed the emotion of what had happened, and put Smith's readers in the middle of what was going on that tragic day.

The next day, Smith's story appeared in some of the country's biggest newspapers, including the *St. Louis Post-Dispatch*, the *Los Angeles Times*, and the *Dallas Times-Herald* and *Houston Chronicle* in Texas. The story won Smith the Pulitzer Prize.

After the story was written and edited, Smith and some coworkers went to the National Press Club bar, on the top floor of a building that housed the Washington bureaus of UPI and other newspaper and broadcast outlets. There, the story goes, Smitty complained that his back hurt. He pulled up his shirt, and colleagues saw the welts on his back made by Jack Bell's fists.

How hard Bell hit Smith is disputed. Al Spivak doubts Bell had the strength to hit Smith hard enough to leave any welts. Smith himself clouded the issue in a January 1967 letter to the editors of *Look* magazine, which was about to publish advance excerpts of William Manchester's book *The Death of a President: November 20– November 25, 1963*. Smith's aim was to correct Manchester's notion that he and Bell engaged in a "furious fistfight" in the wire car. In the wire car, Smith wrote, "Bell was grabbing for the telephone over my shoulders and I certainly would have done the same thing if I had been in the back seat. I bent over the dashboard so I could hear the read-back over the yelling and the sirens and quite naturally Bell kept grabbing for the phone. Then I handed it to him.

"If this is a 'furious fistfight,' Mr. Manchester must be a quite delicate soul who has never seen competitive press association reporters at work."[296] Manchester apparently accepted Smith's correction. The phrase "furious fistfight" does not appear in the final version of his book.

Patrick J. Sloyan, who in 1963 was a Washington-based UPI editor, reported the welts in a 1998 article in *American Journalism Review*. He stands by the story today. Sloyan wrote: "The welts were proof that it was Smith—not Bell—who had administered an unforgettable beating."[297]

SIDEBAR • REWRITE

Hours after the assassination, long after Smith and Air Force One left for Washington, UPI's Dallas staff was still reporting and writing the story.

Jack Fallon was the top UPI editor in Dallas. Fallon was a top-notch rewriter. Rewriters gather notes and information from other reporters and turn them into coherent stories. Earlier in his career, Fallon was a rewriter on the United Press's foreign desk in New York. His skill helped the UP win a Pulitzer Prize for its reporting on the 1956 Hungarian uprising.

Fallon's rewrite expertise was one reason UPI led the AP on the assassination story. He worked "like a human machine," recalled Mike Rabun, a young UPI Dallas staffer. Fallon kept up the pace hour after hour, writing fresh, clear copy.

Several Teletype operators—punchers—took turns putting Fallon's copy on the wire. One puncher, Betty McClure, was known to everyone in the bureau as "Aunt Betty."

After several hours of writing assassination news, Fallon paused and looked up from his typewriter toward McClure.

"Aunt Betty," he said, "I still can't believe this happened."

Then he turned back to his typewriter and went back to work.[298]

Chapter 10 ✦ Shooters

Every reporter knows people like Jack Ruby. They're news-hounds. They need to be where the action is. They show up at murder trials, at public events at city halls and state capitols, and anyplace else the media gathers. Reporters tell themselves: "I wouldn't be here unless I was getting paid. So why are these people always hanging around?" Ruby was a publicity-seeking Dallas nightclub owner known to many of the city's cops and some of its reporters. He hung around cops and reporters because he liked being where news is made.

Seth Kantor was one of the reporters who knew Jack Ruby. Kantor was a feature writer at the *Dallas Times Herald,* from September 1960 to May 1962, and wrote several stories about Ruby's night-clubs. "I think by the nature of the stories I wrote, I sort of attracted Jack Ruby," Kantor told the Warren Commission, which President Johnson established to investigate the assassination.

Ruby approached Kantor at the *Times Herald* one day and "said he owned a club or clubs in town, and that he thought he might have some stories for me from time to time, and he did." One story was about a Dallas-area housewife who performed at Ruby's club. She charmed snakes while she was stripping. Another was about a limbo dancer from the Caribbean who was getting Ruby's help in obtaining citizenship. "We got a picture of him at the U.S. Naturalization Service office in Dallas passing under a low bar," Kantor said. Kantor also recalled seeing Ruby around the *Times Herald* newsroom. One of the paper's photographers often took publicity shots for Ruby's club.[299]

In his later writing about Ruby and the assassination, Kantor made much of Ruby's mob connections—or, at least, his mob aspirations. Ruby admired the mob leaders of the day, and certainly had mob associations, but was never found in government investigations to be a member of any organized crime family. Kantor didn't think the government investigations went far enough. He wrote a book that explored the possibility that Ruby was involved in a plot to cover up President Kennedy's assassination.

Merriman Smith put no stock in assassination conspiracy theories and didn't buy the idea that Ruby was involved in any cover-up. He was content to write of Ruby's "sleazy, crawling nature" and label him a "strip club loudmouth."[300]

After Kantor left the *Times Herald,* he moved to Washington to cover Texas political news for the Scripps Howard News Service. Kennedy's Texas trip was important news to the newspapers Scripps Howard owned in the state, so it was natural that Kantor went along. On November 22, Kantor was aboard the second press bus in President Kennedy's motorcade.

After Kennedy was shot, Kantor made his way from the Dallas Trade Mart to Parkland Hospital with several other reporters in a station wagon driven by a man who had been waiting to hear President Kennedy speak.

Kantor was with Smitty and Kennedy press aide Malcolm Kilduff as they ran from the emergency room outdoors and around to another hospital entrance on their way to the nurses' classroom where Kilduff was to announce Kennedy's death. Smith was "incessantly asking for whatever news there was. . . . I knew it was a rather grim situation, but I didn't know how grim," Kantor said.

They were barely back inside the hospital when Kantor encountered Ruby. "I apparently walked right past him . . . as I was walking, I was stopped momentarily by a tug on the back of my jacket.

And I turned and saw Jack Ruby standing there. He had his hand extended."

"I very well remember my first thought. I thought, 'Well, there is Jack Ruby.' I had been away from Dallas eighteen months and one day at that time, but it seemed just perfectly normal to see Jack Ruby standing there, because he was a known goer to events."

"Isn't this a terrible thing?" said Ruby.

"He had quite a look of consternation on his face," Kantor recalled. "He looked emotional—which also seemed fitting enough for Jack Ruby."[301] Kantor thought Ruby appeared miserable—grim, pale, with tears brimming in his eyes.[302]

Ruby was deeply troubled by Kennedy's assassination. "He cried harder when President Kennedy died than when Ma and Pa died," his sister Eva told author Vincent Bugliosi.[303] He worried when he read in the newspaper that Jacqueline Kennedy might be called to testify at Oswald's trial. He was also moved by a Dallas citizen's open letter to Caroline Kennedy in the *Times Herald:* "No one can erase this day. . . . You will cry. . . . You will miss him. . . . You will want to know why anyone would do a thing like this to your father." Bugliosi said the letter had a "devastating effect on Ruby."[304]

"Should I close my places for the next three nights, do you think?" Ruby asked Kantor at the hospital.

"Yes, I think that is a good idea," Kantor answered.

By Kantor's account, this encounter took place around 1:30 p.m., an hour after the shooting and a half hour after Kennedy's doctors declared him dead. After his brief talk with Ruby, Kantor headed to Kilduff's momentous press conference.[305]

The Warren Commission didn't believe Kantor's story about meeting Ruby. Warren investigators found that Ruby's itinerary that day included a visit to the advertising department of the *Dallas Morning News* that lasted to just after 1:00 p.m., and a stop at the Carousel Club, one of his strip joints, where he made a phone call at 1:45 p.m. The Commission's investigators figured he simply didn't have time to stop at Parkland Hospital, which was several miles out of his way through heavy traffic. Also, Ruby firmly denied visiting the hospital.

But Kantor was confident enough of what he saw to report the encounter in a newspaper story he wrote three days after the assassination.[306] And minds eventually changed about Kantor's tale. Subsequent investigations found that Ruby's 1:45 p.m. phone call and another call at 1:51 p.m. from the Carousel Club were made by one of his employees.[307] There was another witness—her recollection was a bit vague—who claimed she saw Ruby at Parkland at about the same time as Kantor.[308]

In 1979, the House Select Committee on Assassinations decided that Ruby was in the hospital when and where Kantor said. It based that finding on testimony by a Warren Commission investigator, Burt W. Griffin, that "in light of evidence subsequently brought out, that the Commission's conclusion about Kantor's testimony was wrong."[309] Besides, Ruby had motive to deny he was there: his hospital visit would have been evidence for a jury that he had thought out Oswald's killing in advance, increasing the severity of his punishment.

Kantor's story opens a window on Ruby's character as a man who liked being with reporters, with cops, or anyplace where he thought the action was. That's how Kantor remembered him from his time as a reporter in Dallas—"a known goer to events." That he might have shown up at Parkland Hospital was no surprise.

And there's no doubt that Ruby showed up at another place where assassination news was made—Dallas police headquarters, where Oswald was being questioned the night of November 22. Many people saw Ruby amid the media scrum that crowded the police department's hallways and offices. Ruby even gave a business card to Ike Pappas, a reporter for WNEW radio in New York who'd hurriedly flown to Dallas that afternoon with other New York media types.

Pappas began November 22 in a dentist's chair in Manhattan— it was a day off. When the dentist was done, he took the subway to the West Fourth Street station, on Sixth Avenue in Greenwich Village.

"This woman came running up to me as I came out of the subway. She was screaming to me that the president was shot. Her face was wet with tears. She was crying, screaming hysterically," Pappas said. He wasn't sure what to make of the woman's behavior—someone in New York is always yelling and upset about something. But this was different. People were talking, gathering by radios, listening to news. "I looked around. I said, 'Something is very wrong,'" Pappas said. "I ran across the street to a telephone booth."

Pappas called his editor at WNEW. "What is this about Kennedy?" he asked.

"Get your ass up here right now," the editor answered.

"My heart sank," Pappas said. It was true.

He got a cab to his office. Pappas's editor gave him $500 in cash, a tape recorder, and a pile of wire service copy. "Get to Dallas," the editor said.

Pappas took a cab to Idlewild Airport and ended up on an American Airlines charter that took aboard New York–based FBI and Secret Service agents and New York reporters. Jimmy Breslin, Robert Bird, and Mickey Carroll from the *New York Herald Tribune* were on the plane. So were people from the *New York Times* and the *New York Daily News*. Bob Considine, a famed syndicated newspaper columnist of the day, was also on the flight. The plane flew the agents and journalists to Washington, where it took on more passengers before it headed on to Dallas.

At Love Field, Pappas got a cab and went straight to Dallas police headquarters. A man at the elevator asked him for ID. Then Pappas rode up to the building's third floor, which housed the department's administrative offices and detective bureaus. It was, he said, "pandemonium." Carroll said it was "chaos . . . a lot of noise, a lot of people shouting." The cops could barely open their office doors. FBI agent James Hosty—who had been monitoring Oswald for months before the assassination—told the Warren Commission that the police station was something like "Grand Central Station at rush hour, maybe like the Yankee Stadium during the World Series, quite noisy. . . . The place was swarming with people."[310]

Henry Wade, the Dallas County district attorney, thought there were three hundred reporters at police headquarters; the Warren Commission says only that there were "upwards of 100 newsmen and cameramen" present. Crews stretched cables to two TV cameras in the corridor. "Men with newsreel cameras, still cameras, and microphones, more mobile than the television cameramen, moved back and forth seeking information and opportunities for interviews," the Warren Commission said. "Newsmen wandered into the offices of other bureaus located on the third floor, sat on desks, and used police telephones; indeed, one reporter admits hiding a telephone behind a desk so that he would have exclusive access to it if something developed."[311] The journalists packed in tightly—the third floor corridor was 110 feet long and six feet wide, and an intersecting lobby was twenty-seven feet long and ten feet wide. Those hundreds of reporters and photographers were jammed in to 840 square feet of space. And they were all jostling for whatever information they could get.

When Oswald was brought from the police station's fifth-floor lockup to the homicide bureau, he had to be walked about twenty feet down the third-floor corridor in the journalists' presence. The reporters yelled questions to him. Captain Will Fritz, who was leading the Dallas police investigation and was among a number of cops and federal agents questioning him, believed Oswald got upset every time he was paraded through the corridor. "The number of people in the interrogation room and the tumultuous atmosphere throughout the third floor made it difficult for the interrogators to gain Oswald's confidence and to encourage him to be truthful," the Warren Commission said. The commission quoted Dallas Police Chief Jesse Curry: "We were violating every principle of interrogation."[312]

Reporters and photographers from around the world crowded the police headquarters. Carroll said the Dallas cops simply didn't know how to handle all the media attention. "If there'd been a normal murder, a few reporters would have shown up. They'd let them in and handle it," he said. "They just did the same thing [for the assassination]. But this time, there were people on every airplane coming to Dallas. The place was just mobbed. There's no protocol for how you cover a presidential assassination. They shouldn't have let us in. There's no doubt about that."[313]

The only rule, said Pappas, was that reporters were not to enter the homicide detectives' office. "They had a guard outside to make sure of that," he said. The reporters had no trouble using phones in other offices on the third floor—but there weren't enough for everyone. About forty-five minutes after he arrived, Pappas left the building and ran to a hotel across the street, from where he called his office in New York. Then he went back to police headquarters.

That evening, Jack Ruby stopped by a delicatessen and bought some sandwiches and soft drinks, which he said he wanted to take to KLIF, a Dallas top-forty radio station. One of its disc jockeys had given him "some free plugs," Ruby said. Then, he drove to the police station, hoping to find Joe Long, a KLIF personality who he believed was there covering Oswald's arrest as a news story. Inside, he encountered the media scrum—and he happened to be present while Oswald was being moved about. Ruby said he was just two or three feet away from the prisoner.[314]

At midnight, just after he was charged with killing Kennedy, Oswald was displayed to the reporters at a news conference in the police station's basement. The Warren Commission estimated that from seventy to one hundred people were there, including "Jack Ruby and other unauthorized persons."[315] "I felt perfectly free walking in there. No one asked me or anything," Ruby said.[316] Police chief Curry had asked the reporters not to ask Oswald any questions, but they yelled questions at him anyhow. "We didn't have the luxury of behaving like gentlemen," Carroll wrote in a memoir. He added: "The world screamed for information."[317]

At one point, Ruby recalled, a reporter asked District Attorney Henry Wade the name of a political organization Oswald belonged to. "Free Cuba," Wade answered. Ruby corrected him: "Fair Play for Cuba." "Oh yes—Fair Play for Cuba," Wade said.[318]

The press conference was so noisy that no one could hear either the questions or Oswald's answers. Curry ordered Oswald taken back to the lockup because the reporters "tried to overrun him."[319]

Wade wanted to go home. He was on his way out the door when "this guy stood up, ran up to me, and he said, 'Henry, I'm Jack Ruby.'"

"What are you doing here?" Wade asked.

"I represent the *Jewish Press*," Ruby answered. He also mentioned that he was the man who corrected Wade's press conference statement about Oswald's political affiliation.

"I knew who he was by name," Wade said years later. "But I hadn't seen him before. . . . That was the first time I got acquainted with him."[320]

Ruby told Wade that he was wanted on the phone. So, prodded by Ruby, the district attorney stayed at police headquarters longer than he'd intended, giving interviews to reporters in the department's records bureau. Pappas heard Wade give "one or two statements" to the reporters present, and then saw him speak on the phone with others. "I decided that I would try to get Henry Wade on the telephone directly to my office in New York," Pappas said.

He picked up a phone next to one Wade was using, called his office in New York, and then turned to Wade. "Could you do this interview with me?" he asked.

"Yes," said Wade, "but I have another phone call over there." He pointed across the room, where another reporter had called for him. "This disturbed me," Pappas said. He'd promised his editors an interview, "and I wasn't coming through with it immediately, and this is always frustrating."

"It was at this point that I ran into Ruby," Pappas said.

"Where are you from?" Ruby asked the reporter.

"New York," Pappas said.

"How long are you going to be in town?"

"As long as it takes to do this story."

Ruby reached into his pocket and pulled out a card that advertised the Carousel Club. "Jack Ruby, your host," the card said.

What was this guy doing at police headquarters? "I was amazed," Pappas said. "I didn't know who he was or what he was. My immediate impression was that he was a detective."

"Come on over to the club if you get a chance—you can get some drinks. . . . There are girls there," Ruby said.

"I was astounded," Pappas recalled years later. "Here is the president, dead, and this person Lee Harvey Oswald is arrested. The Mexican border is closed. We don't know if we are going to be attacked. There was a feeling in this country very much of uncertainty. . . . And here is this guy trying to hustle me into his nightclub. This is very weird. And what is he doing here anyway, in the middle of this story?"

Pappas took his card.

"He was in a very animated mood. He moved quickly, and he spoke quickly. . . . Maybe this is the way he is naturally. . . . He appeared very worked up by the happenings, by the activity, by the people, by the reporters, by the cameras, by the flashguns, and everything else. He seemed, as I said before, very animated."

Ruby put it in his own words: He was "carried away by the excitement of history."[321]

Pappas had a phone line open to New York, and he still wanted to talk to Henry Wade. Ruby noticed that Pappas seemed frustrated. "What's the matter?" Ruby asked him.

"I am trying to get Henry Wade over to the telephone."

"Do you want me to get him?"

"Yes, I would like to have him over here," Pappas said. He didn't know anything about Dallas and appreciated whatever help he could get.

Ruby walked over to Wade, spoke to him, and pointed at Pappas. A few minutes later, Wade walked over to Pappas's phone, and they did an interview.[322]

"Now I'm saying, 'I'm the luckiest guy in the world. . . . I figure this little guy Jack Ruby is pretty connected," Pappas said. "I did the interview and I hung up the phone, and I went about my business."[323]

Glen Duncan, a newsman at radio station KLIF, was also trying to get an interview with Wade. Duncan had spoken to Wade on the telephone but didn't get a tape recording of the interview needed for the station's morning news broadcasts. So he sent disc jockey Russell Lee Moore—who went by the on-air name "Weird Beard"—to get a few words from Wade on tape.

Moore walked the several blocks from the radio station to police headquarters. When he arrived, Ruby met him and took him to Wade. Moore was generally known around Dallas. When Ruby introduced Moore to Wade, the district attorney said: "Oh—the Weird Beard. My kids listen to you."[324]

Ruby had given Moore a question to ask Wade: Was Oswald sane? Wade answered that Oswald was not insane, and that the shooting was premeditated. The interview lasted less than a minute.

Pappas, needing a place to file his copy and audio to New York, headed to KLIF. It was around 2:00 a.m., and Pappas was hungry. And there was Jack Ruby, bearing sandwiches and soft drinks for KLIF's staff. "He says, 'Hi guys—I saw the lights on . . . I thought you guys might be working late and you might want some coffee or Cokes. . . . I got some sandwiches here for you.'"

"There is that weird guy again," Pappas said to himself. "He is everywhere."

Pappas didn't take any of the sandwiches. "I didn't trust him . . . I'm a New Yorker," he explained. "We are very suspicious. But I did open a Coke."[325]

During KLIF's 2:00 a.m. newscast, "Weird Beard" Moore described his interview with Wade and gave Ruby a blind shout-out by saying: "Through a tip from a local nightclub owner, I asked Mr. Wade the question of Oswald's insanity."[326] Ruby had moved on from being someone merely interested in news events. That night, in the chaos of Dallas police headquarters, he influenced how the biggest story in the country was being reported.

Oswald was paraded again before the reporters on November 23, a Saturday. He told them he wanted to talk to a man in New York, who the reporters assumed was a lawyer. Asked if there was anything he wanted, Oswald said: "I'd like to have the basic fundamental hygienic right of a shower."[327] That was a fine quote for some of the journalists. But their biggest question that day was: When would Oswald be moved from the police station to the county jail? Prisoner movements are a chance for photographers to get pictures and reporters to yell questions.

It crossed the minds of some Dallas officials that it might be a good idea to move Oswald during the early-morning darkness, when the reporters and public would not be around. Curry discussed the idea with Captain Fritz, his top investigator. Fritz pointed out that darkness would aid anyone who tried to attack Oswald or the officers as they moved about downtown Dallas. So Curry decided the move would take place around 10 a.m. on Sunday, November 24. When reporters asked Curry when Oswald would be moved, he told them: "I believe if you are back here by 10 o'clock you will be back in time to observe anything you care to observe."[328]

Dallas Sheriff Bill Decker suggested that Curry break his promise to the reporters and move Oswald earlier in the morning, at around 5 a.m. But Chief Curry didn't change his mind. Wade said Curry had given his word, "and he said that he was going to keep his word to the press."

"I wouldn't," the district attorney told the police chief. He didn't care whether Curry kept his promise to let the reporters view Oswald's transfer, so long as the operation was carried out safely. "But he did keep his word," said Wade. "He was afraid he'd aggravate a few members of the Fourth Estate. . . . I wasn't as sensitive as he was."[329]

On Sunday morning, the reporters, photographers, and broadcast news crews were ready. They set up TV cameras in the basement garage of Dallas police headquarters with big cables that went to remote trucks outside. Like the wire services' Teletype machines, the TV cameras were bulky and crude by twenty-first-century standards. But like Teletype machines, they could transmit news instantaneously. Newspaper and wire service reporters and photographers ringed the basement, notepads and cameras ready.

For some reporters, waiting in the basement was not enough. Pappas and Jeremiah O'Leary, a reporter for the *Washington Star*, together planned to wait for Oswald to emerge from the homicide detectives' offices on the third floor in hopes of asking him a question. After Oswald was walked the twenty feet from the detectives' offices to the elevator, they would sprint down a stairway to the basement in hopes of seeing him again before he was driven to the Dallas County jail. "We went to the extent of practicing running up and down the steps in case we lost him," Pappas said.

It turned out that Pappas and O'Leary weren't the only reporters with "the same brilliant idea," as Pappas put it. Mickey Carroll joined them in the third-floor police department corridor.

Several minutes after 11:00 a.m.—more than an hour after Chief Curry had promised—Oswald and an entourage of detectives emerged. "They treating you all right, Lee?" someone asked. Oswald mumbled an answer. Then Pappas approached Oswald. "I went up to him, and I tried to say, 'Do you have anything to say in your defense?'"[330] The detectives pushed Pappas aside as Oswald leaned toward him. "He said something about, 'I want to see the American Civil Liberties Union,' or something. And then they pushed him in an elevator."

The plan didn't work as the reporters hoped. "I missed the story," Pappas said. "I mean, here is Oswald coming out of the office and he's now going to be taken out [of the police station] . . . and I don't have a description of his departure. All I have is a detective pushing me away from him. . . . My first thought was that I would never work in the news business again, because I had blown a story. My heart was leaping out of my chest. I was saying, 'How could I do this? How could I have allowed this? . . . My boss was going to say, 'You were there and we paid you to go down there and you didn't get the story, you dope.'"

All he and the other reporters could do was dash to the basement garage. "I flew down the steps. We all ran like hell. I don't remember hitting the steps at all. I just went right down." A police sergeant encountered them in the stairwell. "Where are you going?" he asked. "Press, press," Pappas answered as he and the other reporters "practically ran right over him."

They got down to the garage in plenty of time. Pappas was astonished at the access he and the other reporters had in the police station. "In New York, they never let you near the guy," he said. "A prisoner like Oswald would have been put into an armored car in the basement. We would have been outside. . . . All you would have seen was a van leaving. Here we were, amazingly, allowed to be in this basement during the movement. I looked around, and the scene was still set. The scene was still people crowded around, waiting for Oswald."

"I saw a little opening right next to the fender of a car," Pappas said. "I went over there and squeezed in with my New York City elbows. I was squeezing in right in front of Jack Ruby."[331]

There he was, again.

"Here he comes!" some journalists shouted when they first saw Oswald in the garage.

It was 11:21 a.m. Only one TV network—NBC—broadcast the transfer live. Tom Pettit of the network's Los Angeles bureau was at the microphone, several steps away from the scene.

"There is Lee Oswald," Pettit told his viewers.

Pappas was closer. He shouted to Oswald again: "Do you have anything to say in your defense?"

Just then, Jack Ruby stepped forward with a .38 caliber Colt pistol. The reporters heard him yell "You son of a bitch!" as he shot Oswald point-blank in the stomach. By some accounts, those words were really spoken by a Dallas police officer yelling for Ruby to back off.[332]

"He's been shot! He's been shot!" Pettit told his audience. "Lee Oswald has been shot. There's a man with a gun. It's absolute panic, absolute panic here in the basement of Dallas police headquarters. Detectives have their guns drawn. Oswald has been shot—there's no question about it. Oswald has been shot. Pandemonium has broken loose here."

Pettit sounded surprisingly calm as he described the first murder broadcast live. NBC was better than lucky that morning. Instead of live coverage of Oswald's transfer, CBS viewers heard journalists Roger Mudd and Harry Reasoner read essays about the fallen president over images of the scene in Washington as President Kennedy's body was about to be moved to the Capitol—huge crowds, an honor guard, a long shot of the Capitol itself. CBS was on the air with the news of the shooting less than a minute after it happened and had live pictures soon afterward. The network showed live images of Oswald being loaded into an ambulance. CBS was about ten minutes late in displaying pictures of the shooting itself.[333]

Two Dallas newspaper photographers shot dramatic pictures of the murder. *Dallas Morning News* photographer Jack Beers photographed Ruby, gun drawn, as he ran toward Ruby. At the AP's photo office in the *Morning News* building, Harold Waters prepared to transmit Beers's picture to the world. He compared Beers's shot to the picture his colleague James "Ike" Altgens had taken of Kennedy's limousine on Dealey Plaza two days before.

"Man, Ike has lost his Pulitzer Prize," Waters thought to himself.

Then Waters' boss told him to head over to the *Times Herald* building. Bob Jackson, the *Times Herald*'s photographer at the police station, hadn't developed his pictures yet.

By the time Waters arrived, Jackson had already seen Beers's picture on the news wires. He was nervous about his own shot. "Harold,

I don't know if my flash went off or not," Jackson said. "Things were happening so fast, I don't know what I've got."

About eight minutes later, a whoop erupted from the *Times Herald* darkroom so loud it was heard across the newsroom. It was Jackson. "I got it!" he yelled.

Waters looked at the now-famous picture, which captured the exact moment Ruby fired. Ruby's back is to the camera. Oswald grimaces in pain as the bullet hits his gut.

"I saw three Pulitzers that weekend," Waters said.[334] Bob Jackson's close-up of Ruby shooting Oswald won the prize.

Months later, the Warren Commission said the media had to take some blame for Oswald's death. "The crowd of newsmen generally failed to respond properly to the demands of the police. Frequently without permission, news representatives used police offices on the third floor, tying up facilities and interfering with normal police operations. Police efforts to preserve order and to clear passageways in the corridor were usually unsuccessful. On Friday night the reporters completely ignored Curry's injunction against asking Oswald questions in the assembly room and crowding in on him. On Sunday morning, the newsmen were instructed to direct no questions at Oswald; nevertheless, several reporters shouted questions at him when he appeared in the basement. . . . The general disorder in the Police and Courts Building during November 22–24 reveals a regrettable lack of self-discipline by the newsmen. The Commission believes that the news media, as well as the police authorities, who failed to impose conditions more in keeping with the orderly process of justice, must share responsibility for the failure of law enforcement which occurred in connection with the death of Oswald."[335]

By firing that one shot in the basement of the police department garage, Jack Ruby advanced. At Parkland Hospital, he was a mere "goer to events." When he corrected District Attorney Henry Wade and suggested questions to Weird Beard at Dallas police headquarters on Friday night, he became a news influencer.

When he killed Lee Harvey Oswald live on TV, Jack Ruby made himself the story. He became news.

SIDEBAR · THE EAST ROOM

Doctors at Bethesda Naval Hospital finished President Kennedy's autopsy early on Saturday, November 23, and released his body to his family. Kennedy's coffin was then brought to the White House's East Room, a space big enough for parties, stage performances, and presidential funerals.

Reporters were brought to the East Room at 10:00 a.m. so they could describe the scene. President Kennedy's body laid in repose in a closed, flag-draped coffin. Pairs of Catholic priests took shifts kneeling in silent prayer, and a military honor guard of four enlisted men—one from each armed service—stood by the coffin's corners.[336] The coffin was to be taken to the Capitol to lie in state on Sunday. On Monday, it was to be moved to St. Matthew's Cathedral for a funeral. Later that day, Kennedy was to be buried at Arlington National Cemetery.

Henry Brandon, the socially connected reporter for the *Sunday Times* of London, returned from Dallas late Friday and worked through the night on his story for that week's newspaper. He was filing his copy at 11:00 a.m. Saturday when Robert Kennedy, the late president's brother, called to invite him to visit the East Room.

At the North Portico, Sargent Shriver, Kennedy's brother-in-law, greeted Brandon "with a slight welcoming smile." "I felt like having entered a cathedral," Brandon wrote in his diary. "The blinds had been lowered, the curtains and white marble fireplaces were covered with black crepe. . . . When I entered the East Room, there were six people, two kneeling at the casket . . . candles were flickering and a guard of honor was holding watch. . . .

"I suddenly felt very close to the President. I saw him laughing and joking. It was a sad farewell."[337]

CHAPTER 11 • GETTING BEAT

GOOD REPORTERS HATE GETTING BEAT. Jack Bell was a good reporter, and getting beat by Smitty on November 22 hurt more than his ego. After the assassination, Bell spent several days in a Washington hospital for a "checkup," according to a brief item in the December 14 issue of *Editor & Publisher*, a newspaper business trade magazine. President Johnson sent flowers.[338] There's no evidence Bell's frustration and stress over the assassination was a factor in his hospital stay, but it's hard to imagine otherwise.

Bell's anger over how Smith treated him in the wire car got worse after he learned of a column by Leonard Lyons in the December 18 issue of the *New York Post*. Lyons, a gossip columnist, put in print for the first time the story of what happened in the wire car—of how Smith grabbed the phone, and how another reporter in the car "started clawing and pummeling him." Lyons wrote that to avoid the blows, Smith "ducked under the dashboard." Lyons did not identify Bell by name. He also was wrong in one important detail—he wrote that Smith and the pummeling reporter were the only journalists in the car.

Lyons quoted Smith saying of the incident: "He'd have done what I did, and I'd have done what he did."[339]

Bell heard of the column a few days later when it was discussed on WTOP, a Washington radio station. It infuriated him. He had good reason to suspect Smith planted the item. Not only did Lyons quote Smith, but it was printed a day after Smith traveled to New York to cover a Johnson appearance at the United Nations. Bell knew Smith was never above a bit of self-promotion.

So on December 23, Bell put a piece of Associated Press letterhead into a typewriter and wrote Smith a nasty note.

"Dear Smith," it began—note he didn't call him Smitty. "I think you've milked this for about all the personal publicity you can get out of it," Bell wrote. "I'm getting a little tired of this krap about how I 'pummelled' you and you have the bruises on your back to prove it. Also about the 'world beat' that you got which doesn't seem to have showed up on your wires. Now you add a filip that I never got the phone."

Bell went on to say he had forwarded to his lawyers a transcript of the WTOP radio broadcast based on Lyons' item. "They may be interested in who told Lyons this imaginative version," he wrote.

Smith forwarded a copy of Bell's letter to his bosses in New York. Earl Johnson, UPI's editor, wrote back on January 3. "Jack Bell is obviously burned up by not getting enough recognition for his work in Dallas," Johnson said. He'd heard Bell was in the hospital. The note, Johnson said, "indicates that he was still under the weather."

"I don't think you can ignore Bell's churlish note," Johnson wrote. "But please do treat him gently and sympathetically."

If Smith hadn't leaked the story to Lyons, Johnson suggested, "I think you should say Oh my dear Jack not any of these things were my doing and in fact when I had the opportunity I did my best to water them down." UPI promoted its assassination coverage to its clients, but it avoided mentioning the fact Smitty and the Dallas bureau reported the story minutes ahead of the AP. "I think there was one reference in a U.P.I. ad to the fact that most newspaper editors preferred U.P.I.'s version of the assassination story," Johnson wrote. "However, we did not advertise a world beat because our people would not want to capitalize competitively on such a grievous event as the assassination."[340]

Smith stood up for Bell three years later, when he wrote the editors of *Look* magazine to complain that William Manchester would inaccurately describe what happened in the wire car. "Bell is a fine, tough, competitive reporter," Smith wrote.[341] If Bell ever learned of this compliment, he did not care to return it. "Smith didn't apologize for keeping the phone. Smith never apologizes," Bell said.[342]

Bell wasn't the only Associated Press person steamed over Smith's behavior in the wire car. Bob Johnson, the AP's Dallas bureau chief, came to believe Smith deliberately cut off Bell's phone call to the Dallas bureau by tapping the phone's cradle. In 1997, several years after he retired, Johnson wrote a letter to AP archivists stating that UPI had confirmed that Smitty had cut Bell's call.[343]Bell, in the backseat, did not himself see Smith tap the cradle, Johnson admitted. Smith's colleagues also doubt the story. Helen Thomas, one of Smith's closest colleagues, classed it as "apocryphal."[344]

Some at AP had no hard feelings about Smith's behavior. Among those who did not need an apology was Wes Gallagher, the AP's general manager and top executive. "You know, I don't blame Smitty," Gallagher once told Johnson. "I probably would have done the same thing."

"I'm not sure I would," said Johnson.

Except, Johnson had to admit, he had done such things himself as a reporter. "Fact is, I had beaten UPI staffers to the phone and kept it until they—until I knew they were going to be well behind," he told an interviewer in 2005.[345]

Gallagher was effusive in his praise for photographer James Altgens and his initial report of the assassination. In the AP's annual report in February 1964, Gallagher credited Altgens with "the first break on the No. 1 story of the year, both news and photo."

Altgens' quick eyewitness account gave his bosses an excuse to claim they beat the competition on the assassination story. "The AP was ahead of UPI on everything that happened after the first phone call from the pool car," Johnson declared in his 1997 letter to AP archivists.[346] In an oral history eight years later, Johnson insisted:

"The fact is that because of Altgens we weren't really—we were not behind as far as the news that the president had been shot. We were right on."[347]

But Johnson's recollection that the AP was "right on" is simply incorrect. A careful look at the record clearly shows that UPI was ahead of the AP at nearly every turn that day.

UPI first reported the shooting at 12:34 p.m. At 12:39 p.m. UPI moved Smith's report that Kennedy had been wounded "perhaps seriously perhaps fatally." AP's first bulletin about the shooting, based on Altgens' eyewitness account, also moved at 12:39 p.m., but only west of Kansas City. It wasn't until 12:40 p.m.—six minutes after Smith's first report—that the AP bulletin finally reached East Coast newsrooms.

UPI moved Clint Hill's "He's dead" quote at 12:44 p.m., which it followed with four additional updates in the next seven minutes that could be chained together into a coherent story of about 425 words. During those same minutes, AP moved garbled dispatches impossible to use, and a disjointed series of short dispatches totaling about 250 words that would have been difficult to join together.

UPI reported Father Huber's administration of the last rites to President Kennedy at 1:23 p.m., four minutes before the AP. At 1:35 p.m., UPI was first to report "FLASH PRESIDENT KENNEDY DEAD," based on Malcolm Kilduff's official statement. AP moved its flash of Kennedy's death at 1:37 p.m.

AP also made a serious factual mistake at 1:18 p.m., when it moved an "unconfirmed report" that Vice President Johnson was "wounded slightly" in the mayhem. This simply wasn't true. But because of this erroneous report, House Speaker John W. McCormack, who was next in the line of succession after the vice president, believed for a few minutes that he was about to become president. McCormack, then seventy-one years old, suffered an attack of vertigo when he heard the news in the House restaurant.

Six minutes later, AP moved another item that quoted Lady Bird Johnson saying her husband "is fine," and reported that she shook her head in the negative when asked if he had been shot. McCormack felt better when a colleague told him of the correction.[348]

Years later, Bob Johnson said he was not sure where the Dallas bureau got the story that Johnson was hurt, and admitted it was "embarrassing" that the mistake "slipped through."[349] At least, he said, it was quickly corrected.

AP made another big mistake at 2:08 p.m., when it reported from Hyannisport, Massachusetts, that President Kennedy's parents were informed of the assassination by a workman at the Kennedy compound. This was not true. But at least this story did not come from the Dallas bureau.

Six minutes later, at 2:14 p.m., came another blundering AP dispatch with a Dallas dateline: "A Secret Service agent and a Dallas policeman were shot and killed today some distance from the area where President Kennedy was assassinated." About an hour before this report, Lee Harvey Oswald shot dead Dallas police officer J. D. Tippit. But it's unclear if this story refers to Tippit's shooting. In any case, no Secret Service agents were shot in Dallas.

Despite the AP's bungles, Johnson felt the Dallas staff did a good job getting the story out quickly. He believed the dispatch he wrote based on Altgens' eyewitness account of the shooting surpassed Smith's initial report, which merely said shots were fired and did not mention that Kennedy was hit. He also noted the awkwardness of UPI's cautious "perhaps seriously, perhaps fatally" flash, calling it "a jumble of words."[350]

Bell made a series of bad decisions on November 22. He should have focused less on trying to write his color story and more on gathering information. He wasn't even in the room when Kilduff announced Kennedy's death. He should have gone back to Air Force One with the White House pool. Maybe he should have left the wire car duty to Frank Cormier in the first place. But his colleagues think his problem was much simpler: Bell was just no match for Smitty.

Bell's performance the day of the assassination did not get him in any trouble with his bosses. "Everybody understood the pressure that Bell was under . . . there was no big commotion about that," said Johnson.[351]

But Bell, a proud man, understood that he'd been defeated. "I should have yanked the goddamn phone out of its socket," he told colleagues.[352] He took his anger and frustration to his grave. When he died in 1975, his official AP obituary did not mention that he had been in Dallas.

Unlike Johnson and Gallagher, Bell did not rationalize what happened that day. He never tried to claim that he was ahead. And he knew better than anyone that most of the beating he and his colleagues took on November 22 came from Merriman Smith.

Sidebar · A loose end

Back in Washington soon after the assassination, Sid Davis had business at the White House press room. Smitty was there too. He seemed angry.

In Dallas, Davis had written in his fifteen-cent notepad that President Johnson took the oath of office at 2:38 p.m. Central time. That's the time Davis gave when he delivered the pool report.

"You son of a bitch!" Smith said to Davis. "You son of a bitch! I told you 2:39!"

Smith grabbed the younger reporter. "He practically put a hammer lock on me," Davis said.

Some newspapers on November 23 said Johnson took the oath at 2:39 p.m. It's possible Johnson began the oath at 2:38 and finished twenty-eight seconds later at 2:39. But history has settled upon 2:38 p.m.

Not even Smitty could adjust that.

Whether the oath happened at 2:38 or 2:39 was a big worry to him. "Smitty was always very concerned about times and sequences," Davis explained.

CHAPTER 12 ✦ NIGHTMARES

MERRIMAN SMITH'S COLLEAGUES EFFUSIVELY PRAISED his coverage of the tragedy in Dallas. "The performance was magnificent! This is the sort of a reportorial team you dream about," wrote Frank Bartholomew, UPI's chairman of the board. "You were great all the way, Smitty! You have always led the way on every story you have been on and this time you excelled all past performance records," wrote Mims Thomason, UPI's president. "If you do not win a Pulitzer Prize, I am going to be sadly surprised," Jack Fallon wrote.[353]

Smith was anything but ebullient in the late hours of November 22. Back in Washington, he telephoned his twelve-year-old daughter Allison. "He sounded like he had witnessed something horrible, and it changed him forever. He sounded like a different man," she recalled. "I will never forget the tenor of his voice and the somberness and that sensation of just the wind being out of his sails."[354]

He covered Kennedy's funeral rites in typical Smitty style, wearing the required formal black mourning clothes while toting a canvas-cased walkie-talkie that allowed him to provide instant updates to UPI's Washington bureau. Smith thought this was necessary, even though UPI's editors and writers were getting a lot of what they needed for their stories by watching the ceremonies on TV. Finally, on the afternoon of November 25, Smith filed a story about Kennedy's interment at Arlington National Cemetery. "John Fitzgerald Kennedy went to rest today on a grassy hillside. . . . Present in death on the nearby slopes were thousands of other heroes who died in the country's wars," he wrote.[355]

The official ceremonies were over. Smith was worn out by the long hours he put in covering the assassination, the funeral, and the burial. "I dragged home, pulled off my formal clothes and fell into bed," he wrote. "There began night after night of the most horrible dreams I have ever endured."

The nightmares went on for months. "Not a night passed without my hearing in troubled sleep those three sharp rifle shots from the Texas State Book Depository building . . . the scream of sirens . . . the skidding stop in the hospital driveway . . . brown bubbles coming from the chest wound of Gov. John Connally [. . .] The dark stain spreading down the suit of the face-down Kennedy. . . .

"I seldom slept for more than an hour at a time. There was no effective opiate."[356]

Usually, Smith was diligent about keeping in touch with his mother. But after the assassination, he went twelve days without writing her. "Yes, I was in Dallas . . . I'm awfully tired and would like to get away for a spell," he finally wrote her on December 4.[357]

He did get away, but the travel was for work. Smith was in New York on December 17 when Johnson promised the United Nations General Assembly that he would carry on Kennedy's foreign policy. And over Christmas, Smith and colleague Al Spivak traveled to the Johnson ranch near Stonewall, Texas, sixty miles west of Austin, where the president planned an extended holiday vacation.

Johnson proudly showed off his property to the visiting journalists. On Christmas Day, a busload of about fifty photographers traveled from their hotel rooms in Austin to the ranch. Smith was among a group of about a dozen reporters who tagged along in hopes of asking a few questions. Johnson seemed glad to see them.

"When the picture-taking was over and they started to leave, he wouldn't let them go," wrote historian Robert Caro.[358] Johnson offered each journalist in the group an ashtray bearing a picture of the ranch. He signed autographs, introduced the journalists to his family, and offered tours of his house. UPI moved a picture that day of Johnson showing off a set of miniature steers on the desk of his study. The steers represented the University of Texas football team. Usually, reporters avoid appearing in such pictures. But Smith showed up in this shot—and he was such a celebrity, his editors identified him in the photo caption along with the president.[359]

Johnson and his family celebrated Christmas "around a big home-cut tree," Smith wrote in a story for that day's afternoon newspapers. Holiday festivities weren't all that was going on; the same story went on to report Johnson's prediction that the federal budget deficit was running lower than the public expected, and it delved into details of a proposed tax cut.[360] Smith and Spivak worked that Christmas from 8:30 a.m. to 1:30 a.m. "Johnson has had three press conferences in the past three days," Smith wrote in a letter December 26. "We were out at the ranch quite a while yesterday afternoon and damned if he didn't pop a big story about cutting federal personnel. . . . [T]here was so much stuff to handle that Spivak and I got miserably behind. It was just dreadful."[361]

The following days brought a Texas summit with German Chancellor Ludwig Erhard. People in Stonewall, a small town about four miles from the ranch, did their best to spruce up the aging high school gymnasium for a state dinner prepared by Johnson's favorite caterer, who traveled all the way from Fort Worth and "laid in 600 pounds of beef and 200 pounds of potato salad," Smith reported.[362] It was a grand affair. The menu included "piled-high plates of bar-becued beef, pork spareribs, ranch beans, cole slaw, and fried fruit pies."[363] Smitty was impressed with the preparations for the "rootin' tootin'" barbecue.

Kennedy's press events were carefully planned, and transcripts of his TV news conferences were provided to reporters immedi-ately. Johnson was more freewheeling in his dealings with the press. One day, Smith said, Johnson held five unscheduled press confer-ences—two of which press secretary Pierre Salinger did not know about. Compared to Kennedy's Florida vacations, LBJ's ranch holiday was hectic. "Texas makes Palm Beach look like a picnic. He's always on the move," Smith said in a speech several weeks later in Lexington, Kentucky. "How long this can keep up is debatable. But the President says it is normal for him."[364]

Just as Smith was unsure about Harry Truman after Roosevelt's death, he was also unsure about Johnson. He couldn't help but compare Kennedy's smooth, urbane, and wealthy manner with Johnson's cornpone rural background. "In JFK's death, my sense of loss has taken the form of simply being unable to accept in my guts the coarse image and patois of LBJ," he wrote in personal papers a year after the assassination. "This is really no slam at LBJ. He can't help being what he is."[365]

But Smith the newsman saw something appealing about the new president. Johnson was an outsize personality who made interesting copy. "Never before in history has a president held a press conference using a bale of hay for a podium and then made his exit on horseback," Smith told Washington columnist Drew Pearson.[366] Something about Smith appealed to Johnson too. Smith became an LBJ favorite. Patrick Sloyan, a UPI desk editor, said LBJ "doted" on Smith.[367] Johnson never stayed mad for long when Smith wrote or said unflattering things about him. Bill Moyers, a top Johnson aide, said Smith and the President "had some personal tie that I never figured out the basis of, except possibly their experience in Dallas on November 22."[368]

The new president's policies also gave Smith plenty to write about. Early on in his presidency, Smith reported, Johnson began plotting to pass the civil rights and tax cut programs Kennedy had been pushing in the face of strong opposition in Congress. This proved to be one of the biggest stories of the coming months. Thanks to his years in Congress, Johnson was an expert at maneuvering legislation through the House and Senate. In the months after Kennedy's death, he pursued a complicated legislative strategy that resulted in both the tax cut and in passage of the 1964 Civil Rights Act, which outlawed racial, ethnic, and sexual discrimination in education and public accommodations and fortified the right to vote.

Johnson followed the news media closely—he even had UPI and AP Teletype printers in the Oval Office. He readily complained when he felt a story was inaccurate or unfair. Sometimes he telephoned his gripes to AP and UPI reporters before their stories had been printed in full on the Teletype machines.[369]

Days after he returned to Washington from the ranch, Johnson took umbrage at a story under Smith's byline that said Senator James Eastland, the powerful chair of the Senate Judiciary Committee, gave a "cool response" at a White House meeting about plans to revamp immigration laws. The January 13 story reported that Eastland was seen "quickly turning away from the newsreel and television microphones set up for the occasion."[370] Without being specific about Eastland's thinking, the story implied that he didn't care much for Johnson's ideas. But Johnson believed Eastland, a conservative Southerner, was interested in his immigration proposals. He didn't think the senator's response was detached at all. "I know his attitude, and I know what he said," Johnson told press aide Andrew Hatcher. He ordered Hatcher to find out why the story implied Eastland was uninterested in his program. But even in his anger, Johnson was ready to let Smith off the hook. "I don't believe Merriman wrote that story," he said.[371]

Outwardly, Smith's career seemed at a high point during the first months of 1964. A story in *Esquire* magazine assessing the Washington press corps noted that of 1,200 reporters with White House press credentials, "the best-known correspondent is doubtless Merriman Smith of the United Press International, who practically holds a patent on the phrase 'Thank you, Mr. President.'" The story went on to say that Smith had turned the words he used to close presidential news conferences into "the title of a book, a nice reputation and a special niche in the interstices of the Establishment."[372] Smith was annoyed that a graphic accompanying the article identified him as a friend of presidents. "He did not like the thought of being dismissed as just a crony," his son Tim said.[373]

In May, the news came from the Pulitzer board at Columbia University in New York: Smith won the Pulitzer Prize for the story he wrote for morning newspapers on November 23 about the assassination. His editors had entered the story in the breaking news category, even though the entry did not include Smith's breaking news dispatches from the wire car or from Parkland Hospital. UPI was careful not to seek credit for being first to break the assassination news. At the Pulitzer office, Smith's story was moved from breaking news to the national reporting category.

When Johnson heard about the Pulitzer, he arranged immediately to have his picture taken shaking hands with Smith. The picture ran on many front pages with news stories about Smith's award. Smith got dozens of congratulatory letters from friends and colleagues, and so much fan mail from readers that UPI struggled to help him acknowledge it all. One piece of mail stands out. It is from Francis A. Bridges Jr., a member of the Florida Probation and Parole Commission, who apparently was an old friend of Smith. "I know that you would have much rather gained recognition through some other news reporting, but you did a tremendously good job during that troubled time," Bridges wrote.

"You are quite right," Smith replied. "There are a thousand ways I would have rather received the award."[374]

Despite the prize, its accompanying $1,000 check, the praise from his colleagues, and the useful connections he was building with the new president, Smith fell into a dark mood in the six months after the assassination. He went to a psychiatrist for help coping with his nightmares.[375] He was depressed, and drinking heavily.

Around the time of the Pulitzer announcement, Smith traveled with Johnson on two whirlwind tours of Appalachia that were primarily aimed at promoting the president's antipoverty programs. At one stop, Johnson stopped to speak to a child who was overwhelmed by the appearance of the White House entourage.

"I was just like you," Johnson told the boy. "Go to school, work hard and someday you can be just like me."

Patrick J. Sloyan, one of Smith's UPI colleagues, says that as Johnson stepped away, Smith approached the boy and said: "Bullshit, kid, you'll always be poor."[376]

Later in May came the fiftieth-anniversary dinner of the White House Correspondents' Association. Smith was the association's president that year. Early in June, Smith was back in the Atlanta area to give the commencement address at Oglethorpe College. Though he'd dropped out, Oglethorpe considered him a member of the class of 1936. Smith also received an honorary doctorate. His son Tim attended, and observed his father was "very emotional, possibly drunk."[377]

Smith was soon hospitalized at Washington Medical Center. Dorothy Kilgallen, the New York gossip columnist, wrote that the cause was "a burst blood vessel between the eyes." It could have been fatal, she said.[378] "We miss you. Hurry back," President Johnson wrote on June 18.[379] Smith was away from the White House for more than a week.

The burst blood vessel was just one of Smith's problems. His physical ailments led him to stop drinking. He described his dark mood in a letter to his girlfriend in California, Gailey "Lenni" Johnson. Smitty and Gailey first met during one of President Kennedy's California trips, said Smith's son Tim. By now, Smith's marriage to Ellie was beyond repair.

"My cabin fever knoweth no limitations . . . I see the doctor tomorrow, then, if he approves, I'll have a try at working," he wrote Gailey on June 27. "I'm not at all afraid of going back to work—that is, afraid in terms of the blood-letting starting up again," the letter said. But he wasn't looking forward to the 1964 presidential campaign. "[W]hat is lacking in me is zest for a campaign year or for that matter, zest for anything. . . .

"I have absolutely no answer except that I'm in a lack-lustre or depressed period; part of it is an easy-to-spot backlash from the complete stop on drinking, a stop which I knew had to come one way or another." He recalled that when he quit drinking in 1958, he went months without wanting to speak to anyone. "I'm in essentially the same state now, although part of it has to be attributed to a state of lethargy and debilitation caused by that heavy loss of blood. Part of that lethargy is emotional in origin because I was feeling it long before I had my hospital encounter and this in itself accounted for a good bit of my drinking. Thank heavens something took the hooch problem out of my hands.

"So, sweetie, be it self-centered or not, my behavior these next few months will be oriented to self-survival and I can ask only that you bear with me."[380]

In May, it seemed that Smith was on top of the world. By the end of June, he had hit an emotional bottom.

It got worse. Smith couldn't stay away from the "hooch." Lyle Wilson, UPI's Washington bureau manager, once had asked Al Spivak to keep an eye on Smitty's drinking. "If you don't let us know that Smitty's drinking, you may wind up contributing to a your colleague's death," Wilson warned Spivak. The request put Spivak in an awkward spot, since he was not inclined to snitch on Smith or any other colleague.

The issue came to a head in an embarrassing incident on August 26, a miserably hot Washington day. President Johnson had kept reporters in suspense over his choice of running mate in the 1964 election. At the peak of the day's heat, Johnson held a walking press conference on the White House's South Lawn. It was ninety degrees, Johnson's kind of weather but supremely uncomfortable for reporters and photographers who had shown up at work in coat and tie. Johnson circled the South Lawn fifteen times—four miles. Spivak called the group of reporters a "panting throng." Go home and shave, Johnson told the journalists. Later that afternoon, they'd all fly to Atlantic City, where the Democrats were holding their convention. All would be revealed.

So, later that afternoon the reporters gathered at Andrews Air Force Base, anticipating a big story. Two planes would make the quick flight to Atlantic City. A press plane carried reporters, photographers, and broadcast technicians. The other plane was Air Force

One, which would carry Johnson, his staff, and a press pool that included Smith. Two helicopters would fly from the White House to Andrews—one carrying Johnson and his immediate entourage, the other carrying the Air Force One press pool and anyone else needing to make the trip.

Spivak was settling in on the press plane when Malcolm Kilduff approached him. "Al, you've got to go over to Air Force One," Kilduff said. "The President is going to be on his way very shortly with the press pool. We don't want Smitty to go, because he had too much to drink." Kilduff reported that as Smith boarded the press helicopter for the flight from the White House to Andrews, he "almost walked into the rear helicopter blade."

"He's my boss," Spivak answered. If this went wrong, Smith could make Spivak's life miserable. "I can't tell him he can't go on your airplane. You tell him he can't go," Spivak pleaded.

But Kilduff was firm: he wanted Spivak to deliver the bad news. "You have to tell him," Kilduff said.

"You are putting me in an impossible position," Spivak said.

"He just won't be allowed," Kilduff answered.

So Spivak walked over to Air Force One, climbed aboard, and waited. When Smith showed up, he told him: "Look—Kilduff said they don't want you to go. You've been drinking, and they are concerned about your own safety."

"Get the hell off the airplane," Smith said. He was going to stay with Johnson in the press pool.

Spivak pointed out that Johnson's arrival in Atlantic City would be shown on TV and that Wilson, their bureau chief, would be watching. It would not do for Smith to be seen stumbling off the plane drunk.

So Smith agreed to stay behind—but only after he delivered a subtle threat to Spivak. "OK, buddy, it's your ass," he told his colleague.[381]

Just two days after the Air Force One incident, Smith was back on TV in New York, sitting next to Johnny Carson on *The Tonight*

Show, as if nothing had happened. He and Carson talked about the silly demonstrations at that year's political conventions. "It makes the demonstrators feel better. . . . It does very little for the candidate because the delegates aren't swayed by these things," Smith said. They also talked about campaign buttons. "Gosh the button thing is wild this year," Smith said, noting that some political button makers set up shop right at the conventions. Carson asked him what to do about the Soviet Union's failure to pay its United Nations dues. "Well, I guess you could tax vodka?" Smith asked. "I don't know how you make them pay up!" The audience chuckled at these banalities, which could not have offended anyone in or out of power.[382]

But if Smith's trip to New York involved any meetings with executives at UPI headquarters, it must have been unpleasant. Soon after his visit, his bosses slashed his pay on the grounds of "failure to perform the services specified" in his employment contract. "When we have your proper assurances that you will fulfill your part of the agreement we will review the matter," wrote Earl J. Johnson, UPI's top editor.[383] The letter, dated September 2, was addressed to Smith at the home of C. Edmonds Allen in Mattituck, New York, on the eastern end of Long Island. Allen was a top UPI executive, and Smith sometimes stayed with him and his family.

That Ed Allen hosted Smith during this time was a sign that amid their anger, UPI executives were also worried about their star reporter. Smitty's drinking was a severe problem for them. Smith was a big asset to UPI, someone who helped sell the service to newspapers and broadcasters, and who raised the company's profile through TV appearances, speeches, and books. He'd just won a Pulitzer Prize. His bosses liked him personally. But it seemed as if Smitty's whole life was about to be washed away by a river of vodka, scotch, and gin.

Yet Smith—who needed to work about as much as he needed to drink—soon resumed his breakneck pace. He freelanced magazine pieces, wrote sketches for the NBC comedy show *That Was the Week That Was,* and filed news stories and "Backstairs at the White

House" columns. Late in September, he wrote about complaints of mudslinging in that year's presidential campaign. "Politicians involved in the presidential campaign are beginning to behave like politicians. . . . Any student of campaign '64 knows, for example, that Sen. Barry M. Goldwater has called President Johnson a liar. The Chief Executive in turn obviously regards his opponent as a 'raving, ranting demagogue' . . . [T]his sort of thing happens in every national political campaign. The unusual aspect this year is that it became so bitter so soon. Cries of liar and warmonger ordinarily are not heard from the principals until about mid-October."[384]

Next Smith and several colleagues holed up for several days in UPI's Washington bureau writing stories off of an advance, embargoed copy of the Warren Commission report on President Kennedy's assassination. Smith wrote about his nightmares in a lengthy dispatch offered to newspapers as a sidebar to UPI's coverage of the report. It was as close as he ever came to going public with his despair:

"Reading the Warren Commission report on President Kennedy's assassination was like ripping the bandage from a still-fresh wound.

"Or staring into an awful nightmare being played back in painful slow motion on a mottled gray screen.

"It was almost a hypnotic experience for one who was riding along Elm Street in Dallas in the fourth car behind the President when he was shot—the hypnosis of re-living through the report's 888 pages a dreadful but still historic happening. . . .

"As we pored over the report in these recent hours, I recalled how the impact of the assassination, the flight home on the White House plane with the new President, sober and in control, the dead President in his casket and then the moving funeral—how all of these things did not crash down upon me until later. . . .

"This awful nightmarish period passed eventually, but it comes back again occasionally. And now the Warren Report. Dear God, may I never dream again. At least, not this dream."[385]

The wrecked state of Smith's marriage made things even worse. His wife Ellie's relationship with their children was a very sore point.

Their son, Merriman Jr., was in the Army. In October 1964, soon after he finishing a tour of duty in Germany, Merriman Jr., his wife Jean, and their young children spent three days visiting Ellie in Washington. The visit was brief. Merriman Jr., Jean, and their kids soon headed home to North Carolina. Merriman Jr. said he "was not going to subject Jean again to such a painful time."[386]

"A few nights later, she [Ellie] called me every 15 minutes from 2:30 a.m. to 4:30 a.m. to denounce me for having poisoned M. Jr.'s mind against her," Smith wrote to a friend. Smith was deeply bothered by his wife's emotional abuse, and was especially worried that their two younger children, Tim and Allison, "must take the front-line brunt of this."

He was also stressed about his finances. He sent Ellie $150 each week. He also had to pay the family's other expenses—"taxes, school tuition, bills, bills, bills . . . [S]he wants a total, crushing victory with which she can stand before the world and crow, I brought the bastard to heel, didn't I?" Maybe he was at fault, he admitted. "But never in history has there been a human relationship completely black and white. This is something E cannot get through her head."[387]

And then Smith's drinking brought a new crisis. Late in October, he was back in the hospital, this time in Manhattan. "I got souped-up in New York, developed quite some evidence of hyper-tension and entered Gracie Square Hospital for two weeks," he wrote a friend. "The therapy, entirely medical, was most beneficial, but in talks with my doctors, we determined and I made the final decision, that I had fooled around long enough with this darned hooch problem and some deep digging was indicated."[388]

His bosses pushed Smith to deal with his drinking decisively. They saw that once he was out of Gracie Square, he would need extended therapy. "The consensus here is that when Smitty gets through this treatment, he should probably be sent to some place like the Hartford Retreat or Menninger's for some four to six months," Ed Allen wrote to Smith's girlfriend, Gailey Johnson. The Hartford Retreat and Menninger's were well-known rehabilitation facilities of the day. UPI executives were weary of Smith's repeated failed efforts to deal with the issue and hoped to find him a treatment that would stick. "We certainly aren't winning anything with these on-and-off deals," Allen wrote.[389]

After he checked out of Gracie Square, Smith returned to Washington for two nights to pack some warm clothes and collect files for a book project that ultimately was never published. During this visit, UPI executives insisted that Smith steer clear of his apartment and stay instead in a hotel in Virginia. Smith said this was to avoid harassment from his estranged wife. "Ellie's position was that I had no need whatever for hospitalization . . . that what I needed was to come back to Washington, get to work on the book, the TV show, magazine pieces and the lecture circuit so as to provide more cash for her." She made her case directly to Smith's bosses. "With the management, she was alternately cajoling, threatening and non-sensical. Because of her harassment, I stayed particularly out of sight."[390]

Then he headed back to New York. In mid-November, Smith entered High Point Hospital in Port Chester, New York, a rehab and psychiatric hospital in an old hilltop estate in Westchester County, near the Connecticut state line. Earl Johnson wrote a letter introducing Smith to Dr. Alexander Gralnick, High Point's founder. "I believe you will find Merriman Smith to be a most cooperative patient. His complete recovery will be a major contribution to our profession." UPI would pay whatever bills Smith ran up that were not covered by the company's health insurance, Johnson wrote.[391]

Smith kept his bosses up-to-date on his progress and told them about hospital life. "What a magnificent place this must have been 40 years ago," he wrote to Johnson.[392] "I have a pleasant, small room to myself on the third floor, the lights of which seem to serve as beacons for aircraft landing at the Westchester County airport. In the evenings and for a few mercifully brief periods during the day, the floor is frightfully noisy due to two young men who're obviously in here because of their addiction to Cannonball Adderly, Joan Baez and Peter, Paul and Mary. At every opportunity, they play their radio to the point of making my dental fillings vibrate. One of them also plays the guitar and sings along with the radio."[393] Once a week, he took a train to Manhattan for group counseling. When the sessions were over, he caught a train back to Port Chester right away. The idea, he told newly promoted Washington bureau manager Julius Frandsen, was "to find out why I fall victim to recurrent alcoholism and how to stop it."[394]

He explained his situation more carefully to his mother. "My hospitalization is not the result of my having suffered a 'break-down,'" he wrote her. He went on: "I am not at all ashamed or sensitive about undergoing psychotherapy, which certainly should carry with it less stigma than being overly fond of hooch. . . . The fact that my earnings are greatly reduced because of cancelled lecture, TV dates, etc. is sad, of course. But not as sad as I—and you—might have been if I had continued in the direction I was headed during the summer."[395]

For the next few months, Smith immersed himself in his treatment. Besides the group therapy, he took Antabuse, a drug that made drinking alcohol physically unpleasant if not impossible. Taking one drink while on Antabuse would make a patient sick. Several drinks would "produce nausea, noticeable skin flushing, vomiting, a very rapid heart beat and the third or fourth [drink] might produce unconsciousness."[396] Antabuse caused him no side effects, but "for some patients, it makes them smell like they've just polished off a half-pound of Italian salami."[397] The smell was a sign the dosage needed to be reduced.

Smith's biggest complaint was lack of exercise. He sought permission to walk the hospital grounds, which would have been an exemption from High Point's rule that patients were not to leave the hospital building without an escort. Smith argued to the hospital staff that he was at High Point voluntarily, unlike other patients committed by their families or the courts. But "no dice," he wrote. "To permit this for me would be to extend privileges not granted other patients."³⁹⁸ He pressed the matter by persuading his Manhattan doctor to speak up on his behalf. Finally, after a few days, the High Point doctors began letting him walk outdoors each morning.

Smitty kept busy. He walked the hospital grounds and participated in the hospital's mandatory arts-and-crafts program and other group activities. He read four New York newspapers every day: the *New York Times,* the *Daily News,* the *World-Telegram,* and the *Journal-American.* "If I can stand clear of the minutiae of psychiatric hospital life—and believe me, this is difficult—and make the absolute most of the therapeutic opportunities, I have every belief that I'll come out of here rock-solid as far as drinking is concerned and far more able to cope sensibly with my personal problems," he wrote to Gailey early in his stay.

Smith didn't want to advertise to anyone that he was in treatment, but he didn't intend to hide his problem either. During a group counseling session in Manhattan, he saw other patients "craftily addressing each other only by their first names or even assumed nick-names. When I had to sign a register, I spelled out my name and said, 'If my own name was good enough to get drunk under, I have no misgivings about using it as I try to stay sober.'"³⁹⁹ Some of his non-UPI colleagues knew where he was—Smith corresponded with Bill Lawrence, a former *New York Times* reporter who worked at ABC News. His disappearance from newspapers and TV was noticed by those who didn't know. Dorothy Kilgallen wrote in mid-December that Smith was "seriously ill." Gossip columnists in Chicago and Kansas City asked UPI executives what was going on. Smith's bosses successfully tamped down further reports of his condition.

Smith was a prolific letter writer during his hospital stay. He sounded optimistic in letters to his youngest children, Tim and Allison, late in December. "Maybe next year will be better and, for me, brighter. Overall, I feel in good physical shape except for a weight problem," he wrote Tim. To a friend, he confided that his weight gain made him "look like Porky the Pig." He also wrote a series of love letters to his girlfriend Gailey, who he called "Kissy-face." "Darling—who needs to drink, Kissy-face? You're a potent brew in yourself."

Late in January, Mims Thomason took him to a gun club near Bridgeport, Connecticut. Smith shot four rounds of skeet.

Finally, on March 8, he was back at work. "Everybody at the White House couldn't have been nicer—messengers, stenographers, police—all going out of their way to tell me how glad to see me back," Smith wrote to Gailey on a piece of reporter's notebook paper.

He also wrote: "I must say, my joy is confined."[400]

Smitty was ready for the hard work of staying off the "hooch," and enthusiastic about maintaining his sobriety. He probably seemed too enthusiastic to some. Smith was such a fan of Alcoholics Anonymous and its group counseling meetings that he felt obliged to correct misstatements about AA "when such ignorance manifests itself in print or on the air. For example, when I hear a TV comic use AA as the butt of a joke, I drop him a note, explaining that a lot of people in show business today are sober because of AA. When I see a distorted news story about alcoholism and its treatment, I try to write briefly to the editor of the publication."[401] He also worked with a freelance writer to develop magazine and news articles about alcoholism and its treatment.

Despite his enthusiasm for beating his problem, Smitty's troubles with "hooch" were far from over.

Chapter 13 ✦ Close to home

Merriman Smith's eldest son faced a moral dilemma. Albert Merriman Smith Jr.—friends and family called him Bert—was strongly influenced by the philosophy of nonviolence he learned at the George School, a Quaker boarding high school near Philadelphia. Later, at Knox College in Illinois, Smith Jr. realized he was called to a military career. He enrolled in the Army Reserve Officer Training Corps program. ROTC also seemed to help him with his academic struggles.

In 1960, after he graduated from college, Smith Jr. hashed out the contradictions with Richard Clark, his roommate at a Quaker residence in New York City where he lived while working as a page at NBC's studios in Rockefeller Center. "We were far from being philosophers and our Quaker backgrounds presented problems as to what Bert was expected to do about the military service," Clark wrote. "This was Bert's major concern, should he as a Quaker, object? We both rightly knew he wouldn't. His love for the Army was evident early in college and his work with the R.O.T.C."402

Smith Jr. soon moved from the reserves to the full-time US Army. He served in Germany in the Signal Corps, and then sought training as a helicopter pilot. His brother, Tim, believes he could have had a cushy desk job, but he "wanted to be in the fight as a pilot." Smith Jr. was excited about learning to fly the Army's UH-1—the Huey, the workhorse US military helicopter in Vietnam. "What a thrill it was to get into that ship and take her up by myself," he wrote his dad after his first solo flight in 1964.

The younger Smith was on a career path unpopular with others his age. American involvement in the Vietnam War grew rapidly during Lyndon Johnson's presidency. Johnson sent more and more young Americans to Vietnam, and more and more of them died there. In 1963, the last year of the Kennedy administration, 16,300 US troops were deployed to fight the Viet Cong; of those, seventy-eight died in battle.[403] By 1966, the third full year of Johnson's presidency, the number of US troops in Vietnam had grown to 385,300; of those 5,008 were killed.[404] Though it was fought far away on the other side of the Pacific Ocean, the war touched every city and town in America. Everyone knew or knew of someone in the fight.

When he shipped out, Smith Jr., by then a US Army captain, was happily married to a schoolteacher from North Carolina. He and his wife Jean had two young sons. "I never thought that life with another person could be so wonderful . . . I kick myself sometimes when I think that I waited so long in marrying her," he said in a letter to his dad.

Smitty expressed pride in his son in a letter to President Johnson in June 1965, a few weeks before Smith Jr. shipped out to Vietnam. "This boy was trained and educated by Quakers in his pre-college years. Their deep devotion to peace remains with him," Smith wrote. "But also, he is intensely dedicated to a simple belief that his country is right; that there is a messy, sad and sometimes deadly job to be done for a larger gain; that his job is necessary lest the things and ideas and life we regard so highly are overrun by something alien and harsh, or destroyed by a wider, inglorious and senseless conflict."[405] To Merriman Smith, America's war against Communism in Vietnam was a just cause.

Captain Smith's wife and father were nervous that he'd be flying helicopters in Vietnam's war zones. "I know chances of his safe return are less than some combat personnel," Smitty said in his letter to the president. "But I'm glad that he goes without bravado, with no firebreathing lust for war, with no gung-ho desire to destroy. He's simply a well-trained man going to work. He expects to return in a year or so to resume schooling with the Army. During that year, he hopes the work he does will have helped the aims and purposes of his country."

Smitty's letter to Johnson was unusual for a reporter who took pride in his objectivity. Instead of thinking like an impartial journalist, Smitty wrote to Johnson as a friend. He explained to his son that he wrote the letter out of concern for Johnson's emotional state over the Vietnam War, which was growing more and more unpopular. "Presidents sometimes become so caught up in operating detail and strategy that they lose sight of the individual," he wrote. "Mr. Johnson is not that way. He takes the assignment of troops to Viet Nam as a highly personal matter and literally grieves to the point of sleepless nights over casualties. I therefore felt a low key recital of one case history might be helpful.

"The example of you also gave me an opportunity to say something which I feel deeply, but say it politely: he's been paying far too much attention to snippets of criticism, barks of dissent and political sniping. There have been times when he has not paid, to my way of thinking, sufficient attention to well-deserved and qualified criticism."[406]

Johnson liked Smith's letter. He replied that he'd have Captain Smith in mind when he saw his father at news conferences. "I am sure that every time I make an announcement about our decisions or actions in Viet Nam and see you sitting there in the front row, I will be thinking about your son—and about what you have told me about him," the President wrote to Smith a week later. He asked Smith to bring his son around to the White House some time.

Smith did not do so. "He didn't want to for two reasons," Johnson said later. "He wanted the boy to be on his own. And number two, if something happened, he didn't want the President to feel responsible."[407]

Nonetheless, his father's connections eased Captain Smith's way in Vietnam. He became friendly with reporters in UPI's Saigon bureau. Vice President Hubert Humphrey met Captain Smith during a visit to Vietnam early in February 1966. Smith was interested in the Vietnamese people, his father said; he and his buddies spent some of their downtime playing with children in Vietnamese orphanages. He was particularly interested in the peasants. "[H]e told me how sorely they wanted more than anything else to be left alone in some semblance of freedom to grow their rice and raise their families," Smith wrote.[408]

Often, Smith's helicopter flying involved being "a glorified taxi driver." He and his colleagues ferried troops and equipment around the country. One letter described what he said was an unusual day. "We picked up an ARVN [Army of the Republic of Vietnam] battalion and dropped them in position where they nailed the VC [Communist Viet Cong rebels]. We kept bringing in reinforcements all morning.

"Early in the afternoon the gun ships took off and were just climbing out when a terrific fire fight started about 500 yards away from the field [where the helicopters were landing]. Apparently the VC had broken off from the ARVN and moved up near the field where we would have been sitting ducks when we took off—fully loaded. If war weren't so terrible, the firing rockets would have been beautiful. Our sense of pride came—I'm sure—from knowing that it was our ships that were slamming hell out of the VC. We had just nailed them before they had the chance to get into position and get us."

He signed that letter, "Stay high, M." In a footnote, he explained the "Stay high" signoff: "You either fly here above 2500' or balls to the wall at tree level."[409]

At 8:30 a.m. on February 16, 1966—days after he met Vice President Humphrey—Captain Smith teamed up with Lieutenant Colonel Charles M. Honour at the controls of a US Army Huey UH-1 at Tan Son Nhut Airbase near Saigon. Honour was in the right pilot seat, and soldiers on the ground observed him to be in control when the chopper lifted off. Smith was in the copilot seat. They had five passengers aboard, including two woman nurses, Lieutenant Carol A. Drazba and Lieutenant Elizabeth Jones, who worked at Tan Son Nhut's field hospital. The nurses were due leave, and the chopper's final destination, Nha Trang, was a popular rest-and-recreation spot for US soldiers. The chopper also carried one of the hospital's doctors, a gunner, and a crew chief.

The morning sky was hazy, but with enough sun to affect the pilots' vision as they headed east-northeast. They flew at over 90 miles per hour at an altitude of about 100 feet—treetop level. Army helicopter pilots in Vietnam liked the view they got at the treetops. Smith or Honour may have sought to impress their passengers with some scenery.

About ten miles northeast of Tan Son Nhut, the Huey sliced into an electric power line. A sergeant attached to a special forces group witnessed the crash from a mile away. "I noticed a helicopter in a slow spin," he said. "I saw it for approximately three to four seconds before it went behind a barn which obstructed my view. At this point I heard a loud metallic crash and observed black smoke rise from the general area where the aircraft disappeared." The impact and the intense fire instantly killed all seven aboard.

Honour and Smith were still strapped to their seats when rescuers arrived. The US Army ultimately blamed the crash on the pilots' decision to fly "at low level for no apparent reason."[410] Investigators never figured out which pilot was in control of the helicopter when it crashed. In any case, Lieutenant Colonel Honour, the ranking officer, was ultimately responsible—even if it was Captain Smith who piloted the chopper at treetop level. A Smith family friend said Smith had complained to his father that Honour was a "hotshot . . . always showing off."[411]

Because of Smitty's fame, his son's death made the news. By the news values of the day, the fact that Lieutenants Drazba and Jones were the first female US fatalities of the war by itself would have been enough to bring wide coverage to the tragedy. But editors thought the death of a prominent man's son was more important. UPI's copy reported Captain Smith's death just above those of the nurses.

President Johnson sent Smith a note of condolence. "Dear Smitty," he wrote:

"I don't know how to say what in my heart I feel. The death of any man's son is cause for grief, but I feel this loss—of the son of a man I admire so much—more deeply than I can express. The war in Vietnam is a thousand contradictions, and the death there of your boy seems even more tragic. But I do not believe, I genuinely do not believe, he died for a senseless or empty cause."[412]

Smith's reply deeply moved Johnson and his aides.

"While it is hard to explain to his younger brother and sister, and at this point, beyond rationalization for his young wife and her two babies, we all know and accept with some degree of comfort the purpose of his mission," he wrote.

"This young Army captain, husband and father was a professional, but he was no killer. As I wrote you when he shipped out last year, he was anything but gung ho, but a well-trained young American going to work. . . .

"Please try not to take these things personally, Mr. President. Yours is the awesome responsibility of command and we want you to exercise it as surely and confidently as possible.

"My boy did not die for an empty cause nor was he a war-maker. His hope was yours, Mr. President—peace and at least a chance at a better life for others."[413]

Johnson was so taken by Smith's letter, he read it aloud at a National Security Council meeting. "By God, I cried," Johnson said. "And nearly everybody around the table cried. It's the most beautiful letter you ever read from a human being about what his boy died for." In a phone conversation hours later, Johnson told a newspaper editor that Smith's letter "has got real guts and cause and purpose in it, and it's something these American people need right now, from a guy who's just given the only thing he had, his boy. His letter is news." Johnson wanted everyone to hear what Smith had written. "It's the most effective damn thing I've ever seen," he said.[414]

Johnson hoped Smith's letter would help rally support for the American war effort. He quoted from the letter during a speech February 23 at the Waldorf-Astoria Hotel in New York that was meant to assure Americans that he did not intend a "mindless escalation" of the war with Chinese- and Russian-backed Communists fighting to dominate Vietnam.

Johnson said the purpose of the war "is, simply put, just to prevent the forceful conquest of South Vietnam by North Vietnam." He quoted Smith's words about his son near the close of the speech: "This good young American and thousands like him was not on the other side of the world fighting specifically for you or me, Mr. President. He was fighting in perhaps our oldest American tradition—taking up for people who were being pushed around."

"The young captain described in this letter is dead tonight," Johnson told his audience. "But his spirit lives in the 200,000 young Americans who stand out there on freedom's frontier in Vietnam."[415]

Smith was reluctant to have Johnson use his letter publicly, so Johnson quoted him without mentioning his name. But everyone knew the President was talking about Captain Smith. UPI even moved a story saying so. In the end, Smitty didn't mind being associated with the Waldorf speech. He thought Johnson's performance was "magnificent. I've never heard him better," he wrote the next day to Bill Moyers, Johnson's press secretary. "I was honored that he included a few lines from my letter, although this was not my intent when I wrote him. I know you people tried to keep our names out of it, but I suppose the putting of two and two together was inevitable."

Smith was also pleased that his son's death brought attention to the Vietnam War. He said he heard from "people too many to count saying this was the first time they had realized any involvement in the war." He received more than one thousand letters and telegrams of condolence. "So it all adds up to the fact that while Bert may not have taken out a Viet Cong stronghold when his helicopter was sliced in half by an unseen wire, he accomplished one thing to be sure—the fighting in Southeast Asia and more importantly, the need for peace have become quite real for many of his fellow countrymen."[416]

Plenty of Americans did see a "need for peace"—but not in the manner Johnson and the government intended. While Johnson spoke at the Waldorf, four thousand antiwar protesters gathered outside. "Hey, hey, LBJ, how many kids did you kill today?" was the most popular chant. It was just the kind of protest Smith worried would upset the president. Smith's letter mourning his son, "the most effective damn thing" Johnson had ever seen, didn't change many minds.

Five days later, on February 28, Johnson and his wife sat with more than two hundred other mourners at Merriman Jr.'s funeral at Arlington National Cemetery. Captain Smith, twenty-seven years old, was buried about one hundred yards downhill from President Kennedy, among the rows of graves of other fallen American soldiers.

Captain Smith was the son of a man President Johnson liked and admired. His death brought the war home to Johnson and everyone else in the White House. "The death of Merriman Smith's son constituted what can only be described as a death in the White House family, and it was treated as such," the *New York Herald Tribune* reported. The White House family "is a tight little group," the paper said. "They all travel and work together, the President knows them all on a first-name basis, and no one has been around longer than Merriman Smith."[417]

Smith's closeness to Johnson is evidenced by how the White House trusted him to get its message across. Soon after Captain Smith's funeral, Johnson and his staff weighed involving Smith in another effort to advance his policies and improve his image.

Jack Valenti, a former Texas advertising executive who was a special assistant to Johnson, sent Johnson a memo in March 1966 outlining his fears that several negative books about the president

would be published later that year. Syndicated newspaper columnists Rowland Evans and Robert Novak planned one—"No telling
what this book will say, but suffice it to say we won't like it." Philip
Geyelin, a journalist at the *Wall Street Journal,* was working on a
book about Johnson's foreign policy—"Possibly a minus, but it
might be somewhat objective."

"We need to have some pro-LBJ books on the stands this fall,"
Valenti wrote. He offered several ideas. One was a collection of
Johnson speeches. Another was a recounting of Johnson's successful
handling of a presidential crisis based on "the news stories of that
moment, as well as reprints of columnists." The third was a book of
photographs by Yoichi Okamoto, Johnson's official photographer.
Valenti suggested enlisting Smith to write the book's captions and
text. Johnson thought that was a viable idea.[418]

Valenti's picture book proposal festered for more than a year.
Smith was interested in the project. He was looking to write a book
about Johnson—after all, he'd covered the Roosevelt, Truman,
Eisenhower, and Kennedy administrations in five earlier books. But
he thought getting Johnson's help would be a lot of trouble. "His
mood swings are such that he would promise cooperation one day,
take it all back the next," Smith wrote to his literary agent in April
1967. He also feared Johnson's wrath if he wrote anything that displeased him. "Any book that portrays this man with even kindly
accuracy will arouse great anger in him, possibly quite punitive
anger. . . . As White House correspondent for U.P.I. I can live with
a certain amount of this and do from time to time, but I must be
careful not to destroy my professional usefulness entirely."

Smith also thought a Johnson book would be dull. He pointed
out to his agent that the Evans and Novak book Valenti had feared
a year earlier "was something less than a best-seller, possibly because
Rollie and Bob never brought off Lyndon the person." And what
would be the market for an LBJ book if, as Smith suspected,
Johnson didn't run for reelection in 1968? "Pending his decision
on 1968, the only type of book about Johnson which would receive

wide circulation would be a complete tear-down and I don't think the man deserves anything like that."[419]

Smith nonetheless told his agent he was working on an outline of a Johnson book. It was never published.

Johnson put his closeness to Smith to work in other ways. In a curious incident on the night of May 26, 1966, the president enlisted Smith to defuse a potentially damaging—and untrue— story about his health.

Johnson that evening hosted a reception for African ambassadors. Later, he held another reception for representatives of the Mexican-American community. Johnson left the second reception around 9:00 p.m. to meet with some aides.

Over the next hour, something happened that led newsrooms to believe Johnson was either sick or dead. "Bells were ringing on the [wire service] tickers and newspapers were holding the presses," Johnson's official diary states. At around 10:00 p.m., Smith telephoned Bill Moyers, Johnson's press secretary, to check out the reports. Soon, Smitty was on the phone with Johnson. "The President insisted on having Smith come to the White House. Smith protested and said he had guests. The President told him to bring the guests along."

So Smitty; his girlfriend, Gailey; and their four houseguests all headed to the White House, where Johnson; his wife, Lady Bird; and their daughter Lynda gave them a tour of their private quarters. They then watched movies in Johnson's private theater. Johnson's official diary says the rumors that he was sick or dead were "finally traced to the fact that someone had seen the President leave the African Ambassadors reception appearing pale, shaky, and distraught, and thought he was feeling poorly."[420] Soundly disproved with Smith's help, the rumor was not reported the next day.

Johnson also used Smith as a conduit for routine information meant to enhance his image. For example, in August 1966 Moyers fed him some tidbits about the White House wedding of Johnson's daughter Luci. "There's a touch of sadness that any father feels when he sees his little girl leaving the family circle," the press secretary told him. Instead of naming Moyers in his story, Smith told his readers his source was "one of the chief executive's intimates."[421]

Johnson genuinely liked Smith. He envied his abilities as a writer—"My letters don't amount to anything," he said when he discussed Smith's letter about his son's death.

Smith obviously liked Johnson too. But his real allegiance was to the White House—to the beat he covered every day.

Smith sought to promote his White House–centric view of the world with a pitch for a TV series pitch he circulated in the summer of 1966. The show was called "Thank You Mr. President," after the title of Smith's first book and the words Smith had used to close presidential press conferences during his decades as the most senior White House wire service reporter. "The show is an in-depth view of Washington and the world as seen from the top—the White House. . . . Merriman Smith will host and tie the show together through narration. . . . We take you inside Blair House when an Arab king arrives and show his colorful retinue. We go for a walk with the White House electrician who takes care of the President's dogs. Another week we talk with a handsome, snobbish butler who has a good thing going on the side—a small business which furnishes social know-how for parties." Such fluff would ensure that "the show will not be limited to the frequently flat facade of officialdom."[422]

A bit more than a year after Johnson's speech explaining his Vietnam policy—a year in which the number of troops and US combat deaths continued to rise—it was Smith's turn to deliver a speech of his own, also at The Waldorf-Astoria in New York. He spoke in defense of Lyndon Johnson. Smith didn't directly support Johnson's policies—that would have cut against his need to maintain journalistic objectivity. He was always careful to avoid taking sides on policy matters. But he did protest the manner in which some Americans challenged Johnson's positions.

"President Johnson these days is the object of some of the worst vilification—even obscenity—that I've seen or heard in more than twenty-five years on the White House assignment," Smith told the gathering, the April 1967 convention of the American Newspaper Publishers Association.

"There have even been buttons and printed placards around the country saying, 'Lee Harvey Oswald, where are you now?'" Smith noted that Johnson had even been accused of engineering Kennedy's assassination. He also said that in a protest days before in New York's Central Park, "there were grown men carrying signs which openly and plainly challenged the President's normalcy—mentally and sexually."

"This is not enlightened social change, or legitimate dissent or revolution," he said. "It is anarchy, born of a highly permissive atmosphere in this country; a strangely paradoxical, pejorative atmosphere in which freedom, at times, seems to be working against the very things for which freedom supposedly stands."

Smith worried that "vicious personal attacks on government leaders could have only one motivation that would make any sense at all—and that is to tear down public confidence in the establishment—and by establishment, I mean authority on almost any level." Of Johnson, Smith said: "No President deserved the indignities being heaped upon him these days in the name of peace or civil rights. Criticism and challenge have their rightful place in our political system, but not the scrawls from the rest room walls."

The speech before the eight hundred publishers was widely reported, and so popular that UPI distributed its text as a pamphlet. Several newspapers backed Smith's thinking in editorials. The *Nashville Banner* wrote that Smith "is shocked at the filthy-mouthed and reckless torrent of abuse which, in the name of peace, has been turned on President Johnson and all others who disagree with them in their greedy hunger for chaos."[423]

Some of Smith's "Backstairs" columns railed against Americans who went against the establishment's view of the Vietnam War as a just cause. "Government professionals, careermen who have no stake in domestic politics or the fortunes of President Johnson, are appalled by the number of fellow Americans who, if given the choice, believe strictly stories from Hanoi or Peking over diametrically opposite versions of Washington, be it from the White House, the Pentagon or the State Department," Smith wrote in October 1967.[424]

A few days later, Smith reported on a big weekend antiwar demonstration outside the Pentagon. "If one personal impression came from rubbing shoulders and sometimes notes with the peace demonstrators here Saturday and Sunday, it was one of dismay at their apparent disregard for fact," the story began. Smith doubted the protesters' claims that 250,000 people showed up. "Police and reporters accustomed to crowds week after week thought 50,000 was generous, and this included untold numbers of sightseers and teenyboppers from the Washington area," he wrote.

He also doubted demonstrators' complaints that on Saturday night, they were "brutally clubbed by rifle butts" by law enforcement. Discussing protesters' claims that no reporters were present during this assault, Smith quoted an anonymous reporter—perhaps it was himself: "I was there the whole damned night, outside with you people, and what you're describing . . . is pure fiction. It never happened."

To which "a pretty young girl with autumn flowers in her long golden hair smiled patronizingly and murmured, 'We would expect you to say that.'" A small newspaper in California headlined this piece "Reporter Tells of Exaggerations by the Flower People."[425]

Smith was anguished that the turbulence of the 1960s—the anti-Vietnam War movement, civil rights protests, college students demanding change by occupying campus buildings—challenged the Washington establishment. Smith didn't just cover that establishment; he was unabashedly part of it. He feared anything that might undercut the establishment's ability to take its policy in one direction or another.

Though Smith never wrote or said that the war was a good idea, he gladly reported the Johnson administration's complaints about the antiwar demonstrators. "President Johnson and ranking members of his administration have no doubt about Communist involvement in some of the so-called peace protests," he wrote in November 1967. Linking the protesters to Communists was tantamount to accusing them of treason. Johnson's people were afraid to be open about these beliefs, Smith reported. But they evidently didn't mind leaking their views to him under cloak of anonymity: "Some Americans, according to high government sources, are in frequent touch with Hanoi. And it seems nothing short of stupid for those participating in such contacts not to realize they are being monitored and their messages copied, what with the resources of surveillance and detection available to the executive branch of government."[426]

US involvement in the war peaked in 1968, Johnson's last year in office. That year, 536,100 troops were deployed in Vietnam; 14,592 did not come home.[427]

It seemed to much of the public that the Vietnam War was vicious and unwinnable. Amid the protests and the ascension of antiwar challengers in the Democratic party, Johnson announced in a televised speech in March 1968 that he would not seek reelection. During the same speech, he also announced a halt to most bombing of North Vietnam.

Official Washington did not back away from the faraway conflict quickly enough to suit many Americans. The war dragged on for five years more and took thousands more American lives as generals, diplomats, and politicians struggled to find a way out. By the time US involvement in the war ended in 1975, more than 58,000 American soldiers had died in Vietnam. That's more than eight times the 6,878 US soldiers killed in Afghanistan, Iraq, and Syria from 2001 to 2015.[428]

Smith's connections in the White House greatly helped him in Dallas on November 22, 1963. During Lyndon Johnson's presidency, those connections narrowed his view of what was going on in the country. His sources helped him understand Johnson's policies and thinking, but his closeness to the president and his administration blinded him to Americans' frustration and anger over a war that was killing too many of their sons and daughters. Smitty failed to see beyond the establishment he covered.

Sidebar • A fishing trip

Hal Pachios, a young White House assistant press secretary during Lyndon Johnson's presidency, liked Smitty. Pachios went to work at the White House after the 1964 campaign, around the time Smith was being treated at High Point Hospital. "I never saw him drink," he said.

Smith seemed like a loner. His colleagues liked him, Pachios said. But he noticed Smith didn't go out to lunch with them.

Smith was, of course, among the reporters who regularly traveled with Johnson to Texas. One sunny Sunday, Smith joined a group of his colleagues in a press gaggle as Johnson worshiped in a church near Lake Lyndon B. Johnson. The lake was named for the president in 1965, and the Johnsons had a home on its shore. After the church service ended and Johnson had left, Smitty asked Pachios to join him on a fishing trip that afternoon.

"I told him I didn't like to fish," Pachios said. "Nonetheless, he suggested I could relax and sun myself on the boat while he fished and then enjoy the catfish he was going to fry."

Pachios thought to himself: "This is a side of Smitty I haven't seen. We are going to have a lovely relaxing afternoon which has nothing to do with journalism or managing the press. We'll have a lovely boat ride, Smitty will catch fish, and I'll get a tan."

After church, Smith and Pachios drove to the lake. Smith rented a small boat and put his fishing rod and a small bag inside.

"I assumed the bag contained fishing tackle," Pachios said. "But once we got out into the lake Smitty opened it and out came powerful binoculars.

"Sure enough, within a half hour a speeding boat came down the lake with LBJ at the wheel and several guests aboard. The boat went up the lake and down the lake several times during the afternoon."

Each time the boat passed, Smith used his binoculars to see not only who was onboard but how they interacted with Johnson.

Pachios feared he'd be reprimanded—or worse—by his boss, the President of the United States. He tried his best to duck out of Johnson's view. He was grateful that Smith kept the boat far enough away that probably no one would recognize him.

"I was there because, I think, he wanted company," Pachios said. "He was engaged in his profession the entire afternoon.

"He caught a couple of fish. We had a nice fish fry afterwards."[429]

CHAPTER 14 ✦ CONSPIRACIES

IT WAS AFTER MIDNIGHT AT Rickey's in Palo Alto, California, a popular bar and restaurant where the Rotary Club met and Stanford University students dined with their parents. Several reporters gathered for a boozy bull session. Smitty had a highball. In the years after his stay at High Point, Smith went through periods of sobriety and periods of drinking. This was not one of his sober periods.

The talk that late 1960s night turned to the Warren Commission report. How could one assassin fire so quickly and accurately at a moving target? "I've been around guns most of my life," said Smith. Even as a boy he could have hit the target—"I would have been accurate up to 150, maybe 200 yards." He pointed out that Lee Harvey Oswald, a Marine Corps–trained marksman, hit President Kennedy from less than one hundred yards away.

But what about the bullet the Warren Commission said passed through Kennedy's neck and continued on to wound Governor Connally? Conspiracy theorists called it the "magic bullet," because they found its path improbable. And what about the possibility someone fired from the grassy knoll to the right of the presidential limousine, or from the railway tracks atop the Triple Underpass to the limo's front?

Smitty slammed his glass to the table. He hated the conspiracy talk. It was all wild gossip, some of it implicating people high in the government. He didn't believe any of it. "Not a word of it can stand against the overwhelming weight of the findings of the Warren Commission," he said. "Remember—I was there."

Smith resolutely believed the Warren report's conclusion that Oswald acted alone. The legions of conspiracy buffs and theorists were "these great, self-anointed detectives," Smith said. They didn't even know what the weather was like in Dallas that day. Their ideas were nothing against the weight of a government investigation carried out by Washington establishment men Smith respected. That investigation concluded Oswald acted alone—and Smith believed it.[430]

The conspiracy talk started the moment the gunshots rang out in Dealey Plaza on that warm November day. A few people thought shots came from the grassy slope just west of the Texas School Book Depository. Cops sprinted up the slope to the railway tracks just to its west, fearing someone in the area fired at the front of Kennedy's limousine. They found nothing.

The officers' fruitless search was reported in the media right away. Smith and UPI put it on the wire at 12:46 p.m.—sixteen minutes after the shooting. This report, widely repeated by Walter Cronkite and other broadcasters, said motorcycle cops ran up a "grassy hill" next to the Book Depository. In a follow-up dispatch ten minutes later, at 12:56 p.m., Smith and UPI rewrote the description of the incident to say the cops ran up a "grassy knoll." Smith worked with Dallas UPI colleague Jack Fallon on these dispatches. But Smith is sometimes credited with coining the term "grassy knoll" to describe the place where some conspiracy theorists believe shots were fired. The idea that something happened on or near the grassy knoll has hung in the air for decades like a lingering smell of gunpowder. In reality, nothing happened there.

The Warren Commission determined that Oswald fired three times from the sixth floor of the Book Depository.

One of the three shots missed. The Warren Commission was not sure which one, but investigators later settled on the idea it was probably the first shot.

The second shot—the conspiracists' magic bullet—passed through Kennedy's neck from back to front and traveled onward to wound Connally. Federal investigators found that this bullet had the right trajectory and enough velocity to hit both men.

Oswald's third bullet smashed open Kennedy's skull and scattered some of his brains on the back hood of the limousine. The president was as good as dead when the third bullet hit him.

That Oswald fired three times is supported by 88 percent of the two hundred witnesses at Dealey Plaza whose opinion on the number of shots they heard was recorded in the National Archives or the Warren Commission, according to author Gerald Posner, whose book *Case Closed* soundly debunks the conspiracy theories.[431] By Posner's count, just 5 percent of witnesses thought they heard four or more shots, and 2 percent thought they heard shots from more than one location. Since nearly nine of ten people there heard three shots, it was reasonable for the Warren Commission and other probers to conclude three shots were fired. But conspiracists conflated the minority belief that more than three shots were fired—maybe from multiple locations—into the backbone of their theories.

The conspiracists were boosted by the confused news conference given by Parkland Hospital doctors soon after Kennedy died. The doctors told reporters that the wound at the front of Kennedy's neck appeared to be an entrance wound, indicating that someone shot Kennedy from the front. The doctors were mistaken: The wound at the front of Kennedy's neck was, in fact, the exit wound caused by the second bullet that continued on to wound Connally. The doctors never turned Kennedy over in the emergency room, so they never saw the real entrance wound in the back of his neck.

After the press conference, the Parkland doctors acknowledged their mistake. But their admission was too late. The doctors' misstatements helped the conspiracists push their ideas further. If the wound at the front of Kennedy's neck was an entrance wound, they said, there must have been four or more shots. Maybe the extra shot or shots came from the grassy knoll, or from atop the Triple Underpass, or from someplace else.

The conspiracy theorists got yet another boost two days after the assassination, when Jack Ruby killed Oswald in the basement of Dallas police headquarters. That led to the idea that Ruby killed Oswald as part of a cover-up. This line of thinking was backed up by Ruby's flimsy links to organized crime.

Moreover, Oswald's life story—dug up by reporters and investigators in the hours and days after the assassination—offered all kinds of possibilities for those who thought the Soviet Union or Cuba put him up to the plot.

Oswald's hatred for the American system led him to defect to the Soviet Union, where he lived from October 1959 to June 1962. Oswald found the Soviet system didn't suit him either. Disillusioned again, he returned to the United States. In Dallas in April 1963, he tried to assassinate former General Edwin Walker, a right-winger who thought America wasn't tough enough with the Soviets. Oswald's bullet missed, and only after the assassination did he become a suspect in the Walker shooting.

Then Oswald lived for a time in New Orleans, where he publicly protested US efforts to fight Communism in Cuba. Two months before he killed Kennedy, Oswald traveled to Mexico City in hopes of getting permission to travel to Cuba. From Cuba, he hoped to make his way back to the Soviet Union—he'd changed his mind again. But he was denied the visas he needed to make the trip. The Soviets wanted nothing to do with him. So Oswald returned to Texas. He took a job at the Book Depository on October 15, five weeks before the Dallas motorcade.

A week after the assassination, President Johnson established the Warren Commission in the hopes of getting to the truth of who killed his predecessor and why. The Commission was led by Chief Justice Earl Warren. Four members of Congress were named to the Commission, including Republican Representative Gerald Ford, who a decade later became president. The other commissioners included former Central Intelligence Agency director Allen Dulles and former World Bank president John J. McCloy. Johnson hoped the distinguished panel's findings would be beyond reproach.

The Commission's ten-month investigation uncovered plenty of witness and physical evidence to support the idea that Oswald acted alone. But it could not figure out why Oswald committed the crime. So the Commission settled on the idea that his motive was rooted in his emotional state: "Oswald was moved by an overriding hostility to his environment. He does not appear to have been able to establish meaningful relationships with other people. He was perpetually discontented with the world around him. . . . He sought for himself a place in history—as the 'great man' who would be recognized as having been in advance of his times."[432]

The Commission's theory fits Oswald's biography—his inability to hold a job, his confusion about what political system he wanted to live under, the problems he faced in his personal relationships, his arrogance, and his boastfulness. But it was a hard story to sell. Why would he do such a thing without a clear motive? And why did Ruby kill Oswald? Those questions stem from the most basic question of all about the assassination: How could one man pull off such a monstrous crime without help?

Even Lyndon Johnson came to doubt that his own Commission got to the bottom of the story. "I can't honestly say that I've ever been completely relieved of the fact that there might have been international connections," the former president said in a 1970 CBS News interview. His fears were eased by the messages of condolence sent by the Soviets and other world leaders after Kennedy's death, which he felt were genuine. But Oswald "was quite a mysterious fellow and he did have connections that bore examination, and the extent of those connections on him I think history will deal with much more than we're able to now."[433]

Public interest in the alternate theories was insatiable. Mark Lane, a New York lawyer, questioned whether Oswald had the shooting skill required to fire the deadly bullet at Kennedy. Lane also doubted whether Oswald really killed Dallas police officer J. D. Tippit. Lane's 1966 conspiracy book *Rush to Judgment* spent twenty-nine weeks on the *New York Times* best-seller list. "Some publishers estimate that more than 20,000 Americans will buy any book relating to the late President," Smith reported. [434]

Smith kept up with the conspiracy books and theories. He called the public's belief in them "almost mystic," and observed that from the conspiracy theorists' "torrent of words spread tributaries of rumor." He was dismayed by the theories' wide public acceptance. "None of this mixture of theory and hokum appears to have any basis of provable fact, but that has not stopped the clamor," he wrote in a long *Washington Post* story in November 1966 that picked apart the different conspiracy ideas. [435]

Richard Popkin, a university philosophy professor, authored *The Second Oswald,* a convoluted book that said Lee Harvey Oswald was a decoy whose arrest was set up to take the heat off the real assassin. "Oswald played his role well," Popkin wrote. "The police chased him and found him, and ignored all other clues, suspects and possibilities." [436] The real killer, Popkin said, was an Oswald look-alike who fired at Kennedy from the grassy knoll.

Among other things, Popkin doubted the real Oswald's rifle, found on the sixth floor of the Book Depository, was capable of making the deadly shot. In his *Washington Post* piece, Smith quoted Popkin: "He (Oswald) had to fire a cheap rifle with a distorted sight and old ammunition, at a moving target in minimal time, and shooting with extraordinary accuracy." [437]

"This simply is not fact, but the opinion of a college professor," Smith wrote. "Fact: A weapon's price does not necessarily indicate its accuracy. Fact: There is no evidence whatever that the sight was 'distorted' when Oswald fired at Mr. Kennedy. Fact: As to 'old ammunition,' the age of a rifle load does not necessarily control its accuracy or power." Smith had no doubt that Oswald's Marine training gave him the skill required to shoot Kennedy in the head.

Smith also slammed Lane's take on the Warren report. Lane's book picks apart the report's findings in the same manner a criminal defense lawyer might take apart a prosecutor's case. Smith explained: "[H]is technique is to take tiny variations in evidence before the Commission and build a mountain of doubt. Lane believes that while the Commission suppressed 'a vast amount of material of paramount importance,' there was enough in the published evidence 'to question, if not overthrow, the Commission's conclusions.'"

To Smith's mind, the main problem with the conspiracy theories was that they could not be proved or disproved. He expressed that idea in dismissing the claims of Edward Jay Epstein, whose 1966 book *Inquest: The Warren Commission and the Establishment of Truth* suggested that more than three shots were fired at Kennedy's limousine.

"To disprove that more than three shots were fired would be impossible," Smith wrote. "Nor would it be possible to prove more than three, beyond a shadow of a doubt. Therefore the Commission had to settle for what the burden of evidence showed—three shots." That the conspiracy theorists didn't concur with the Warren Commission's three-bullet conclusion "is a classic example of the almost Puckish impossibilities on which some of the current assassination books are built," Smith said.[438]

Smith remained certain he heard three shots, exactly as he reported in his first bulletin from the wire car. "The shots were fired smoothly and evenly," he wrote. "There was not the slightest doubt on the front seat of our car that the shots came from a rifle to our rear (and the Book Depository at this point was directly to our rear)."

In February 1967—three months after his *Washington Post* article ran—Smith went to New Orleans to report on Jim Garrison, the city's politically ambitious district attorney and the most prominent conspiracy theorist of all.

Smith arrived in New Orleans amid a media frenzy over Garrison's investigation. Garrison had tried to keep the probe secret. But reporters at the *New Orleans States-Item* heard rumors of what he was up to. They poked around Orleans Parish court records, and learned that Garrison's office had spent $8,000 on the investigation from November 25, 1966, to February 1967. The paper reported its findings February 17 in a front-page story.

Reporters from everywhere descended upon Garrison's office. They came from the French magazine *Paris Match* and TASS, the Soviet Union's news agency, and they telephoned from across the United States and around the world.[439] On February 24—a week after the *States-Item* disclosure—Garrison announced he had "solved" the assassination. "I wouldn't say this if we didn't have evidence beyond the shadow of a doubt," he said. "We know the key individuals, the cities involved and how it was done."[440]

Garrison boasted that assassination suspects and witnesses had no hope of eluding his investigators. "The only way they can get away is to kill themselves," he said. [441]

Garrison had several theories about who killed Kennedy, and why. One was that the assassination "was a homosexual conspiracy," and that the plotters sought "the thrill of staging the perfect crime."[442] Another was that the killing was orchestrated by CIA operatives working with Cubans angry over Kennedy's failure to depose Fidel Castro from Cuba in the disastrous 1961 Bay of Pigs invasion. This theory runs counter to the fact that when Oswald lived in New Orleans, he presented himself as a Castro supporter. Garrison's ideas are full of such anomalies.

Smith was invited to an interview at Garrison's home. While they spoke, Garrison sipped a mixture of cream soda and gin—Smitty thought this choice of beverage was "nauseous." That wasn't all that bugged him about the crusading DA. He wrote in his notes: "Bombastic—publicity hungry as adjunct to political ambition—reportedly would like to run for lt gov [lieutenant governor] this fall. . . . Made at least one trip to Vegas, bills paid by gambling mobster." Smith also noted that while Garrison "triggered and enforced crackdown on French Quarter joints," he once owned a piece of a bar and befriended a stripper.[443]

"Garrison, an enormous man, paced around his study with his suit jacket off and an empty .38 revolver holster flapping on his hip," Smith wrote in a "Backstairs" column two and a half years after their meeting. "Garrison explained that because of threats in the case, he and his top staff members were wearing concealed weapons for self-protection; that they even held occasional practice sessions on a target range, but that he had an awful habit of forgetting the gun and wearing the holster."[444]

"We have definitely found out how they killed President Kennedy and we're going to prove it," Garrison assured Smith. At most, Garrison said, Oswald fired one bullet that wounded Governor Connally and hit Kennedy in the throat. He believed the fatal shot came from somewhere else—"another gun, another assassin," Smith wrote. Garrison did not make clear who the other shooter was.[445]

When Smith returned to his hotel room after the interview, he got a phone call from one of the principal figures in Garrison's case. "He wanted to warn me that I was being slowly gassed to death by enemies unknown with deadly fumes seeping in through tiny holes hidden in the wallpaper design," Smith reported. When Smith told the caller his room had no wallpaper, the man replied: "They're getting more clever all the time."[446]

On March 1, 1967, Garrison's investigators arrested Clay Shaw, a New Orleans businessman who had been managing director of the New Orleans International Trade Mart. Shaw was well known in New Orleans as a champion of the restoration of the city's famous French Quarter. He was also a playwright. Garrison said Shaw conspired with Oswald and with David Ferrie, a pilot who was fired from Eastern Airlines for homosexual activity. A week before Shaw's arrest—on February 22—Ferrie was found dead, "wearing a red wig and mascara eyebrows," Smith reported. Smith described Ferrie as a "sexual deviate." The coroner said Ferrie died of natural causes. Garrison insisted it was suicide.

Smith wrote a long story about his New Orleans trip, which many UPI newspaper clients used on Sunday, March 5. It reported that Garrison's case seemed based on alleged conversations between the plotters that were overheard by various "oddball" witnesses.

One Garrison witness claimed Ferrie sent Oswald to Dallas under a hypnotic spell. Another witness, bus-station baggage handler David F. Lewis Jr., claimed he knew four or five people in on the assassination plot. "Lewis is supposed to have overheard some of those bound together in their hatred of Castro communism by a mutual wish for Kennedy's death," Smith explained in his March 5 story. Lewis invited UPI to bid $1,000 for a tape recording "naming names." "It hardly seemed worth it," Smith wrote.

After the story ran, Lewis threatened to sue Smith. According to unpublished UPI copy with Smith's personal papers, Lewis asked Garrison to have Smith arrested and held on bond of $1,837,500 for an alleged seven hundred instances of "criminal defamation and public intimidation." This was a joke to Smith's bosses. "Smitty—700 instances! Why do you always do things so big?" Washington bureau manager Julius Frandsen wrote his star reporter in a note.[447] Nothing ever came of Lewis's silly allegations.

Smith believed Garrison's case was "based on the words and deeds of men and women of known instability." "With all respect to the hard-driving, hard-living 45-year-old district attorney, his case so far has to be described as flimsy. In his currently powerful position, he can arrest almost anyone for anything. But proof will come harder, particularly considering the credibility of some of his sources," Smith wrote.

"At this point, it seems doubtful that the investigation and promised court trials will produce much more than the fact that some Cubans in New Orleans in 1962–63 and some American oddballs did indeed speak wishfully of seeing Kennedy killed."[448]

Smith's reporting on the Garrison case could be seen as beyond the realm of objective wire service journalism. He cast doubt on a criminal case before it was tried—a daring stance for a journalist who was supposed to analyze facts coldly and treat all sides equally.

He was not the only Garrison skeptic. Gerald Ford vehemently denounced Garrison for declining to share his evidence with the federal government. "I am amazed that public officials would refuse to cooperate with federal authorities," Ford said.[449] Garrison dismissed federal officials' criticism. "I am running this investigation, not the President, not the Attorney General. Now if they want to help me, I'll welcome their assistance. But I'm not reporting to anyone."[450]

Henry Wade, the Dallas district attorney who would have tried Oswald had he lived, said he suspected the assassin "had some advice, some moral support, maybe, but we had no evidence of it that we know of." He doubted Garrison could win his case.[451]

Wade proved right. Shaw's trial stretched over January and February of 1969. When the jury got the case on March 1—exactly two years after Shaw's arrest—it needed less than an hour to find Shaw not guilty. Despite the acquittal, Garrison would not let the case go. Two days later, he filed perjury charges against Shaw, claiming Shaw had lied when he said he didn't know Ferrie or Oswald. The perjury case ended two years later when a federal court ordered Garrison to stop prosecuting Shaw.

Garrison's completely bogus case bankrupted Shaw. Shaw sued, alleging that Garrison wrongly pursued him. Shaw died of cancer in 1974 before the case got to court. Garrison paid no price for bringing the crushing weight of his prosecutorial power down upon an innocent man. Despite this abuse of his discretion, he is a hero to assassination conspiracy theorists. Oliver Stone lionized Garrison and his case in the 1992 movie *JFK.*

Though Smith had no regard for the conspiracy theories, he knew the government withheld information about Kennedy's death. "They—the government, LBJ, RFK [Robert F. Kennedy], Jackie et al—simply cannot release for public perusal and publication complete results of the JFK autopsy, X-rays and post-mortem photographs," he wrote UPI executive C. Edmonds Allen in May 1967.

Releasing the information wouldn't change the findings of the Warren report, Smith said. But it would show that Kennedy was in poor health, "a truly sick man with an unfavorable prognosis, suffering from Addison's disease with no crap about it being merely a mild form of adrenal insufficiency; that he was, in lay terms, a sick man who never would have been elected had the true state of his health been known." If the public knew this truth, Smith believed, "the question of his re-election in 1964 would have been ridiculous. There are enough doctors who gossip about this guardedly that I think it is more than medical gossip.

"Two of the most respected doctors in America have told me this year that they had treated Kennedy, they had examined him and they hope the hell the autopsy reports are never released in toto. A doctor who treated him in 1955 and 1956 told me before JFK's death that he was surprised that he was 'still around.'"[452]

Thanks to Garrison, the public got more details about Kennedy's autopsy. In 1969, before testimony began in Clay Shaw's trial, a panel of four doctors appointed by Attorney General Ramsey Clark issued a review of the autopsy reports, X-rays, and autopsy photographs. Smith reported that the evidence eliminated "with reasonable certainty" any possibility that Kennedy was shot through the head "from any direction other than from back to front."[453] That contradicted Garrison's belief that Kennedy was shot from the front. The issuance of this report also kept the government and the Kennedy family from releasing the full details of the slain President's autopsy during Shaw's trial. The report dealt with the questions raised by Garrison's case, and nothing more.

For years, the media kept probing the assassination. CBS News spent $1 million on a reinvestigation of the Warren report that resulted in a four-part documentary broadcast in June 1967. It included an elaborate test that showed how easily Oswald could have shot President Kennedy. CBS built a sixty-foot-tall tower to simulate Oswald's sniper perch in the Texas School Book Depository building, and mounted a moving target on a track that simulated the route of Kennedy's limousine. CBS asked marksmen of varying skill to fire at the target as it rolled down the track at about the speed

Kennedy's limo rolled through Dealey Plaza. The shooters easily got off three shots as quickly as Oswald. Most had no trouble hitting the target.

CBS went into the project thinking that its reporting might prove others besides Oswald were involved in the assassination. That would have been a much better story than the investigation's result—that the Warren Commission was mostly right, and that Oswald indeed acted alone. Cronkite was disappointed. "We got nowhere," he said.

"We really thought, of course, that with our million dollars we might break the story as to who assassinated our President," Cronkite said in 2004. "Instead, all we did was establish that the Warren Commission had done its job well and that indeed there were not these holes in the story, that everything could be explained."[454]

Cronkite admitted a gap in the network's research: CBS didn't dig into the failure of FBI and CIA officials to tell the Warren Commission all they knew about the possibility Fidel Castro might have been involved. "What we did not know was the same thing the Warren Commission did not know," he said. What the CIA and the FBI knew about Oswald remains an open question more than fifty years after the assassination. But it seems unlikely the agencies' intelligence about Oswald will change what is now understood about his motive—that he was a disgruntled loner who sought a bizarre kind of fame by shooting the president.

Despite its journalists' conclusions, CBS News executive Don Hewitt continued for years to discount the Warren report's findings. Hewitt—who created the show *60 Minutes*—suspected Jack Ruby killed Oswald at the behest of someone in the Mafia. Like Garrison, he also wondered if the assassination was orchestrated by Cubans angry over the Bay of Pigs invasion. "Whether there were shots fired from the grassy knoll, we're never going to know that. Maybe someday we will," Hewitt said in 2002. As for Oswald, Hewitt said: "That kid was not smart enough to have figured all this out all by himself."[455]

A Congressional investigation in 1979 revived the idea that more than three shots were fired. Experts cited a recording of Dallas police radio transmissions that appeared to include a fourth shot. Based on this finding, a Congressional committee said Kennedy was "probably" assassinated in a conspiracy that involved a second gunman. But further testing by the National Academy of Sciences found the Congressional investigators were mistaken.[456] It turned out the police recording of a fourth bullet was made a minute after Oswald fired. This result, made public in 1988, closed the door on government investigations of the assassination—though conspiracy theories abound to this day.

In prepared text for speeches he gave in 1967, Smith elaborated on his belief that the Washington establishment—the Warren Commission and the people he covered for UPI—was a more credible source of assassination information than Jim Garrison or any other conspiracy theorist.

"If indeed there was a sinister plot to kill John F. Kennedy; if, indeed, Lee Harvey Oswald was part of an apparatus; if, indeed, the Warren Commission was part of this plot in that it suppressed or failed to explore pertinent evidence, then you must remember that the Attorney General of the United States during the commission investigation—the attorney general of the United States who was the boss of the FBI—was Robert F. Kennedy," President Kennedy's brother, Smith said.

"So, who do you want to believe—the Attorneys General of the United States from Robert Kennedy to Ramsey Clark; do you want to believe the FBI and the Secret Service; do you want to believe the Chief Justice and the President of the United States, or do you want to believe a politically ambitious county prosecutor who is riding to a curious sort of glory on the jumbled, irrational stories of pitiable human trash?"[457]

CHAPTER 15 ✦ A FATAL SHOT

"I DO NOT INTEND TO become a Willy Loman," Merriman Smith wrote to his family in a 1967 pre-Christmas letter that asked everyone to curb their holiday spending.

Willy Loman is the downtrodden, middle-aged protagonist in Arthur Miller's play *Death of a Salesman*. In some ways, Smith had it better than Willy. Unlike Willy, he had the respect and support of his bosses and colleagues. He was not a man who denied reality, including his drinking problem and the other woes of his life. Unlike Willy, Smitty didn't live in the past. His job required him to keep up with what was happening in the world.

But in other ways, Smith and Willy were alike. Smitty was aging, yet he kept a brutal pace, covering the White House for UPI, freelancing for magazines, giving speeches, and appearing on *The Merv Griffin Show*. Money problems gnawed at him: tuition, expenses, taxes. The bank foreclosed on the Smiths' vacation home in Pennsylvania. The lawyers sent bills for his legal battle with Ellie. "I am forced to do little but work," Smith said.

"I want nothing quite as much from life as an untroubled, happy and productive existence for this family, individually and collectively," he wrote in his pre-Christmas letter. "But I think it would be unwise for me to sink any deeper into guilt for not being able to provide better. I happen to think we have a darned good level of existence."[458]

Two years before this letter—late in 1965—Smith embarked on a new phase in his personal life when he moved from his Washington apartment to a big rented house in Alexandria, Virginia. His girl-friend, Gailey, moved into the house with him. Under Virginia law, divorce was automatic after a couple separated for two years. So the following year, Smith was finally able to divorce Ellie with a mini-mum of legal fuss. On October 14, 1966—the day the divorce was final—Smitty and Gailey got married. "I'm getting a great wife in this girl," Smith wrote to his mother after they wed.[459] It was a sec-ond marriage for both.

Smith's relief about the divorce was clear—and he expressed it directly to his ex-wife. "I won't pay your bills, nor will I be respon-sible for any debt contracted by you," he wrote her. "You'd better believe this." He also said he'd no longer fully support her, and urged her to work out a financial settlement with him. He was tired of covering what he thought were her needless expenses. "You have cost me a lot of money unjustifiably. It stops right now," he said.[460]

At first the marriage promised to finally give Smith a happy relationship, his son Tim recalled. The couple adopted a daughter, Gillean. But Gailey, eighteen years Smith's junior, had demons of her own, including an alcohol problem. Her enjoyment of par-ties and nightlife hindered Smith's unending effort to stay sober. Also, his new wife was used to living expensively. "Gailey is not used to being without money," Smith wrote in another letter to his mother.[461] Smith's daughter Allison often lived with Gailey and her father in the big house in Alexandria. "He probably needed some-one more grounded and financially stable and emotionally stable and biochemically stable," Allison said. "That wasn't Gailey."[462]

Outside of the UPI job and the flow of freelance and TV work he already enjoyed, Smith had few chances for more income. "Professionally, I may not earn as much as many men, but in my field I earn a lot more than most," he said. In a memo related to his divorce case, Smith reported that late in 1966 UPI paid him $500 a week, or $26,000 a year. Adjusted for inflation, that sum would equal $192,000 per year in 2016. His outside work added to this income.[463] It wasn't enough.

Even Lyndon Johnson felt sorry for him—to Smith's surprise. In a private interview on Johnson's fifty-eighth birthday in August 1966, Smith asked the president how he could enjoy the day given the "painful accumulation of crises" he faced—Vietnam, racial violence, and a bout of rising prices then hitting American pocketbooks.

"You've got to remember that a President can concentrate on his official problems with almost no thought of daily personal detail," Johnson replied. "Hell, I don't have anything like the troubles you have. You lost your boy in Vietnam when you were going through a divorce from your first wife, behind in your taxes, poor-mouthing me on the Merv Griffin show to make money for big tuition bills—I've got it a lot better than you have." Smith wasn't sure if Johnson had ordered some kind of government check on him, or if he'd learned of his woes by asking around.[464]

Although Smith personally liked Johnson, he had no trouble writing articles and columns critical of him. Johnson was peeved by a May 1968 "Backstairs" column in which Smith reported that the president took "detailed interest in plans for the Democratic National Convention" even though he was not seeking reelection. White House aides tried to find out who had leaked the details of this story to Smith. Larry Temple, a presidential aide, wrote a memo to Johnson stating that he questioned two other aides, Horace Busby and George Christian, about whether they were Smith's sources. Both denied it.

A few weeks after that, Smith got a note from Harry Truman saying he was glad Smith could attend his eighty-fourth birthday party in Missouri in June 1968. Johnson took note of Smith's appreciation of Truman. "Looks like the only way a President can get Smitty's affection is when he leaves office," he quipped.[465]

Perhaps Johnson should have been glad that during his last year in office, Smith was holding back on the idea of writing a book about him. He had plenty of material, he told his agent—but "it is not the type of material that can be printed while he is in the White House."[466]

Smith might not have had time to write a book anyhow. He had a lot of news to cover. Late in the summer of 1968, Smith hit the road to cover that year's political conventions and presidential campaigns.

Early in August, Smith traveled to Miami Beach for the Republican convention at which Richard Nixon won the party's presidential nomination. Nixon knew Smith since his days in the Eisenhower administration, and this helped Smith get a bit of up-close-and-personal material. In the hours after he secured the nomination, Smith wrote, Nixon, "somewhat fidgety," took a pair of wire-service reporters on an impromptu car ride through Miami Beach. Smith doesn't say it directly, but he writes as if he was one of the reporters on this trip. "With no sirens or flashing lights, Nixon's car slipped out into the traffic shortly before 11:30 p.m. During a thirty-minute drive, he took his nomination as a foregone conclusion and talked largely of his plans for the future."

"Richard M. Nixon was a changed man today—he was a winner," Smith wrote for newspapers of August 8. "He was the undisputed possessor of the Republican presidential nomination over such glamorous opponents as Gov. Nelson A. Rockefeller of New York and Gov. Ronald Reagan of California.

"But more importantly for his self-esteem, he was a man who had clawed and climbed from the depths of political despondency after two terrible beatings—for the presidency in 1960 and for the California governorship in 1962."[467]

Three weeks later, Smith was in Chicago, for the tumultuous Democratic convention. He reported on the Yippies, a war protest group that tried to run a pig for president. "They brought Pigasus to Chicago's Civic Center for his 'nomination' and 'acceptance' speech under the shadow of a five-story-high piece of statuary by Pablo Picasso, a Spaniard who pioneered far-out art three generations before most hippies were born," Smith wrote disdainfully. But he thought the nomination of Pigasus was pretty funny. "There were cries of 'Pork Power' and 'Vote Pig' from his delegates." Poor Pigasus flopped on his belly as soon as he hit the pavement. "It was a disappointing opening for a campaign and the candidate's image suffered greater damage when Cmdr. James Riordan of the First Police District ordered his delegates to move in. Pigasus was hauled off before he could grunt the first sentence of his acceptance speech."

During the convention, Smith watched Chicago police spray tear gas and mace on antiwar demonstrators. That gave him an opportunity to write about what he considered antiwar protesters' irresponsibility and futility—it had become one of his favorite themes.

Smith said the Chicago cops behaved "miserably" toward reporters and photographers—they often seized journalists' notebooks, "as if this would somehow prevent the reporter from getting into print details of police behavior." Contrast that with his views of the Chicago cops' response to the protesters—which was in line with his support of the Washington establishment. Smith admitted that at times, the police use of force was "needless." Despite this, he maintained that "the police performance does deserve a certain amount of understanding."

"Most police in every major American city have a highly derogatory attitude toward young men with long hair, bizarre clothing and such costume items as beads, iron cross medallions, German helmets and the like," Smith wrote. Most cops, Smith said, think a man in such attire "has to have something wrong with him.

"Also, a great many police officers are former members of the armed services and thus are conditioned emotionally to strong negative feelings toward those advocating an end to the draft and general opposition to what U.S. soldiers are doing in Vietnam.

"Police are trained from the first day of their recruit training to respect established authority. When a great many demonstrators assume a raffish anti-establishment stance, most police are almost certain to react negatively."[468]

Smith complained in the following weeks that the protesters were disrupting Vice President Humphrey's campaign appearances. "The so-called peace demonstrators making life miserable for Vice President Hubert H. Humphrey in city after city have a simple purpose: prevent him from delivering his speeches or in any case, turn his meetings into a shambles," Smith wrote. He saw some of the same demonstrators in different cities on different days. Their motive, he said, was to "punish Humphrey for having been part of the Johnson administration and secondly, bring public attention to their belief that as far as the Vietnam war is concerned, the voters have no choice between Humphrey and Nixon."[469]

By early October, Smith saw Nixon as the "overwhelming favorite," though he thought Humphrey "is coming up and will make a better showing than current polls indicate." Smith got it about right. A Gallup poll in October had Nixon at 44 percent, Humphrey at 32 percent and third-party candidate George Wallace at 15 percent. On Election Day 1968, Nixon ended up with about 43.7 percent of the popular vote to Humphrey's 42.7 percent; Wallace got 13.5 percent.

In a story newspapers printed on November 7, Smith recalled Nixon's election defeats in 1960 and 1962. "Seldom, if ever, in American political history has a man suffered the jolting defeats Nixon did. . . . The fact that Nixon has come out of the shadows to victory seems certain to produce some changes in his political personality. He may be more magnanimous as chief executive than many of his political enemies would believe."[470]

Nixon's win put Smith on the road to Florida "to watch RMN (Nixon) like a hungry seagull." "After getting to know RMN better than I ever had before, I'm convinced he's going to try like the devil to be a genuinely good President," Smitty wrote to friends. "But the dice are so loaded against him, so many ugly situations facing him at home and abroad, so many people simply waiting . . . before pounding on him, that I doubt seriously whether he gets the chance he deserves."[471]

Then, Smith took sick, again. In mid-November, he ended up at Mercy Hospital in Miami, suffering from high blood pressure. "I came down with a crash. . . . Three weeks in a Catholic hospital and they let me out only on the understanding I would remain in the Miami area under constant supervision of a team of cardiologists," Smith wrote to friends in the same letter in which he discussed watching Nixon. In typical fashion, he addressed his friends as "Mary and what's-his-name."

He was out of Mercy Hospital just a week before he ended up in another hospital, "this one Jewish, just to cover all bets with the Lord." The doctors at the second hospital removed cysts under his right eyelid "which I didn't even know I had."

After two more weeks in the hospital, he moved to a hotel room. He had vision trouble, and his eye doctors told him to be careful moving around. His heart doctors told him he needed exercise. Smith laughed off the contradiction. "Smitty, we love you," President Johnson wrote him on December 24.[472] Gailey and Gillean came to visit him at a hotel over Christmas.

"By the end of December, I was simply tapped out. Too young for Medicare, too transient for welfare, too old for the Peace Corps," he wrote to "Mary and what's-his-name." Around New Year's, he was back home in Alexandria, still an invalid. He began an exercise regime, and ate just one thousand calories a day. Gailey served him no-fat, no-salt meals. He went out every morning for two and a half miles of roadwork, with weights on his wrists and ankles. "I look, I'm told, like an aging fighter training for That Last Bout," he wrote. Over the following weeks, he lost forty pounds.

"Seriously, I feel simply great, but bored, bored, bored with taking eight different kinds of medicine a day, then taking that awful morning mixture" designed to make sure the medicines didn't lodge in his digestive system, Smith wrote. The doctors were trying to wean him off these drugs by the time of Nixon's inaugural. "It <u>would</u> be awkward, going back to work and right in the middle of the Inaugural Ceremony, to cry out over four [TV] networks, 'Where's the can' or 'I need a glass of water for my noon medicine.'"[473]

Even though he was away from work, he filed a few UPI stories. One was a long essay about Johnson's impending departure from office. "Millions of his fellow countrymen, instead of being grateful and admiring, are glad to see him go," Smith wrote. He went on to describe Johnson's emotions, saying he was leaving Washington in a "mixed mood of pride, nostalgia and downright bitterness." The story noted that Johnson did not feel he got "a fair shake or proper credit" from the news media.[474]

Smith was due to stop by the White House in January 1969 for a "final warm handshake and bawling out from LBJ." He figured Johnson would give him an earful for writing that he was bitter. But Johnson was not angry. Smith underestimated the president's affection for him. On January 20, his last day in office, Johnson awarded Smith the Presidential Medal of Freedom, which along with the Congressional Gold Medal is considered the United States' highest civilian award. "I was shocked," Smith said. Johnson wrote Smith a gracious note: "Mrs. Johnson and I look forward to seeing you in the good years ahead."[475] Johnson could never stay mad at Smitty.

Richard Nixon was the sixth president Smith covered since he went to work at the White House in 1941. Nixon's slow-moving effort to draw down US involvement in Vietnam allowed Smith to keep writing cranky copy about the antiwar protesters—though as usual he remained careful not to judge the war itself. Smith also wrote plenty of breaking news stories, about White House Cabinet meetings, disaster declarations, bill signings, and presidential announcements. Smitty traveled with Nixon to Europe in February 1969, and in the following months he regularly wrote under such datelines as Key Biscayne, Florida, and San Clemente, California, places where the President liked to vacation. He also traveled with Nixon around the country—to Colorado Springs for an Air Force Academy graduation ceremony, to Los Angeles to cover a dinner for the Apollo 11 astronauts, to New York for a United Nations speech.

He kept up funny correspondences with his friends. Molly Allen—the daughter of UPI executive C. Edmonds Allen—was a child when she met Smith. "A brilliant man. A loving man," she said. She kept in touch with Smitty after she graduated from college in 1969. Allen got a letter or postcard from him every week. Once she told Smith she was upset with her college grades. "Grades, schmades," she recalled Smith writing her. "Who cares whether you got an A or a B when you've got a swinging shape and can play the guitar."

Smith was regularly in and out of rehab hospitals. In 1968, Molly Allen recalled, Smith went on a bender and disappeared for several days. When it was over, he turned up sober. Another time, according to June Lockhart, Gailey got so frustrated with his drinking she whacked Smith in the head with the butt of one of his pistols. She called an ambulance. Smith took eighteen stitches in the emergency room, Gailey told Lockhart. Smith could be a mean drunk, Gailey said.

Sometimes, friends and family say, Helen Thomas or other UPI colleagues helped cover Smith's drinking by writing stories under his byline. There are even stories that White House aides wrote some of Smith's copy. On his way back to Washington from a trip to Asia and Europe in August 1969, Nixon stopped over in England to meet British Prime Minister Harold Wilson. Wilborn Hampton, who'd moved up from the Dallas bureau to become a foreign correspondent, was one of two UPI reporters assigned to help Smith cover the story at the Mildenhall air base. "He was pretty much wasted on the plane. . . . We ended up having to cover for him," Hampton said.[476]

Early in April 1970, Smith was back in rehab. His inability to deal with his drinking depressed him greatly, friends said. It was a big change in attitude from how he felt after he left the rehab program at High Point Hospital five years earlier. On the night of April 12, after he got home from his latest rehab stint, Smith called Helen Thomas, just to talk. Thomas knew of his drinking problem, and she viewed his marriage to Gailey as "difficult." "I think he saw no way out from the demons that beset him. . . . While in the past nine years I had seen and heard him in his 'down' moments, I never heard him sound so low as in that telephone call," Thomas said.[477]

The next day, April 13, Smitty began to come down with a cold. The Smiths had a tradition: when Smitty was coming down with a cold, they went out for dinner at a Chinese restaurant. So he and Gailey got ready to go out. They teased each other. "Go to hell," Gailey said before her husband went into the bathroom to wash up. The words were a gag, she told friends later—they meant nothing.

At 4:55 p.m., Gailey was dressed and ready to leave for dinner. She heard the bathroom fan. "I will be a few minutes before my coat is on," Smitty called to his wife. Another of their regular gag lines. Gailey went off to another part of their big house. She didn't hear any noise. It was several more minutes before she thought something might be wrong. So around 5:15 p.m., she went to the bathroom to check on him.

She found her husband's remains in the bathtub. He had blown his head off with a .357 Magnum revolver. He was fifty-five years old.

His friends and family had seen Smith struggle with his alcoholism, his money problems, his physical health, and his mental health. According to Smitty's friend June Lockhart, UPI editor in chief Earl Johnson always thought Smith was suicidal. The long hours and incessant travel required by his job also took a toll. "The years of the White House grind chewed Smith up physically. It was simply not the kind of life in which a man took good care of himself," said his friend Robert Donovan.[478]

One of Smith's eulogists was Jim Hagerty, President Eisenhower's press secretary. "Merriman would have been pleased if he knew of the numerous times President Eisenhower would ask me, 'What did Smitty think of it and how did he report it?'" Some of Smitty's other friends, people in the business of writing, editing, and publishing, were at a loss for words. Mims Thomason, UPI's president, was unable to finish his remarks at Smith's funeral. He wrote an apologetic letter to Gailey several days later. "I just simply couldn't go on. . . . I'm still in a state of shock," he said.

Smitty was buried next to his son, Merriman Jr., at Arlington National Cemetery. They share a headstone, just downhill from President Kennedy's eternal flame. Gailey joined them when she died in 1984. Smith and his wife are among the few nonmilitary people buried at Arlington.

President Nixon, no friend of reporters, was moved enough by Smith's death to order the White House flags to half-staff. He even telephoned Helen Thomas to express his condolences. "A wonderful, brilliant journalist was gone and it was journalism's loss. They don't make them like Smitty any more," Thomas wrote. "He taught me well about being aggressive, being first and being right with a story."[479]

EPILOGUE · FOUR MINUTES

THANKS TO MERRIMAN SMITH AND his coworkers in the UPI Dallas bureau, we know big news stories move four minutes faster today than in 1963.

After Lee Harvey Oswald shot President Kennedy, it took four minutes for Smitty to call the Dallas bureau, for Wilborn Hampton to type the bulletin, for Jim Tolbert to put it on punch paper tape, and for Jack Fallon to order it on to the A-wire. Oswald fired at 12:30 p.m., and the first UPI bulletin moved at 12:34 p.m.

That four-minute delay has been cut to zero by the Internet. Smitty and Jack Bell wouldn't have to fight over the radiotelephone, and there'd be no editors and punch paper tape between them and their readers. Instead, they'd tap out the story quickly on their mobile phones' glass screens and put it on their Twitter or other social media feeds. Then they would use laptop computers to follow up with more elaborate dispatches cleared by their editors.

Smith's friends say he would like social media and other modern ways of delivering news. He liked anything that got news to readers faster. The gossipy tidbits he put in "Backstairs at the White House" columns would be great blog material too.

Many of the thou-shalt-nots that hindered Smith's reporting are gone today. Smith hated wartime censorship rules that kept him from reporting President Franklin Roosevelt's cross-country travels. Presidents today don't go anyplace secretly except perhaps for Baghdad or Kabul. Smitty and his colleagues kept quiet about Roosevelt's health. Today, presidents issue press releases with details of their checkups.

Rules for press conferences and presidential interviews are also freer. President Eisenhower limited what could be reported of his public utterances—"The President may be quoted directly only when he gives special permission or when his statements are released in written form," said an invitation to a 1957 news conference. Today, news conferences are on live TV, and presidents can't cover up their slip-ups.

Eisenhower also imposed limits on one-on-one interviews. He gave Smith an interview for a book, *A President's Odyssey*, a largely laudatory chronicle of the overseas trips he took in the last years of his administration. The interview takes up a whole chapter—and not once does Smith put any of Eisenhower's words between quotation marks. Smith wasn't even allowed to take notes. Reporters today would never agree to such limits on a presidential interview—and presidents, eager for publicity, are unlikely to impose them.

Even the taboo against reporting on presidential sex lives is gone. Smith pushed back against that taboo in a "Backstairs" column that subtly hinted at Kennedy's womanizing. Today, there'd be no subtle hints. Ask Bill Clinton, Gary Hart, or John Edwards if they want the media held to the reporting standards of the 1950s or 1960s in reporting their sex lives.

Smith would be unhappy to see that reporters now are held in lower esteem than in his time. Smitty wasn't America's only celebrity journalist. One day in the late 1950s or early 1960s, when Smith's friend June Lockhart was acting on the set of the TV show *Lassie*, she brought along Ralph McGill, the editor of the bravely desegregationist *Atlanta Constitution*. Even the Hollywood people she worked with were impressed with McGill. "Everyone was all aflutter," Lockhart said. "They knew of the paper even if they didn't know his name."

What newspaper, wire service, or Internet reporter today enjoys the same status as Ralph McGill or Merriman Smith? Who from the Associated Press, the *Wall Street Journal,* or the *New York Times* sits down regularly with Stephen Colbert or Jimmy Fallon, as Smitty did with Jack Paar, Johnny Carson, and Merv Griffin? Even worse, politicians today—especially presidential candidates—score points with voters by scorning the reporters and journalists who cover them.

Not only are reporters held in lower esteem, there are fewer of them. The number of reporters, editors, photographers, and support staff in US newspaper newsrooms fell from 56,200 in 2000 to 32,900 in 2015—a 35 percent decline, the American Society of Newspaper Editors reports. Newspaper newsrooms today employ 23.5 percent fewer people than the 43,000 people they employed when the survey began in 1978, ASNE says.[480] Newspapers have shed reporters who cover city halls, courthouses, police departments, and school boards. State capitols have been hard hit. The number of newspaper reporters assigned to cover governors, legislatures, and state government plunged from just under five hundred in 2003 to about three hundred in 2014. More reporters for digital-only news outlets cover state capitals and some cities, but they don't employ as many journalists as newspapers have lost.[481]

Since Smitty's time, newspapers have slashed Washington coverage. The days are long past when papers from St. Louis, Detroit, Philadelphia, Cleveland, and Baltimore staffed a presidential trip—as they did during Kennedy's trip to Dallas. From 1985 to 2015, the number of US newspapers with Washington bureaus fell by more than 60 percent, from 71 to just 27, according to data gathered by the Pew Research Center. Newspapers in places like San Jose, Providence, Toledo, and Norfolk have shut their Washington bureaus, which focused on covering news of interest to their circulation areas.[482] New web-only general news sites like BuzzFeed and Vox are adding Washington coverage—but they have yet to fill the gap left by the culling of newspaper reporters.

Wire service journalism is also diminished. Smith's employer, United Press International, once had reporters in every state capital and in many world capitals and competed story-for-story with the Associated Press. UPI is still around, but it's a ghost of its former self. It was laid flat in the 1980s by the demise of the big-city afternoon papers that were its biggest customers. A series of ownership changes and two trips through bankruptcy court brought about the shutdown of nearly all its news bureaus. Most of UPI's news report today is rewritten from various web sites.

Before the digital age, the UPI and AP Teletype machines that clattered away at newspapers and TV and radio stations were many cities and towns' only link to outside news. Newspapers, delivered morning and afternoon, were the place to get news stories that are today instantly available on computers, mobile phones, and tablet screens. They had pencil games and puzzles now supplanted by apps and addictive games. In the day of newspapers, you could check the price of your stocks once or twice a day. At best, the newspapers' stock data was several hours out of date. At worst, it was yesterday's news. Now anyone with an Internet connection can follow stock prices in real time. The same goes for sports stats—they're available even as games are in progress.

Millions of newspaper readers have moved to digital platforms that are more up-to-date than the papers' dead tree editions. The trouble is, advertisers and their money have not followed them. From 2004 to 2014, Pew researchers report, yearly revenue from all newspaper advertising—digital and print—fell 65 percent, from $46.7 billion to $16.4 billion.[483] One day during the last week of December 2015, an entire issue of *USA Today*—one of the biggest selling papers in America—had just two display advertisements.

Even in its emaciated state, the news industry still produces good journalism. Excellent specialized web sites like SCOTUSblog, Inside Climate News, and Syria Deeply publish interesting, well-researched stories available for free. Legacy news organizations like the *New York Times* and the *Wall Street Journal* provide well-written news and feature stories from around the world in part by selling subscriptions to online readers. Politico puts out solid reporting on government and politics that is available for free, and it offers specialized, focused reporting on such topics as government regulation and campaign finance to those who pay thousands of dollars per year for subscriptions.

The *Times,* the *Journal,* and Politico are said to make money—evidence that readers will pay for quality. Even amid the revenue decline faced by the news media, their managers grasp what Merriman Smith's bosses knew well: newsgathering is an investment as much as an expense.

United Press International invested heavily in Smitty. It brought Smith to Washington in 1940, tried him out on different beats, and decided he'd do best at the White House. Then UPI kept him there. What he learned over the years about the White House and the presidency gave UPI a valuable edge. Smitty's enthusiasm and knowledge of his beat scored scoops on President Truman's meeting with General MacArthur and President Eisenhower's decision to fire Sherman Adams. That tragic day in Dallas, Smitty was matched against Jack Bell, an Associated Press reporter of similar experience. But Bell wasn't a White House regular. Unlike Smith, Bell didn't have Secret Service friends who would tell him about Kennedy's condition, and he didn't know to go along when the White House formed a press pool. On November 22, 1963, UPI's investment in Smith paid a big dividend: a five-minute victory over the Associated Press on one of the century's biggest stories, and a Pulitzer Prize.

UPI could have fired Smith when President Johnson's staff booted him from Air Force One in 1964. But UPI did not want to toss away his experience and prominence. It sent Smith to rehab and made sure his treatment bills were paid. Smith's bosses sincerely worried about his well-being. They also knew what they had. Helping him through hard times was good for business. Smith's books, freelancing, and TV appearances promoted UPI. His decades on the beat were even valuable to his bosses when he veered from straight news reporting to publicly denounce 1960s radicalism. His widely discussed speech at the newspaper publishers' convention in 1967 enhanced UPI's standing with its customers.

Smitty was a prominent part of the establishment he covered. He looked at the world through the lenses of the people he wrote about—sometimes too much so.

But as much as the conventions of his time allowed, Smith was all about his audience—his readers, listeners, and viewers. He shared funny stories, like the yarn about Eisenhower and the White House squirrels. He'd give you the inside dope on what peeved Lyndon Johnson and his staff, or take you on a drive with Richard Nixon. He'd tell you about a weeping White House aide on a presidential helicopter. All the while, he wrote readable stories on subjects like federal spending, taxes, defense, civil rights, and government policy—the basic news Americans need to stay informed. In the midtwentieth century, Merriman Smith's experience and hustle brought an audience to UPI's newspaper and broadcast clients. And he brought everyone closer to the President of the United States.

Too many of America's Smittys are gone now. The Internet made news faster, but less complete. We have gained four minutes in the decades since Merriman Smith scored his biggest scoop. We have lost a lot more.

Appendix A · Merriman Smith's eyewitness story

Merriman Smith won the Pulitzer Prize for this story, written after he returned to Washington on November 22, 1963.

By MERRIMAN SMITH,
UPI White House Reporter

WASHINGTON, Nov. 23 (UPI)–IT WAS a balmy, sunny noon as we motored through downtown Dallas behind President Kennedy. The procession cleared the center of the business district and turned into a handsome highway that wound through what appeared to be a park.

I was riding in the so-called White House press "pool" car, a telephone company vehicle equipped with a mobile radiotelephone. I was in the front seat between a driver from the telephone company and Malcolm Kilduff, acting White House press secretary for the president's Texas tour. Three other pool reporters were wedged in the back seat.

Suddenly we heard three loud, almost painfully loud cracks. The first sounded as if it might have been a large firecracker. But the second and third blasts were unmistakable. Gunfire.

The president's car, possibly as much as 150 or 200 yards ahead, seemed to falter briefly. We saw a flurry of activity in the Secret

Service follow-up car behind the chief executive's bubble-top limousine.

Next in line was the car bearing Vice President Lyndon B. Johnson. Behind that, another follow-up car bearing agents assigned to the vice president's protection. We were behind that car.

Our car stood still for probably only a few seconds, but it seemed like a lifetime. One sees history explode before one's eyes and for even the most trained observer, there is a limit to what one can comprehend.

I looked ahead at the President's car but could not see him or his companion, Gov. John B. Connally of Texas. Both men had been riding on the right side of the bubble-top limousine from Washington. I thought I saw a flash of pink which would have been Mrs. Jacqueline Kennedy.

Everybody in our car began shouting at the driver to pull up closer to the president's car. But at this moment, we saw the big bubble-top and a motorcycle escort roar away at high speed.

We screamed at our driver, "Get going, get going." We careened around the Johnson car and its escort and set out down the highway, barely able to keep in sight of the president's car and the accompanying Secret Service follow-up car.

They vanished around a curve. When we cleared the same curve we could see where we were heading—Parkland Hospital, a large brick structure to the left of the arterial highway. We skidded around a sharp left turn and spilled out of the pool car as it entered the hospital driveway.

I ran to the side of the bubble-top.

The president was face-down on the back seat. Mrs. Kennedy made a cradle of her arms around the President's head and bent over him as if she were whispering to him.

Governor Connally was on his back on the floor of the car, his head and shoulders resting on the arm of his wife, Nellie, who kept shaking her head and shaking with dry sobs. Blood oozed from the front of the governor's suit. I could not see the president's wound.

But I could see blood spattered around the interior of the rear seat and a dark stain spreading down the right side of the president's dark gray suit.

From the telephone car, I had radioed the Dallas bureau of UPI that three shots had been fired at the Kennedy motorcade. Seeing the bloody scene in the rear of the car at the hospital entrance, I knew I had to get to a telephone immediately.

Clint Hill, the Secret Service agent in charge of the detail assigned to Mrs. Kennedy, was leaning over into the rear of the car.

"How badly was he hit, Clint?" I asked.

"He's dead," Hill replied curtly.

I have no further clear memory of the scene in the driveway. I recall a babble of anxious voices, tense voices—"Where in hell are the stretchers . . . Get a doctor out here . . . He's on the way . . . Come on, easy there." And from somewhere, nervous sobbing.

I raced down a short stretch of sidewalk into a hospital corridor. The first thing I spotted was a small clerical office, more of a booth than an office. Inside, a bespectacled man stood shuffling what appeared to be hospital forms. At a wicket much like a bank teller's cage, I spotted a telephone on the shelf.

"How do you get outside?" I gasped. "The president has been shot and this is an emergency call."

"Dial nine," he said, shoving the phone toward me.

It took two tries before I successfully dialed the Dallas UPI number. Quickly I dictated a bulletin saying the President had been seriously, perhaps fatally, injured by an assassin's bullets while driving through the streets of Dallas.

Litters bearing the president and the governor rolled by me as I dictated, but my back was to the hallway and I didn't see them until they were at the entrance of the emergency room about 75 or 100 feet away.

I knew they had passed, however, from the horrified expression that suddenly spread over the face of the man behind the wicket.

As I stood in the drab buff hallway leading into the emergency ward trying to reconstruct the shooting for the UPI man on the other end of the telephone and still keep track of what was happening outside the door of the emergency room, I watched a swift and confused panorama sweep before me.

Kilduff of the White House press staff raced up and down the hall. Police captains barked at each other, "Clear this area." Two priests hurried in behind a Secret Service agent, their narrow purple stoles rolled up tightly in their hands. A police lieutenant ran down the hall with a large carton of blood for transfusions. A doctor came in and said he was responding to a call for "all neurosurgeons."

The priests came out and said the president had received the last sacrament of the Roman Catholic Church. They said he was still alive, but not conscious. Members of the Kennedy staff began arriving. They had been behind us in the motorcade, but hopelessly bogged down for a time in confused traffic.

Telephones were at a premium in the hospital and I clung to mine for dear life. I was afraid to stray from the wicket lest I lose contact with the outside world.

My decision was made for me, however, when Kilduff and Wayne Hawks of the White House staff ran by me, shouting that Kilduff would make a statement shortly in the so-called nurses room a floor above and at the far end of the hospital.

I threw down the phone and sped after them. We reached the door of the conference room and there were loud cries of "Quiet!" Fighting to keep his emotions under control, Kilduff said, "President John Fitzgerald Kennedy died at approximately 1 o'clock."

I raced into a nearby office. I spotted Virginia Payette, wife of UPI's Southwestern Division manager and a veteran reporter in her own right. I told her to try getting through on pay telephones on the floor above.

Frustrated by the inability to get through the hospital switchboard, I appealed to a nurse. She led me through a maze of corridors and back stairways to another floor and a lone pay booth. I got the Dallas office. Virginia had gotten through before me.

Whereupon I ran back through the hospital to the conference room. There Jiggs Fauver of the White House transportation staff grabbed me and said Kilduff wanted a pool of three men immediately to fly back to Washington on Air Force One, the presidential aircraft.

Down the stairs I ran and into the driveway, only to discover Kilduff had just pulled out in our telephone car.

Charles Roberts of Newsweek magazine, Sid Davis of Westinghouse Broadcasting and I implored a police officer to take us to the airport in his squad car. The Secret Service had requested that no sirens be used in the vicinity of the airport, but the Dallas officer did a masterful job of getting us through some of the worst traffic I'd ever seen.

As we piled out of the car on the edge of the runway about 200 yards from the presidential aircraft, Kilduff spotted us and motioned for us to hurry. We trotted to him and he said the plane could take two pool men to Washington: that Johnson was about to take the oath of office aboard the plane and would take off immediately thereafter.

I saw a bank of telephone booths beside the runway and asked if I had time to advise my news service. He said, "But for God's sake, hurry."

Then began another telephone nightmare. The Dallas office rang busy. I tried calling Washington. All circuits were busy. Then I called the New York bureau of UPI and told them about the impending installation of a new president aboard the airplane.

Kilduff came out of the plane and motioned wildly toward my booth. I slammed down the phone and jogged across the runway. A detective stopped me and said, "You dropped your pocket comb."

Aboard Air Force One on which I had made so many trips as a press association reporter covering President Kennedy, all of the shades of the larger main cabin were drawn and the interior was hot and dimly lighted.

Kilduff propelled us to the president's suite two-thirds of the way back in the plane. The room is used normally as a combination conference and sitting room and could accommodate eight to 10 people seated.

I wedged inside the door and began counting. There were 27 people in this compartment. Johnson stood in the center with his wife, Lady Bird. U.S. District Judge Sarah T. Hughes, 67, a kindly faced woman stood with a small black Bible in her hands, waiting to give the oath.

The compartment became hotter and hotter. Johnson was worried that some of the Kennedy staff might not be able to get inside. He urged people to press forward, but a Signal Corps photographer, Capt. Cecil Stoughton, standing in the corner on a chair, said if Johnson moved any closer, it would be virtually impossible to make a truly historic photograph.

It developed that Johnson was waiting for Mrs. Kennedy, who was composing herself in a small bedroom in the rear of the plane. She appeared alone, dressed in the same pink wool suit she had been wearing in the morning when she appeared happy, shaking hands with airport crowds at the side of her husband.

She was white-faced but dry-eyed. Friendly hands stretched toward her as she stumbled slightly. Johnson took both of her hands in his and motioned her to his left side. Lady Bird stood on his right, a fixed half-smile showing the tension.

Johnson nodded to Judge Hughes, an old friend of his family and a Kennedy appointee.

Outside a jet could be heard droning into a landing.

Judge Hughes held out the Bible and Johnson covered it with his large left hand. His right arm went slowly into the air and the jurist began to intone the constitutional oath. "I do solemnly swear I will faithfully execute the office of president of the United States ..."

The brief ceremony ended when Johnson in a deep, firm voice repeated after the judge "and so help me God."

Johnson turned first to his wife, hugged her about the shoulders and kissed her on the cheek. Then he turned to Kennedy's widow, put his left arm around her and kissed her cheek.

As others in the group—some Texas Democratic House members, members of the Johnson and Kennedy staffs – moved toward the new president, he seemed to back away from any expression of felicitation.

The 2-minute ceremony concluded at 3:38 P.M. EST and seconds later, the president said firmly, "Now, let's get airborne."

Col. James Swindal, pilot of the plane, a big gleaming silver and blue fan-jet, cut on the starboard engines immediately. Several persons, including Sid Davis of Westinghouse, left the plane at that time. The White House had room for only two pool reporters on the return flight and these posts were filled by Roberts and me, although at the moment we could find no empty seats.

At 3:47 P.M. EST, the wheels of Air Force One cleared the runway. Swindal roared the big ship up to an unusually high cruising altitude of 41,000 feet where at 625 miles an hour, ground speed, the jet hurtled toward Andrews Air Force Base outside Washington.

When the president's plane reached operating altitude, Mrs. Kennedy left her bedchamber and walked to the rear compartment of the plane. This was the so-called family living room, a private area where she and Kennedy, family and friends had spent many happy airborne hours chatting and dining together.

Kennedy's casket had been placed in this compartment, carried aboard by a group of Secret Service agents.

Mrs. Kennedy went into the rear lounge and took a chair beside the coffin. There she remained throughout the flight. Her vigil was shared at times by four staff members close to the slain chief executive – David Powers, his buddy and personal assistant; Kennedy P. O'Donnell, appointments secretary and key political adviser; Lawrence O'Brien, chief Kennedy liaison man with Congress, and Brig. Gen. Godfrey McHugh, Kennedy's Air Force aide.

Kennedy's military aide, Maj. Gen. Chester V. Clifton, was busy most of the trip in the forward areas of the plane, sending messages and making arrangements for arrival ceremonies and movement of the body to Bethesda Naval Hospital.

As the flight progressed, Johnson walked back into the main compartment. My portable typewriter was lost somewhere around the hospital and I was writing on an over-sized electric typewriter which Kennedy's personal secretary, Mrs. Evelyn Lincoln, had used to type his speech texts.

Johnson came up to the table where Roberts and I were trying to record the history we had just witnessed.

"I'm going to make a short statement in a few minutes and give you copies of it," he said. "Then when I get on the ground, I'll do it over again."

It was the first public utterance of the new Chief Executive, brief and moving:

"This is a sad time for all people. We have suffered a loss that cannot be weighed. For me it is a deep personal tragedy. I know the world shares the sorrow that Mrs. Kennedy and her family bear. I will do my best. That is all I can do. I ask for your help—and God's."

When the plane was about 45 minutes from Washington, the new president got on a special radiotelephone and placed a call to Mrs. Rose Kennedy, the late president's mother.

"I wish to God there was something I could do," he told her. "I just wanted you to know that."

Thirty minutes out of Washington, Johnson put in a call for Nellie Connally, wife of the seriously wounded Texas governor.

The new president said to the governor's wife:

"We are praying for you, darling, and I know that everything is going to be all right, isn't it? Give him a hug and a kiss for me."

It was dark when Air Force One began to skim over the lights of the Washington area, lining up for a landing at Andrews Air Force Base. The plane touched down at 5:59 P.M. EST.

I thanked the stewards for rigging up the typewriter for me, pulled on my raincoat and started down the forward ramp. Roberts and I stood under a wing and watched the casket being lowered from the rear of the plane and borne by a complement of armed forces body bearers into a waiting hearse. We watched Mrs. Kennedy and the president's brother, Attorney General Robert F. Kennedy, climb into the hearse beside the coffin.

The new president repeated his first public statement for broadcast and newsreel microphones, shook hands with some of the government and diplomatic leaders who turned out to meet the plane, and headed for his helicopter.

Roberts and I were given seats on another 'copter bound for the White House lawn. In the compartment next to ours in one of the large chairs beside a window sat Theodore C. Sorensen, one of the president's closest associates with the title of special counsel to the president. He had not gone to Texas with his chief but had come to the air base for his return.

Sorensen sat wilted in the large chair, crying softly. The dignity of his deep grief seemed to sum up all of the tragedy and sadness of the previous 6 hours.

As our helicopter circled in the balmy darkness for a landing on the White House south lawn, it seemed incredible that only six hours before, John Fitzgerald Kennedy had been a vibrant, smiling, waving and active man.

Reprinted with permission of United Press International.

Appendix B ✦ Dallas timeline

Here's how United Press International and The Associated Press reported President Kennedy's assassination on November 22, 1963. All times are Central Standard Time.

12:30 p.m. – Lee Harvey Oswald fires three shots at President John F. Kennedy's limousine, striking Kennedy and Texas Gov. John Connally.

12:34 p.m. – United Press International moves Merriman Smith's first dispatch on its A-wire: "Three shots fired at President Kennedy's motorcade today in downtown Dallas."

12:36 p.m. – Kennedy's limousine arrives at Parkland Hospital. The car carrying Smith and his Associated Press competitor, Jack Bell, is close behind.

12:39 p.m. – UPI flash: Smith reports that Kennedy is "wounded perhaps seriously perhaps fatally"

12:39 p.m. – AP's first bulletin, based on the account of photographer James W. Altgens, moves to clients west of the Mississippi. At the time, the AP's A-wire is on a split managed by its Kansas City bureau. A story budget moving to East Coast papers keeps the dispatch from reaching New York, Washington, and other eastern points.

12:40 p.m. – AP's Kansas City bureau clears Altgens' bulletin for East Coast points.

12:41 p.m. – UPI moves a new lead saying JFK and Connally were "cutdown by an assassin's bullets"

12:41 p.m. – AP moves a first add quoting Altgens saying there was blood on President Kennedy's head.

12:44 p.m. – UPI moves an add to the 12:41 p.m. lead quoting Secret Service agent Clint Hill saying of Kennedy, "He's dead."

12:45 p.m. – AP begins moving a series of adds to the Altgens dispatch that are garbled by Teletype operators. These adds keep moving until around 12:49 p.m.

12:49 p.m –AP moves ungarbled copy from Bell, saying presidential aide Kenneth O'Donnell is unsure of Kennedy's condition.

12:50 p.m. – AP bulletin says Kennedy and Connally were "shot from ambush" and that it's unknown if they were killed.

12:51 p.m. – By now UPI has moved four adds to its 12:41 p.m. lead, which can be strung together into a coherent newspaper story.

1:18 p.m. – AP moves an "unconfirmed" report that Vice President Johnson was "wounded slightly." In fact, Johnson was not hit.

1:23 p.m. – UPI: "A Father Huber, of Holy Trinity Church in Dallas administered the last sacrament of the church to the President."

1:27 p.m. – AP: Kennedy "was given the last holy rites of the Roman Catholic Church today"

1:32 p.m. – AP flash: "Two priests who were with Kennedy say he is dead of bullet wounds"

1:34 p.m. – AP: "Government sources said today that President Kennedy is dead." Washington dateline. No further attribution.

1:35 p.m. – UPI: "Flash President Kennedy dead"

1:37 p.m. – AP: "Flash Dallas – President Kennedy died at 1 p.m. (CST)"

ACKNOWLEDGMENTS

THIS BOOK BEGAN WITH A phone call in 2013 from Faye Penn, then of the *New York Observer*, who asked me to write a piece marking the fiftieth anniversary of President Kennedy's assassination. That assignment set me on the path of reporting out how Merriman Smith broke the story.

A great many people helped me see this project through.

Smith's family and friends contributed immeasurably. Tim Smith, his son, provided extensive access to family records and photographs, put me in touch with several of his father's friends and colleagues, and helped dig out letters and documents. Allison Smith gave valuable insight into her father's thinking, and Gillean Smith offered recollections of her parents and pointed me toward other sources. Al Spivak, who shared the UPI White House beat with Smith and Helen Thomas during the Kennedy and Johnson years, helped with his recollections.

Among Smitty's other friends, contemporaries, and coworkers aiding this project were Sid Davis, Wilborn Hampton, Robert MacNeil, June Lockhart, Molly Allen, and Mike Rabun. Maurice Carroll, Julian Read, and Clint Hill added details to the story of what happened in Dallas. Former White House staffers Hal Pachios and Bill Moyers helped me understand Smith's relationship with Lyndon Johnson. Tom Johnson, an LBJ staffer and Smitty friend, eased my way in carrying out research at the Lyndon Baines Johnson Presidential Library in Austin, Texas.

Many librarians and archivists helped, in person or via phone and email. They work at the LBJ Library, the John F. Kennedy Presidential Library and Museum in Boston, the Herbert Hoover Presidential Library and Museum in West Branch, Iowa, the Dwight D. Eisenhower Presidential Library and Museum in Abilene, Kansas, the Briscoe Center for American History at the University of Texas in Austin, and the Library of Congress in Washington. I found helpful records about Smith and his Pulitzer Prize at Columbia University's Butler Library. I owe special thanks to the staff at the Wisconsin Historical Society in Madison, Wisconsin, Krishna B. Shenoy of The Sixth Floor Museum at Dealey Plaza in Dallas, and Francesca Pitaro of the Associated Press Corporate Archives in New York.

The best deal going for anyone who lives in New York City is a New York Public Library card.

United Press International graciously gave permission to reprint Smitty's Pulitzer Prize–winning story about the assassination.

Mike Pride, the administrator of the Pulitzer Prizes and my editor at the *Concord Monitor* in New Hampshire the early 1980s, read an early chapter draft and enlisted me to write about Smith for the Pulitzer website. Jane Harrigan, Lauren Kern, Michael Birkner, and Linda Massarella also read chapter drafts and made helpful suggestions. Rebecca Morris, Ginger Adams Otis, and Dan Paisner offered advice and encouragement in navigating the world of book publishing.

I also owe thanks to my supportive friends and coworkers at the *New York Post*—especially Paul McPolin, Steve Lynch, Annie Wermiel, and Joe Illuzzi.

My agent, Rita Rosenkranz, found a publisher for this book at a point when all hope seemed lost. She rightly assured me the book would be in good hands at Skyhorse Publishing. Joseph Craig, my editor at Skyhorse, made the manuscript stronger and better.

Somewhere in the book there may be a factual mistake—maybe more than one. If so, it's my fault alone.

Notes

PROLOGUE

1 Earl J. Johnson letter to Smith, Jan. 3, 1964, in the Merriman Smith papers at the Wisconsin Historical Society, box 2, folder 44.

2 Theodore White, "For President Kennedy: An Epilogue," in Editors of *Life* magazine, *The Day Kennedy Died: 50 Years Later LIFE remembers the Man and the Moment*, New York: Life Books, 2013, p. 153.

3 White's account of his interview with Jacqueline Kennedy can be found in the Theodore H. White Personal Papers, Camelot Documents, Item III-A: Copy of White's 19 December 1963 transcript of interview notes, THWPP-059-013, at the John F. Kennedy Presidential Library and Museum. Available online at http://www.jfklibrary.org/Asset-Viewer/Archives/THWPP-059-013.aspx.

CHAPTER 1

4 Family chronology provided to author by Tim Smith, Merriman Smith's son.

5 Frank Rossiter, "A Savannah Man At White House," *Savannah Morning News Magazine*, Sept. 30, 1962, p. 6.

6 Gerry Van der Heuvel, "Reporter Merriman Smith relishes his role as a chronicler of high level events," *Editor & Publisher*, July 6, 1963, pp. 13, 49–50.

7 Smith family chronology.

8 Donald A. Ritchie, *Reporting from Washington: The History of the Washington Press Corps*, New York: Oxford University Press, 2005, p. 15.

9   A. Merriman Smith, *Thank You, Mr. President: A White House Notebook,* 1946: Harper and Brothers, New York, p. 3.

10 *Thank You, Mr. President,* p. 112.

11 *Thank You, Mr. President,* p. 113.

12 Letter from Eleanor Smith, undated but probably written in March 1945, provided by Tim Smith.

13 *Thank You, Mr. President,* p. 38.

14 *Thank You, Mr. President,* p. 46.

15 *Thank You, Mr. President,* p. 209.

16 *Thank You, Mr. President,* p. 3.

17 Eleanor Smith letter.

18 *Thank You, Mr. President,* p. 13.

19 "Report of President Roosevelt in Person to the Congress on the Crimea Conference," *The New York Times,* March 2, 1945, p. 12.

20 Merriman Smith, "President Kept Going At Top Speed Despite Signs of Failing Health," *The Pittsburgh Press,* April 13, 1945, p. 8. This story gives a full account of Roosevelt's mention of his paralysis in the March 1 address to Congress.

21 *Thank You, Mr. President,* p. 159.

22 *Thank You, Mr. President,* p. 181.

23 Smith, "President Kept Going At Top Speed Despite Signs of Failing Health."

24 *Thank You, Mr. President,* p. 209.

25 *Thank You, Mr. President,* pp. 209–210.

26 *Thank You, Mr. President,* p. 20.

27 Merriman Smith, *Meet Mr. Eisenhower,* New York: Harper & Brothers, 1955, p. 9.

28 *Thank You Mr. President,* pp 255–257.

29 Merriman Smith, "President Expects To Arrive In Capital Tomorrow," *The Freeport (Ill.) Journal-Standard,* Aug. 7, 1945, p. 9.

30 *This Week,* April 26, 1953. Clipping in Merriman Smith papers, box 3, folder 16.

31 *Thank You, Mr. President,* p. 283.

32 *Meet Mister Eisenhower,* p. 45.

33 Harry S. Truman Presidential Library, *Oral History Interview with George Tames,* June 11, 1980, p. 53.

34 Merriman Smith, "U.S., Island Police Hunt Conspirators After Attempt On Truman's Life Fails," *The Sandusky (Ohio) Register,* Nov. 2, 1950, p. 1.

35 *Thank You, Mr. President,* p. 47.

36 *Merriman Smith's Book of Presidents,* p. 20.

THE SCREENING ROOM

37 Merriman Smith, *A President Is Many Men,* New York: Harper & Brothers, 1948, pp 7–8.

CHAPTER 2

38 Merriman Smith, "Truman Wings West To Meet MacArthur," *Tucson (Ariz.) Daily Citizen,* Oct. 13, 1950, p. 1.

39 David McCullough, *Truman,* New York: Simon and Schuster, 1992, p. 806.

40 "The Press: Storm Over Wake," *Time* magazine, Oct. 30, 1950.

41 Public papers of the Presidents: Harry S. Truman news conference, Oct. 19, 1950. On the website of the Harry S. Truman Library, http://trumanlibrary.org/publicpapers/index.php?pid=900&st=&st1.

42 Merriman Smith, "Russia Wants Big Asia War, Truman Says," *The Pittsburgh Press,* Dec. 28, 1952, p. 5.

43 Harry S. Truman Presidential Library, *Oral History Interview with Roy L. McGhee,* January 1992, pp. 5–6.

44 Merriman Smith, "Ike Gives Sherman Adams Surprise Birthday Party," *The Tuscaloosa News,* Jan. 12, 1954, p. 5.

45 A. Merriman Smith, *Reminiscences of Merriman Smith: oral history,* unpublished document, available at Eisenhower Administration project, Columbia University, 1968, p. 31.

46 Jim Hagerty, Eulogy at Merriman Smith's funeral, dated April 17, 1970. Text provided by Smith's family.

47 *Meet Mr. Eisenhower,* p. 71.

48 Mike Conway, "The Origins of Television's 'Anchor Man': Cronkite, Swayze, and Journalism Boundary Work," *American Journalism* 31:4, 2014, pp. 445–467.

49 Author interview with June Lockhart, Oct. 1, 2014.

50 Merriman Smith, "Unpublicized 'Battle Of Squirrels' Raging On White House Grounds," *Daily Independent Journal,* San Rafael, Calif., March 19, 1955, p. 4.

51 "THE PRESIDENCY: And Then the Squirrels," *Time* magazine, April 11, 1955. Downloaded from Time's website Feb. 4, 2015.

52 Hagerty eulogy.

53   Smith oral history, p. 35.

54   Donald A. Ritchie, *Reporting From Washington: The History Of The Washington Press Corps*, New York: Oxford University Press, 2005, p. 124, citing Robert Pierpoint, *At the White House: Assignment to Six Presidents,* New York: Putnam, 1981, pp 29–35, 53, 57.

55   Smith papers at Wisconsin Historical Society, box 1, folder 23: Letter from Smith to his girlfriend, Gailey "Lenni" Johnson, June 27, 1964.

56   Smith oral history, p. 58.

57   Merriman Smith, "Report Adams Will Resign," *The Milwaukee Sentinel,* Sept. 11, 1958, p. 1.

58   The Press: Back from the Minors, *Time* Magazine, Oct. 6, 1958. Downloaded from Time's website Feb. 4, 2015.

59   Family chronology provided to author by Timothy Merriman Smith, Smith's son. Washington columnist Jack Anderson reported this incident in March 1971. See, for example, Jack Anderson, "The Washington Merry-Go Round," *Warren (Pa.) Times-Observer,* March 4, 1971, p. 4. The Secret Service records of this incident remain sealed.

60   Author interview with Tim Smith, Sept. 25, 2014.

61   Lockhart interview, Oct. 1, 2014.

62   Tim Smith correspondence with author, Nov. 5, 2014.

THE GOSPEL SINGER

63   Merriman Smith, "Last of Remaining Slaves to Meet For Annual Christmas Observance," *The San Bernardino County (CA) Sun,* Dec. 24, 1938, p. 1. A shorter version of this piece ran on the front page of *The Atlanta Constitution.*

64   Louis Lautier, "Mahalia Nervous At White House Dinner," *The (Baltimore, Md.) Afro American,* Oct. 24, 1959, p. 3.

65   *The New York Age,* Oct. 31, 1959, p. 1.

66   "Mahalia Jackson thrilled by Eisenhower audience," *The (Baltimore, MD) Afro American,* Oct. 24, 1959, p. 15.

CHAPTER 3

67   Timothy G. Smith, ed., *Merriman Smith's Book of Presidents: A White House Memoir,* New York: W.W. Norton, 1972, p. 10.

68   Helen Thomas, *Front Row at the White House,* New York: Scribner, 1999, p. 55.

69 Gerry Van der Heuvel, "Reporter Merriman Smith relishes his role as a chronicler of high level events," *Editor and Publisher,* July 6, 1963, p. 50.

70 Smith papers, Wisconsin Historical Society, box 2, folder 41.

71 Author interview with Sid Davis, Oct. 21, 2013.

72 A. Merriman Smith, *Reminiscences of Merriman Smith: oral history,* Eisenhower Administration project, Columbia University, 1968, p. 64.

73 Pierre Salinger, *With Kennedy,* Garden City, N.Y.: Doubleday, 1966, p. 138.

74 Robert Dallek, *An Unfinished Life: John F. Kennedy, 1917–1963,* New York: Little Brown, 2003, p. 335.

75 Donald A. Ritchie, *Reporting From Washington: The History Of The Washington Press Corps,* New York: Oxford University Press, 2005, p. 125.

76 *Merriman Smith's Book of Presidents,* pp. 240–241.

77 *With Kennedy,* p. 127.

78 John F. Kennedy Library, *Oral History Interview with Charles Roberts,* April 11, 1968, pp 36–37.

79 See, for example, Malcolm Kilduff oral history interview with Sixth Floor Museum in Dallas, Texas, untranscribed, recorded April 16, 1993.

80 Charles Roberts oral history, p. 35.

81 Charles Roberts oral history, p. 34.

82 Merriman Smith, *The Good New Days,* New York: Bobbs Merrill, 1962, p. 218.

83 Unbylined UPI story, "Salinger Makes TV Debut On Paar Show," Redlands (Calif.) Daily Facts, Jan. 18, 1961, p. 1. Salinger played the piano with Paar's band, causing grief for NBC lawyers who feared the music he performed violated copyrights. They were relieved to learn that Salinger had performed his own composition.

84 Author interview with Tim Smith, Sept. 25, 2014.

85 Unbylined United Press International story, "White House's Secrecy Laid To President," *Chicago Tribune,* November 17, 1962, Part 1, page 4.

86 William Manchester, *The Death of a President: November 20– November 25, 1963,* New York: Little Brown, 1967; republished on Amazon Kindle in 2013. Kindle locations 1151–1152. See also *With Kennedy,* p. 131 and *An Unfinished Life,* pp. 432–433.

87 *With Kennedy,* pp. 130–131.

88 Merriman Smith, "D'Gaulle, Kennedy Agree On West Strategy In Berlin," *Tyrone (Pa.) Daily Herald,* June 2, 1961, p. 1.

89 Merriman Smith, "Deadlock Over Laos May Be Ended," *Redlands (Ca.) Daily Facts,* June 5, 1961, p. 1.

90 Merriman Smith, "JFK Peers Across Berlin Wall," *El Paso (Tx.) Herald-Post,* June 26, 1963, p. 1.

91 Merriman Smith, "Plot Is Reported To Kidnap Caroline," *The Modesto (Ca.) Bee and News Herald,* March 31, 1961, p. 1.

92 Author interview with Sid Davis, Aug. 7, 2014.

93 Merriman Smith, Alvin Spivak and Helen Thomas, "An Illness Of The President Is Major News," *The Laredo (Texas) Times,* June 25, 1961, p. 2.

94 Untitled memo dated Oct. 1, 1961, Merriman Smith papers at the Wisconsin Historical Society, box 2, folder 40.

95 Merriman Smith, "President Kennedy taking special muscle-building exercises," *Redlands (Ca.) Daily Facts,* Oct. 20, 1961, p. 1.

96 *A Confidential Report for UPI Personnel Only,* January 1962, Merriman Smith papers, box 3, folder 5.

97 *Front Row at the White House,* p. 58.

98 Merriman Smith, "Backstairs at the White House," *The (Harrisburg, Ill.) Daily Register,* Feb. 2, 1961, p. 9.

99 *Merriman Smith's Book of Presidents,* p. 117.

100 Merriman Smith, "Demos Would Like First Lady To Be More Active," *Kingsport (Tenn.) Times-News,* May 27, 1962, p. 32.

101 Hal Humphrey, "Out Of The Air," syndicated column in *The (East Liverpool, OH) Evening Review,* July 7, 1964, p. 10. Humphrey does not give a date for this anecdote, but it probably happened in 1962, when Marx filled in on the show between Jack Paar's and Johnny Carson's terms as host.

102 *Merriman Smith's Book of Presidents,* p. 79.

103 Doc Quigg, "Television in Review," *Tyrone (Pa.) Daily Herald,* Aug. 10, 1962, p. 5.

104 FBI memos from C. D. De Loach to Clyde Tolson dated June 10, 1959, in *The Official and Confidential File of FBI Director J. Edgar Hoover,* Wilmington, Del: Scholarly Resources, 1988, reel 1, folder 13.

105 Author interview with June Lockhart, Oct. 1, 2014.

106 Barbara Gamarekian, *Oral History Interview with Barbara Gamarekian,* John F. Kennedy Library, June 10, 1964, p. 18.

107 *An Unfinished Life,* p. 477.

108 Merriman Smith, "Star of Broadway revue interviewed on New Frontier," *Ames (Ia.) Tribune,* Dec. 27, 1962, p. 4.

109 Henry Brandon, *Special Relationships: A Foreign Correspondent's Memoirs From Roosevelt To Reagan,* New York: Athaneum, 1988, p. 186.

110 *An Unfinished Life,* p. 636.

111 Spivak email to author, July 31, 2014.

112 Author interview with Sid Davis, Aug. 7, 2014.

113 *Merriman Smith's Book of Presidents,* p. 221.

114 Oral History with Malcolm Kilduff, untranscribed, Sixth Floor Museum, Dallas, Texas, April 16, 1993.

CHAPTER 4

115 Smith letter to his mother January 22, 1950, cited in family chronology provided by Tim Smith.

116 Smith letter to his mother March 22, 1963, cited in Smith family chronology.

117 Smith letter to Ellie Smith, May 18, 1963, in Smith papers at Wisconsin Historical Society, box 1, folder 22.

118 Smith letter to his mother, October 20, 1963, cited in Smith family chronology.

119 Smith letter to his mother, February 19, 1963, cited in Smith family chronology.

120 Smith letter to Ellie Smith, May 18, 1963.

121 Smith letter to Earl Johnson, Oct. 19, 1961, Smith papers at Wisconsin Historical Society, box 2, folder 40.

122 Smith letter to his mother, believed to be early 1960s, in Smith family chronology.

123 Smith letter to Ellie Smith, Oct. 25, 1963, Smith papers at Wisconsin Historical Society, box 1, folder 22.

124 Unbylined story, "U.P.I. Subscribers Increase by 157," *The New York Times,* April 21, 1964, p. 21.

125 Smith letter to Julius Frandsen, November 20, 1963, in Smith papers at Wisconsin Historical Society, box 1, folder 22.

126 Moe Levy memo to Ray Hassan, "JFK's Dallas Visit," in Robert MacNeil papers at Wisconsin Historical Society, box 10, folder 12, p. 2.

127 Donald Janson, "Jeering Texans Swarm Around Johnson and his Wife on Way to Rally," *The New York Times,* Nov. 5, 1960, p. 1.

128 William Manchester, *The Death of a President: November 20– November 25, 1963,* New York: Little Brown, 1967; republished on Amazon Kindle in 2013. Kindle location 924.

129 Robert Dallek, *An Unfinished Life: John F. Kennedy, 1917–1963,* New York: Little Brown, 2003, p. 693.

130 Henry Brandon, *Special Relationships: A Foreign Correspondent's Memoirs From Roosevelt To Reagan,* New York: Athaneum, 1988, pp. 195–196.

131 *The Death of a President,* Kindle location 1406.

132 Unbylined, unheadlined UPI story, *The (Connellsville, PA) Daily Courier,* Nov. 21, 1963, p. 33.

133 The Citizens Council, founded in 1937, is still in business today. See www.dallascitizenscouncil.org.

134 Moe Levy memo, p. 3.

135 *The Death of a President,* Kindle location 1930.

136 Unbylined UPI story, "JFK Visiting Texas To Heal Party Split," *The (Anaconda) Montana Standard,* Nov. 22, 1963, p. 1.

137 Merriman Smith, "Kennedy Defends Space Program In Texas Address," *The (New Philadelphia, Ohio) Daily Times,* Nov. 21, 1963, p. 1.

138 *The Death of a President,* Kindle location 1678.

139 Unpublished Smith copy dated Nov. 21, 1963, in Smith papers at Wisconsin Historical Society, box 5, folder 20.

140 *The Death of a President,* Kindle location 1900.

141 Latryl Layton, "Jackie Enjoys Texas 'Unbelievably,'" *Fort Worth Press,* Nov. 22, 1963, p. 8.

142 Clint Hill and Lisa MacCubbin, *Mrs. Kennedy and Me,* New York: Gallery Books, 2012, pp. 280–281.

143 Charles Roberts, Oral History Interview with Charles Roberts for the John F. Kennedy Library, April 11, 1966, p. 1.

144 *The Death of a President,* Kindle location 2416.

145 *The Death of a President,* Kindle location 2454.

146 Eddie S. Hughes, "Kennedy, in Fort Worth, Kept Darting Into Crowds," *The Dallas Morning News,* Nov. 23, 1963, p. 11.

147   Robert MacNeil, "Transcript of Reading of 'Dallas Diary,'" Robert MacNeil papers, box 10, folder 12, Wisconsin Historical Society, p. 5.

148   Author interview with Robert MacNeil, Oct. 11, 2013.

149   *Special Relationships,* p. 196

150   *The Death of a President,* Kindle location 2501.

151   Author interview with Sid Davis, Oct. 21, 2013.

152   "JFK Fort Worth Breakfast November 22 1963 TV coverage," YouTube video at https://www.youtube.com/watch?v=Tg6-9Cpt-vyM. Viewed April 14, 2016. This is video from KRLD, a Dallas TV station.

153   MacNeil, "Transcript of Reading of 'Dallas Diary,'" pp. 5–6.

154   CBS News, "Assassination in Dallas," p. 23. Transcript of an interview with Lyndon Johnson aired in May 1970 under the title "LBJ: Tragedy and Transition," with the Walter Cronkite papers at the Briscoe Center for American History at the University of Texas at Austin, call no. 2M732.

155   Merriman Smith, "U.S. Will Test Mighty Booster," *The (Valparaiso, Ind.) Vedette-Messenger,* Nov. 22, 1963, p. 1. The story ran with an editor's note that said, "This story is the final report of President Kennedy's activities in Texas prior to the fatal shot which killed the chief executive as transmitted over the United Press International wires."

156   Henry Brandon, "The Greatest American Tragedy," *The (London) Sunday Times,* Nov. 24, 1963, p. 3.

CHAPTER 5

157   Author interview with Robert MacNeil, Oct. 11, 2013.

158   John F. Kennedy Library, *Oral History Interview with Charles Roberts,* April 11, 1966, p. 2.

159   Timothy G. Smith, ed., *Merriman Smith's Book of Presidents: A White House Memoir,* New York: W.W. Norton, 1972, p. 19.

160   Patrick J. Sloyan, "Total Domination," *AJR,* May 1998. http://ajrarchive.org/article.asp?id=1672. Viewed May 8, 2014.

161   Smith letter to *Look* magazine, January 30, 1967, provided by Gillean Smith.

162   Merriman Smith, *The Good New Days,* New York: Bobbs Merrill, 1962, p. 138.

163 Spivak email to author, July 29, 2014.

164 "Kennedy Drives To Unite Split Texas Democrats," *The Bridgeport (Conn.) Post,* Nov. 22, 1963, p. 1.

165 Merriman Smith, "Eyewitness Account of John F. Kennedy assassination," at http://www.upi.com/Top_News/US/2013/11/22/Eyewitness-account-of-John-F-Kennedy-assassination/UPI-51291385108100/. Viewed July 29, 2014.

166 "The Murder of a President," *New York Post,* Dec. 30, 1963, p. 23. This is a transcript of a broadcast the week before on WINS radio in New York.

167 Wilborn Hampton, *Kennedy Assassinated! The World Mourns: A Reporter's Story,* Candlewick Press, 1997, p. 12.

168 *Report of the President's Commission on the Assassination of President John F. Kennedy,* (better known as the Warren Commission report), Washington: US Government Printing Office, 1964, p. 48. Cited further here as the Warren Commission report.

169 John F. Kennedy Presidential Library, *Oral history of Malcolm W. Kilduff,* March 15, 1976, p. 32.

170 William Manchester, *The Death of a President,* New York: Harper and Row, 1967; rereleased on Amazon Kindle in 2013. Kindle location 3319.

171 Theodore H. White Personal Papers, Camelot Documents, Item III-A: Copy of White's 19 December 1963 transcript of interview notes, THWPP-059-013, at the John F. Kennedy Presidential Library and Museum. Available online at http://www.jfklibrary.org/Asset-Viewer/Archives/THWPP-059-013.aspx.

172 Connally interview with Martin Agronsky, November 27, 1963. This interview was aired by NBC News. A transcript is in the Robert MacNeil papers at the Wisconsin Historical Society, box 10, folder 14.

173 Warren Commission report, p. 50.

174 Clint Hill and Lisa McCubbin, *Five Days in November,* Gallery Books, 2013, Kindle location 897.

175 Theodore H. White Personal Papers, 19 December 1963 transcript of interview notes.

176 Warren Commission report, p. 49.

177 Richard B. Trask, *That Day in Dallas: Three Photographers Capture on Film The Day President Kennedy Died,* Yeoman Press, Danvers, Mass., 2000; republished in 2013, p. 68.

178 *Five Days in November,* Kindle location 915.

179 Theodore H. White Personal Papers, 19 December 1963 transcript of interview notes.

180 "Eyewitnesses Describe Scene of Assassination," *The New York Times,* Nov. 23, 1963, p. 5.

181 *Kennedy Assassinated!* p. 13.

182 Sloyan, "Total Domination."

183 Smith letter to the editor of *LOOK Magazine,* January 30, 1967, provided to the author by Smith's daughter, Gillean Smith.

184 Author interview with Wilborn Hampton, November 3, 2015.

185 Unbylined UPI bulletins of November 22, 1963, reproduced on Texas State Library and Archives Commission's website, at https://www.tsl.texas.gov/sites/default/files/public/tslac/landing/documents/jfk-upi_feed-1.pdf. Viewed July 22, 2014. Accounts of this dispatch often incorrectly include the word "were," so that it reads "THREE SHOTS WERE FIRED . . ."

186 *The Death of A President,* Kindle location 3575.

187 Author interview with Al Spivak, July 28, 2014.

188 Sloyan, "Total Domination."

189 *The Dallas Morning News, JFK Assassination: The Reporters' Notes,* Pediment Publishing, 2013, p. 32.

190 Smith letter of January 30, 1967.

191 The dialogue in the UPI Dallas bureau comes from Wilborn Hampton's oral history interview available at The Sixth Floor Museum at Dealey Plaza, recorded Nov. 23, 2009.

192 Kilduff March 15, 1976, oral history at Kennedy library, p. 34.

193 *The Death of a President,* Kindle location 3450. The Warren Commission says the limousine arrived at about 12:35 p.m.

194 Saul Pett et al., "How The Associated Press Covered the Kennedy Tragedy," *The AP World,* Winter 1963–1964, p. 3.

195 http://www.upi.com/Top_News/US/2013/11/22/Eyewitness-account-of-John-F-Kennedy-assassination/UPI-51291385108100/. Viewed July 29, 2014.

196 Author interview with Hampton. Hampton learned this from colleagues the day after the assassination. Another UPI Dallas staffer, Mike Rabun, confirms that Tolbert typed the dispatch without first preparing a paper tape, which would have delayed him a few seconds. In an email to the author, Rabun said he could not confirm that Payette ordered the addition of the word "perhaps." But Rabun notes that the words "perhaps seriously" appeared on the A-wire on

a separate line. Those words should have been part of the first line of the dispatch, Rabun says—leading him to believe that as Tolbert took the dictation, he accidentally hit a key on the Teletype that added a new line to the text. Rabun said this minor mistake indicates Tolbert was distracted by something or someone as he typed. Also, said Rabun, the dispatch's awkward use of "perhaps" suggests another person besides Fallon was involved in writing it. Rabun does not believe Fallon would have written such an awkward sentence on his own.

CHAPTER 6

197 The AP has published several similar and consistent accounts of its Dallas coverage. AP's corporate archivists provided an article Bob Johnson wrote about the assassination for an employee publication in 1972. See also an AP employee newsletter, *AP Log,* Nov. 20–26, 1963. Johnson mentions his plans to attend the opera in an AP oral history recorded March 28, 2005, p. 13; a transcript is available at the AP's corporate archives.

198 Robert Johnson oral history at the AP's corporate archives, p. 18.

199 *AP Log,* Nov. 20–26, 1963, p. 3.

200 Saul Pett, et al., "How The Associated Press Covered the Kennedy Tragedy," *The AP World,* Winter 1963-1964, p. 4.

201 Robert Johnson oral history, pp 12–13.

202 AP Log, Nov. 20–26, 1963, p. 3.

203 Original AP copy from November 22, 1963, provided by the AP's corporate archives.

204 William Manchester, *The Death of a President,* New York: Harper and Row, 1967; rereleased on Amazon Kindle in 2013. Kindle location 3573.

205 Author interview with Clint Hill, January 14, 2015.

206 Collection AP 39.1, box 1, folder 2, AP corporate archives. This file includes early dispatches about the assassination sent by the Dallas bureau.

207 "The Teletype Story," a promotional brochure, Chicago: The Teletype Corporation, 1957, p. 11. Kent Cooper, an AP manager in Chicago, was assigned to develop Teletype machines for news transmission. He later became the AP's general manager.

208 Richard M. Harnett and Billy G. Ferguson, *Unipress: United Press International Covering the 20th Century,* Golden, Colo., Fulcrum Publishing, 2003, p. 7.

209 "Flash President Dead," web page by Larry Lorenz, emeritus professor at Loyola University, New Orleans. http://www.loyno.edu/~lorenz/jfk.html. Viewed August 13, 2014.

210 *Four Days: The Historical Record of the Death of President Kennedy*, New York: 1964, United Press International and American Heritage magazine, pp. 22 and 23. One of several sources for Smith's initial copy.

211 Unbylined UPI bulletins of November 22, 1963, reproduced on Texas State Library and Archives Commission's website, at https://www.tsl.texas.gov/sites/default/files/public/tslac/landing/documents/jfk-upi_feed-1.pdf. Viewed July 22, 2014.

THE DARKROOM

212 Richard B. Trask, *That Day in Dallas: Three Photographers Capture on Film The Day President Kennedy Died*, Danvers, Mass.: Yeoman Press, 1998, p. 58.

213 Harold T. Waters oral history interview, untranscribed, recorded July 9, 1999, available at The Sixth Floor Museum at Dealey Plaza.

CHAPTER 7

214 Robert MacNeil, *The Right Place At The Right Time*, New York: Harper & Row, 1982, p. 208. MacNeil offered a slightly contradictory account in a Nov. 30, 1963, memo included in his personal papers at the Wisconsin Historical Society in which he does not mention meeting anyone on the building's steps. In an email to the author on Dec. 5, 2014, he confirmed the accuracy of the account in his book.

215 Robert MacNeil, "Transcript of Reading of 'Dallas Diary,'" MacNeil papers, box 10, folder 12, Wisconsin Historical Society, pp. 10–12; author interview, Oct. 11, 2013.

216 Charles W. Roberts, *Oral History of Charles Roberts*, John F. Kennedy Presidential Library, April 11, 1966, pp. 4–5.

217 Author interview with Julian O. Read, Oct. 29, 2014.

218 "The Murder of a President," transcript of a Westinghouse Broadcasting Co. radio discussion, printed in the *New York Post*, Dec. 30, 1963, p. 23.

219 Julian Read interview.

220 Charles Roberts oral history, p. 7.

221 Ruth Adler, ed., *The Working Press: Special to The New York Times,* New York: G.P. Putnam, 1966., p. 26. This book is an anthology of stories from *Times Talk,* an internal *New York Times* newsletter.

222 Julian Read interview. A year later, Jonsson was elected mayor of Dallas.

223 Roberts oral history, pp. 7–8.

224 *The Working Press,* p. 26.

225 Roberts oral history, p. 45. This quote is from his unpublished file that day to *Newsweek,* which the oral history includes as an appendix.

226 *The Working Press,* p. 27.

227 Roberts oral history, p. 9.

228 Roberts oral history, p. 47. This section is from his file to his editors at *Newsweek.*

229 Laura Hlavich and Darwin Payne, eds., *Reporting the Kennedy Assassination,* Dallas: Three Forks Press, 1996, p. 62.

230 Memo from White House Communications Agency CWO Arthur W. Bales, "Statement #1," Record No. 172-10001-1000, downloaded from the National Archives web site on August 31, 2014.

231 Wilborn Hampton, *Kennedy Assassinated! The World Mourns: A Reporter's Story,* Cambridge, Mass.: Candlewick Press, 1997, p. 32.

232 Wilborn Hampton oral history interview, untranscribed, available at The Sixth Floor Museum at Dealey Plaza, recorded Nov. 23, 2009.

233 Hampton oral history at The Sixth Floor Museum.

234 Read interview.

235 Theodore H. White Personal Papers, Camelot Documents, Item III-A: Copy of White's 19 December 1963 transcript of interview notes, THWPP-059-013, at the John F. Kennedy Presidential Library and Museum. Available online at http://www.jfklibrary.org/Asset-Viewer/Archives/THWPP-059-013.aspx.

236 Theodore H. White Personal Papers, 19 December 1963 transcript of interview notes.

237 "Wave of Unbelief Sweeps Over Trade Mart Crowd," *Dallas Times Herald,* November 22, 1963, p. 18.

238 This sequence, including Rep. Brooks' recollection, comes from Johnson's Daily Diary, downloaded from the LBJ Library's website at http://www.lbjlibrary.net/collections/daily-diary.html.

239 *The Death of a President,* Kindle locations 4642–4643.

240 Author interview with Sid Davis, Oct. 21, 2013.

241 *AP World,* Winter 1964, p. 5.

242 Robert MacNeil oral history at Sixth Floor Museum, April 16, 2004; author interview, Oct. 11, 2013.

243 Hampton oral history at the Sixth Floor Museum, Nov. 23, 2009. Untranscribed.

244 Merriman Smith, "President Kennedy Could Have Survived Neck Injury But Head Wound Was Fatal," *Syracuse Herald-Journal,* Oct. 1, 1963, p. 31. In a classic case of unfortunate ad placement, this story was displayed next to a department store ad offering "Italian rifle or carbine 6.5 cal – Your Choice $9.99." Oswald killed Kennedy with a 6.5 caliber Italian carbine.

245 Author interview with Wilborn Hampton, November 3, 2015.

246 Hampton oral history at the Sixth Floor Museum.

247 Malcolm W. Kilduff oral history at the Sixth Floor Museum, April 16, 1993. Untranscribed.

248 Hampton oral history at the Sixth Floor Museum.

249 Richard B. Trask, *Pictures of the Pain,* Danvers, Mass.: Yeoman Press, 1994, p. 408.

CHAPTER 8

250 Walter Cronkite oral history interview with The Sixth Floor Museum, April 14, 2004. This interview is on video and not transcribed.

251 Walter Cronkite, *A Reporter's Life,* New York: Ballantine Books, 1996, p. 304.

252 Harrison Salisbury, "The Editor's View in New York," in Greenberg and Parker, eds., *The Kennedy Assassination and the American Public: Social Communication in Crisis,* Stanford University Press, 1965, p. 37.

253 Tom Pettit, "The Television Story in Dallas," in Greenberg and Parker, eds., *The Kennedy Assassination and the American Public: Social Communication in Crisis,* Stanford University Press, 1965, p. 61.

254 The exact time Cronkite went on the air is noted in "Logs for 1" Coverage of the John F. Kennedy Assassination November 22-25, 1963," an internal CBS News document with the Walter Cronkite Papers at the Briscoe Center for American History, Austin, TX, box 98-331/26. Its pages are not numbered.

255 "Logs for 1" Coverage of the John F. Kennedy Assassination November 22–25, 1963."

256 Cronkite interview with The Sixth Floor Museum.

257 Jack Mann, "Reaction at Aqueduct – Tears, Shock, Disbelief," *New York Herald Tribune*, November 23, 1963.

258 Ike Pappas oral history interview at The Sixth Floor Museum in Dallas, Texas, March 1, 1993.

259 Stephan P. Spitzer and Nancy S. Spitzer, "Diffusion of News of Kennedy and Oswald Deaths," in Greenberg and Parker, eds., *The Kennedy Assassination and the American Public: Social Communication in Crisis,* Stanford University Press, 1965, pp. 102–104.

260 "The Editor's View in New York," p. 37.

261 "The Editor's View in New York," p. 39.

262 Transcript of Nov. 14, 2013 AXS TV conference call featuring Dan Rather with TV journalists, p. 13.

263 Cronkite interview with The Sixth Floor Museum.

CHAPTER 9

264 William Manchester, *The Death of a President: November 20–November 25, 1963,* New York: Harper and Row, 1967; rereleased on Amazon Kindle in 2013; Kindle location 6206.

265 John F. Kennedy Presidential Library, *Oral History of Charles Roberts,* April 11, 1966, p. 12.

266 *Death of a President,* Kindle locations 6334–6338.

267 Vincent Bugliosi, *Four Days In November,* New York: W.W. Norton, 2007, p. 175.

268 Gerald Posner, *Case Closed: Lee Harvey Oswald and the Assassination of JFK,* New York: Anchor Books, 2003, p. 294. Dr. Baxter also told Posner he did not want Dr. Rose to conduct the autopsy: "I am sure he would have missed points that have since come up."

269 Henry Wade oral history at the Sixth Floor Museum, untranscribed video, July 20, 1992.

270 *Death of a President,* Kindle location 6359.

271 Charles Roberts oral history, pp. 12–13.

272 Roberts oral history, p. 50.

273 *Case Closed,* p. 287.

274 Bradley S. Greenberg and Parker, Edwin B. Parker, eds., *The Kennedy Assassination and the American Public: Social Communication in Crisis*, Stanford, Ca.: Stanford University Press, 1965, p. 33.

275 Patrick Sloyan, "Total Domination," *American Journalism Review,* May 1998. Downloaded in January 2015 at http://ajrarchive.org/article.asp?id=1672.

276 Sloyan, "Total Domination."

277 Author interview with Sid Davis, August 7, 2014.

278 Author interview with Sid Davis, August 7, 2014.

279 Sid Davis oral history for Sixth Floor Museum in Dallas, November 21, 2003.

280 Author interview with Sid Davis, October 21, 2013.

281 Davis oral history, Nov. 21, 2003.

282 Davis oral history, Nov. 21, 2003.

283 Davis oral history, Nov. 21, 2003.

284 Ruth Adler, ed. *The Working Press: Special to The New York Times,* New York: G.P. Putnam's Sons, 1966, p. 31.

285 YouTube video, "Inside Media: The Assassination of President Kennedy." Washington: Newseum, April 17, 2013. Viewed at http://youtu.be/0ih5gsaFD9Q on January 28, 2015. The recording of Wicker's dictation is played at the 13:30 mark.

286 YouTube video, untitled, a Wicker interview with the Newseum published on April 3, 2013, viewed at http://youtu.be/IsvTKxtj5gc on January 28, 2015. Wicker died in 2011.

287 Adler, ed., *The Working Press,* p. 31.

288 Max Holland, ed. *The Presidential Recordings [of] Lyndon Johnson, Vol. I,* New York: W.W. Norton, 2005, p. 55.

289 Merriman Smith, "UPI Archives: Merriman Smith's account of JFK's assassination." Viewed on UPI's website on January 31, 2015, at http://bit.ly/1CWq0Ap.

290 Charles W. Roberts, "Assassination – and Aftermath," a speech given to *Newsweek* advertising clients in Chicago on June 8, 1964. Provided by the Herbert Hoover Presidential Library in West Branch, Iowa, where Roberts' papers are kept.

291 Roberts oral history, p. 54.

292 Smith, "UPI Archives: Merriman Smith's account of JFK's assassination."

293 Author interview with Al Spivak, July 29, 2014.

294 "Total Domination."

295 Smith, "UPI Archives: Merriman Smith's account of JFK's assassination."

296 January 30, 1967, letter from Smith to the editor of *Look* magazine, copy provided by Gillean Smith, his daughter.

297 "Total Domination;" also Sloyan email exchange with author, November 2014.

REWRITE

298 Email from Mike Rabun to author, March 10, 2015.

CHAPTER 10

299 Seth Kantor testimony to Warren Commission, June 2, 1964, in Volume 15 of the Warren Commission report's appendices, pp. 72–73.

300 Merriman Smith, "Dallas Recalled – With Assassination." Original UPI copy, dated September 27, 1964, with Smith's papers at the Wisconsin Historical Society.

301 Kantor testimony to the Warren Commission, June 2, 1964, pp. 74–80.

302 Seth Kantor, *The Ruby Cover-up,* New York: Kensington Publishing Corp., 1978, Zebra Books paperback edition, p. 89.

303 Vincent Bugliosi, *Four Days in November,* New York: W. W. Norton, 2007, p. 273.

304 *Four Days in November,* p. 402.

305 Kantor testimony to the Warren Commission, June 2, 1964, p. 80.

306 An unpublished version of Kantor's story turned up in an FBI memo reproduced in the Warren Commission report, Vol. 20, p. 469.

307 Gerald Posner, *Case Closed: Lee Harvey Oswald and the Assassination of JFK,* New York: Random House, 1993; 2003 edition, pp. 372–373.

308 Final Report of the Select Committee on Assassinations, Vol. 9, p. 1103.

309 US House of Representatives, 1979: Final Report of the Select Committee on Assassinations, p. 159.

310 James Patrick Hosty Jr. testimony in May 1964, Warren Commission Hearings, Vol. 4, p. 463.

311 Warren Commission report, p. 202.

312 Warren Commission report, pp. 199–200.

313 Author interview with Maurice Carroll, October 15, 2013.

314 Jack Ruby testimony to the Warren Commission, July 29, 1964, in Volume 5 of the commission's appendices, p. 188.

315 Warren Commission report, p. 208.

316 Ruby testimony to the Warren Commission, p. 189.

317 Maurice Carroll, *Accidental Assassin: Jack Ruby and 4 Minutes in Dallas,* Bloomington, IN: Xlibris, 2013, p. 23.

318 Ruby testimony to the Warren Commission, p. 189.

319 Warren Commission report, p. 208.

320 Wade oral history with the Sixth Floor Museum, untranscribed video of July 20, 1992.

321 Ruby testimony to the Warren Commission, p. 188.

322 Ike Pappas testimony to Warren Commission, July 29, 1964, in Volume 15 of the commission's appendices, pp. 360–365.

323 Ike Pappas oral history with the Sixth Floor Museum, untranscribed video made March 1, 1993.

324 Russell Lee Moore testimony to the Warren Commission, July 23, 1964, in Volume 15 of the commission's appendices, pp. 254–256.

325 Pappas oral history with the Sixth Floor Museum. Pappas gave the Warren Commission a different version of what happened at the radio station that night—he said he was there after Ruby had left. His oral history is backed up by statements given by some at the radio station who said Pappas was there at the same time as Ruby.

326 Moore testimony to Warren Commission, p. 257.

327 Gladwin Hill, "Evidence Against Oswald Described as Conclusive," *The New York Times,* November 24, 1963, p. 1.

328 Jesse Curry testimony to the Warren Commission, April 15, 1964, contained in Vol. 12 of the commission's appendices, p. 35.

329 Henry Wade oral history at the Sixth Floor Museum, untranscribed video, July 20, 1992.

330 *Accidental Assassin,* p. 9.

331 Pappas oral history with Sixth Floor Museum.

332 *Four Days in November*, p. 438. See also Gladwin Hill, "One Bullet Fired; Night Club Man Who Admired Kennedy is Oswald's Slayer," *The New York Times,* November 25, 1963, p. 1.

333 "Logs for 1" Coverage of the John F. Kennedy Assassination November 22–25, 1963," an internal CBS News document with the Walter Cronkite Papers at the Briscoe Center for American History, Austin, TX, box 98-331/26.

334 Harold Waters oral history interview with the Sixth Floor Museum, July 9, 1999. Untranscribed video.

335 Warren Commission report, pp. 240–242.

THE EAST ROOM

336 Jack Raymond, KENNEDY'S BODY LIES IN WHITE HOUSE; JOHNSON AT HELM WITH WIDE BACKING; POLICE SAY

PRISONER IS THE ASSASSIN, the *New York Times,* November 24, 1963, p. 1.

337 Saturday 23 November 1963 entry in Henry Brandon diary, with Henry Brandon papers at the Library of Congress, box 6.

CHAPTER 11

338 "Jack Bell in Hospital Receives LBJ Flowers," *Editor & Publisher,* December 14, 1963, p. 13.

339 Leonard Lyons, "The Lyons Den," *New York Post,* December 18, 1963, p. 43.

340 Merriman Smith papers, Wisconsin Historical Society. The Bell and Earl J. Johnson letters are in box 1, folder 11.

341 January 30, 1967, letter from Smith to the editor of *LOOK Magazine,* copy provided by Gillean Smith, his daughter.

342 "Thank You, Mr. Smith," *Newsweek,* April 27, 1970, p. 94.

343 A December 6, 1997, letter from Robert H. Johnson, AP's Dallas bureau chief in November 1963, is the most detailed document in AP's corporate archives on the topic. Johnson also mentions this in his March 28, 2005, oral history, also in the AP corporate archives.

344 Helen Thomas, *Front Row At The White House,* New York: Scribner, 1999, p. 69.

345 Robert H. Johnson oral history interview, recorded March 28, 2005; transcript available at the AP's corporate archives, p. 17.

346 Johnson letter to the AP, Dec. 6, 1997, in the AP's corporate archives.

347 Johnson oral history, pp. 15–17.

348 William Manchester, *The Death of a President,* New York: Harper and Row, 1967; rereleased on Amazon Kindle in 2013, Kindle location 5254.

349 Johnson oral history, p. 24.

350 Johnson oral history, p. 17.

351 Johnson oral history, p.18.

352 Patrick J. Sloyan, "Total Domination," *AJR,* May 1998. http://ajrarchive.org/article.asp?id=1672. Viewed May 8, 2014.

CHAPTER 12

353 Frank Bartholomew letter of November 26, 1963, and Mims Thomason letter of November 27, 1963, are with Smith papers at

Wisconsin Historical Society, box 2, folder 41. Jack Fallon letter of December 4, 1963, also with Smith papers, box 1, folder 10.

354 Author interview with Allison Smith, January 26, 2016.

355 Merriman Smith, "Kennedy Laid to Rest," *The (Provo, UT) Daily Herald*, November 25, 1963, p. 1.

356 Merriman Smith, "Dallas Recalled – With Assassination." Original UPI copy, dated September 27, 1964, with Smith's papers at the Wisconsin Historical Society.

357 Smith family chronology, provided by Tim Smith.

358 Robert Caro, *The Years of Lyndon Johnson: The Passage of Power*, New York: Vintage, 2012, p. 504. This is a source for some detail about the ranch summit.

359 See for example *El Paso (TX) Herald-Post*, December 26, 1963, p. 6.

360 Merriman Smith, "President Enjoys Ranch-Type Yule, Vows Budget Cut," *The Lawton (Okla.) Constitution*, December 25, 1963, p. 1.

361 Merriman Smith letter to Lennie [Johnson], December 26, 1963, with Smith papers at Wisconsin Historical Society, box 1, folder 22.

362 Merriman Smith, "Erhard Allows as How He Likes Folksy Cow Country Diplomacy," *(Lincoln, NE) Sunday Journal and Star*, December 29, 1964, p. 1.

363 Merriman Smith, unheadlined story, *The (Connellsville, PA) Daily Courier*, December 30, 1963, p. 1.

364 Unbylined UPI story, "Johnson Hardest-Working President, Says Reporter," *The (Provo, UT) Daily Herald*, January 20, 1964, p. 10.

365 Timothy G. Smith, ed., *Merriman Smith's Book of Presidents: A White House Memoir*, New York: W. W. Norton, 1972, p. 221.

366 Drew Pearson, "Presidential Image Changed," *The Emporia (KS) Gazette*, January 13, 1964, p. 2.

367 Patrick J. Sloyan, "Total Domination," *AJR*, May 1998. http://ajrarchive.org/article.asp?id=1672. Viewed May 8, 2014.

368 Bill Moyers email to author, February 23, 2015.

369 Al Spivak says this happened to him once, and that he heard of Johnson calling other wire reporters while they were still filing their stories. At the time, a single wire service story was often transmitted in two or three separate files, which newsrooms called takes or adds. If Johnson saw a take or add he didn't like, he had plenty of time to call a reporter before another was sent.

370 Merriman Smith, "Revamp immigration laws, Johnson urges," *Redlands (Ca.) Daily Facts*, January 13, 1964, p. 1.

371 Kent B. Germany and Robert David Johnson, eds., *The Presidential Recordings of Lyndon B. Johnson, Volume Three,* New York: W. W. Norton, 2005, pp. 457–458.

372 Karl E. Meyer, "The Washington Press Establishment," New York: *Esquire* magazine, April 1964, p. 73.

373 *Merriman Smith's Book of Presidents,* p. 10.

374 Smith correspondence with Bridges in box 2, folder 27 of Smith papers at Wisconsin Historical Society.

375 *Merriman Smith's Book of Presidents,* p. 235.

376 "Total Domination." Sloyan does not give a date or place for this encounter, but his description lines up with two Johnson visits to the region in spring 1964.

377 Family chronology provided to the author by Tim Smith.

378 Dorothy Kilgallen, "The Voice of Broadway," *The (Franklin, PA) News-Herald,* p. 6.

379 Lyndon Johnson note, June 18, 1964, in Smith name file at LBJ Library.

380 Merriman Smith letter to "Lenni," June 27, 1964, box 1, folder 23 of Smith papers at Wisconsin Historical Society.

381 The author interviewed eyewitnesses to the events surrounding Smith's removal from Air Force One. They must remain anonymous.

382 Armed Forces Radio and Television Service, "Tonight 103," broadcast September 1964. The AFRTS issued edited audio recordings of NBC's *Tonight Show* to its radio stations, copies of which ended up in the Library of Congress. This appears to be the only surviving recording of any of Smith's appearances on *The Tonight Show.* The original video was destroyed by NBC.

383 Johnson letter of September 2, 1964, with Smith papers at Wisconsin Historical Society, box 2, folder 14.

384 Merriman Smith, "The Muddy Season," *Tyrone (PA) Daily Herald,* September 24, 1964, p. 1.

385 Merriman Smith, "Dallas Recalled – With Assassination."

386 Smith family chronology.

387 Merriman Smith letter to Mary, October 13, 1964, with Smith papers at the Wisconsin Historical Society, box 1, folder 23.

388 Smith letter to Barbara, with Smith papers at the Wisconsin Historical Society, box 2, folder 41.

389 C. Edmonds Allen letter to Gailey, with Smith papers at the Wisconsin Historical Society, box 1, folder 23.

390 Smith letter to Barbara, op. cit.

391 Earl Johnson letter to Dr. Gralnick, November 17, 1964, with Smith papers at Wisconsin Historical Society, box 2, folder 41.

392 Smith letter to Earl Johnson, November 28, 1964, with Smith papers at Wisconsin Historical Society, box 2, folder 41.

393 Smith letter to Earl Johnson, November 19, 1964, with Smith papers at Wisconsin Historical Society, box 2, folder 41.

394 Smith letter to Frandsen, November 17, 1964, with Smith papers at Wisconsin Historical Society, box 2, folder 41.

395 Smith letter to "Mother," November 30, 1964, with Smith papers at Wisconsin Historical Society, box 1, folder 23.

396 Smith letter to Frandsen, November 28, 1964, with Smith papers at Wisconsin Historical Society, box 2, folder 41

397 Smith letter to Earl Johnson, November 28, 1964.

398 Smith letter to Earl Johnson, November 19, 1964.

399 Letter to Barbara, with Smith papers at the Wisconsin Historical Society, box 2, folder 41.

400 Various letters with Smith papers at Wisconsin Historical Society, box 1, folder 24.

401 Smith letter to the editor of *WAIA Reporter*, May 24, 1965, in Smith papers at the Wisconsin Historical Society, box 1, folder 32.

CHAPTER 13

402 Richard Clark letter to President Lyndon Johnson, undated but undoubtedly written in early 1966. Johnson wrote a brief reply on March 8, 1966. Copies provided to the author by Bill Moyers.

403 US Department of Commerce, Bureau of the Census, *Statistical Abstract of the United States, 1967,* p. 264.

404 US Department of Commerce, Bureau of the Census, *Statistical Abstract of the United States, 1973,* p. 267.

405 Merriman Smith letter to President Lyndon Johnson, June 15, 1965, with Smith papers at the Wisconsin Historical Society, box 1, folder 24.

406 Smith letter to Merriman Jr. ["M"], June 28, 1965, with Smith papers at Wisconsin Historical Society, box 1, folder 22.

407 Recorded phone call between Johnson and Walker Stone, editor in chief of Scripps Howard Newspapers, Feb. 22, 1966, on the web site

of the Miller Center at the University of Virginia at http://miller-center.org/presidentialrecordings/lbjohnson.

408 Smith letter to Johnson, February 19, 1966, with Smith papers at the Wisconsin Historical Society, box 2, folder 37.

409 Letter described in Smith family chronology provided to the author by Tim Smith.

410 Details of the crash come from the US Army accident report, obtained with a Freedom of Information Act request. The report is on file at the US Army Combat Readiness Center at Ft. Rucker, Alabama, identified as Incident No. 0D876ACD.

411 Author interview with Molly Allen, daughter of UPI executive C. Edmonds Allen, December 9, 2014.

412 Johnson note to Smith, February 18, 1966, at LBJ Library, filed under Executive ND 9-2-2.

413 Smith letter to Johnson, February 19, 1966.

414 Johnson call to Walker Stone, Feb. 22, 1966.

415 "Transcript of President's Address on Administration Policy in Vietnam," *The New York Times,* February 24, 1966, p. 15.

416 Smith letter to Bill Moyers, February 24, 1966. Provided to the author by Moyers.

417 Douglas Kiker, "Merriman Smith's Arlington Funeral – President Attends," *New York Herald Tribune,* March 1, 1966.

418 Jack Valenti memo to President Johnson, March 5, 1966, at LBJ Library, filed under Executive PU 2-6.

419 Merriman Smith letter to Perry Knowlton, April 1, 1967, with Smith papers at Wisconsin Historical Society, box 2, folder 11.

420 President's Daily Diary, May 26, 1966, available on the web site of the LBJ Presidential Library at http://www.lbjlibrary.net/collections/daily-diary.html.

421 Merriman Smith, "LBJ Leaves Cares of State Behind for Luci's Wedding," *El Paso (TX) Herald-Post,* August 6, 1966, p. 7. Moyers provided the author with an August 3, 1966, memo to Johnson that confirms his contribution.

422 Smith papers at Wisconsin Historical Society, box 4, folder 14.

423 Unheadlined UPI copy of April 25, 1966, with Smith papers at Wisconsin Historical Society, box 2, folder 4.

424 Merriman Smith, "Viet Propaganda." *The Weirton (WV) Daily Times,* Oct. 21, 1967, p. 4.

425 Merriman Smith, "Reporter Tells Of Exaggerations By The Flower People," *The (Eureka, Calif.) Times Standard,* Oct. 23, 1967, p. 3.

426 Merriman Smith, "Backstairs At The White House," *The (Canonsburg, PA) Daily Notes,* Nov. 22, 1967, p. 4.

427 US Department of Commerce, Bureau of the Census, *Statistical Abstract of the United States, 1973,* p. 267.

428 See www.defense.gov/casualty.pdf; data as of Dec. 31, 2015.

A FISHING TRIP

429 Author interview and emails with Hal Pachios, December 2014.

CHAPTER 14

430 Sterling Bemis, "Thank you, Mr. President ...," *(Long Beach, CA) Independent Press-Telegram,* April 19, 1970, p. 33. The account of Smith's discussion with the reporters comes from this column.

431 Gerald Posner, *Case Closed: Lee Harvey Oswald and the Assassination of JFK,* New York: Anchor Books, 2003, p. 235. Posner notes that a conspiracy theorist, Josiah Thompson, determined that out of 190 witnesses, 83.4 percent heard three shots. Posner disagreed "with Thompson's reading of several witnesses and also with his omission of one," p. 235*n*.

432 Warren Commission report, p. 424.

433 CBS News, "Assassination in Dallas," pp. 35–37. Document with the Walter Cronkite papers at the Briscoe Center for American History at the University of Texas at Austin, call No. 2M732.

434 Merriman Smith, "Dallas 'Exposés' Deflated: An Eyewitness – and Marksman – Heard Just Three Shots and Scoffs at Monstrous 'Plot'" *The Washington Post,* November 20, 1966, p. E1.

435 "Dallas 'Exposés' Deflated."

436 Richard Popkin, *The Second Oswald,* Raleigh, N.C.: Boson Books, 1993, Kindle location 1477. This edition is a new issue of the book, which was originally published in 1966.

437 *The Second Oswald,* Kindle location 268.

438 "Dallas 'Exposés' Deflated."

439 James Phelan, "A Plot to Kill Kennedy? Rush to Judgment in New Orleans," *The Saturday Evening Post,* May 6, 1967, p. 21.

440 Unbylined Associated Press story, "JFK 'Plot' Solved – Garrison," *The (Benton Harbor, MI) News-Palladium,* February 25, 1967, p. 17.

441 Merriman Smith. "Garrison Unfolds New, Weird Chapter In JFK Death; Proof Long Way to Go," the *Bridgeport (CT) Post*, March 5, 1967, p. 94.

442 Phelan, "A Plot to Kill Kennedy?" p. 24.

443 Smith papers at the Wisconsin Historical Society, box 7, file marked "JFK Assassination/Warren Commission."

444 Merriman Smith, "Did Garrison Subvert Law?" *The Bensenville (IL) Register*, August 15, 1969, p. 5.

445 "Garrison Unfolds New, Weird Chapter In JFK Death."

446 Smith, "Did Garrison Subvert Law?"

447 Unbylined, unpublished UPI copy with Smith papers at the Wisconsin Historical Society, box 7, folder marked "Assassination/WC."

448 "Garrison Unfolds New, Weird Chapter In JFK Death."

449 Unbylined and unheadlined Associated Press story, *The (Benton Harbor, MI) News-Palladium*, February 25, 1967, p. 17.

450 "A Plot to Kill Kennedy?" p. 22.

451 Unbylined Associated Press story, "No Evidence Supports Claim Says Dallas DA," *The Odessa (TX) American*, February 25, 1967, p. 3.

452 Smith letter to C. Edmonds Allen, May 7, 1967, Smith papers at the Wisconsin Historical Society, box 7, folder marked "Assassination/WC."

453 Merriman Smith, "Secret Study Shows Two Shots Killed Kennedy," *The (Connellsville, PA) Daily Courier,* January 17, 1969, p. 1.

454 Walter Cronkite oral history interview with The Sixth Floor Museum, untranscribed, April 14, 2004.

455 Don Hewitt, oral history interview with The Sixth Floor Museum, November 9, 2002, p. 8.

456 Christopher Callahan, "Assassination Probes Over, U.S. Says," *The Washington Post,* Sept. 5, 1988. Viewed December 15, 2015, at https://www.washingtonpost.com/archive/politics/1988/09/05/assassination-probes-over-us-says/7fe8b1bf-e881-4088-afe1-5cfd57c83388/.

457 Undated Smith speech, with Smith papers at the Wisconsin Historical Society, box 5, folder 8.

CHAPTER 15

458 Smith letter to Gailey, Allison and Tim of November 24, 1967, with Smith papers at Wisconsin Historical Society, box 1, folder 27.

459 Letter of November 5, 1966, cited in Smith family chronology provided to the author by Tim Smith.

460 Smith letter to Ellie, November 10, 1966, with Smith papers at Wisconsin Historical Society, box 1, folder 25.

461 Letter of December 14, 1967, cited in Smith family chronology provided to the author by Tim Smith

462 Interview with Allison Smith, January 26, 2016.

463 Smith memo to William Koontz, August 1, 1966, with Smith papers at Wisconsin Historical Society, box 1, folder 25.

464 Timothy G. Smith, ed., *Merriman Smith's Book of Presidents: A White House Memoir,* New York, W.W. Norton, 1970, p. 45.

465 Smith family chronology entry of June 3, 1968.

466 Smith letter to Perry Knowlton, March 30, 1968, with Smith papers at Wisconsin Historical Society, box 2, folder 11.

467 Merriman Smith, "Richard Nixon, a changed man, today he's a winner," *Redlands (CA) Daily Facts,* August 8, 1968, p. 2.

468 Merriman Smith, "Gives Examples of Chicago Police at Work in Crisis," *Holland (MI) Evening Sentinel,* August 31, 1968, p. 19.

469 Merriman Smith, "Same Hecklers Taunt HHH At All Campaign Rallies," *The Bridgeport (Conn.) Telegram,* October 3, 1968, p. 36.

470 Merriman Smith, "Nixon May Be More Magnanimous Than His Enemies Believe," *Lebanon (PA) Daily News,* November 7, 1968, p. 48.

471 Smith letter to "Mary and what's his name," January 17, 1969, with Smith papers at Wisconsin Historical Society, box 1, folder 29.

472 Letter from Johnson to Smith, quoted in *Charles Hamilton Auction Number 64,* a catalog for a sale January 11, 1973, p. 26.

473 Smith letter to "Mary and what's his name," January 17, 1969; Smith family chronology, entry for December 1968.

474 Merriman Smith, "Disappointed Johnson Goes With Criticism Ringing In His Ears," *Lubbock (TX) Avalanche-Journal,* January 1, 1969, p. 12-A.

475 Letter from Johnson to Smith, quoted in *Charles Hamilton Auction Number 64,* p. 25.

476 Author interview with Wilborn Hampton, November 3, 2015.

477 Helen Thomas, *Front Row At The White House,* New York: Scribner, 1999, p. 70.

478 Smith, ed., *Merriman Smith's Book of Presidents,* p. 25.

479 Thomas, *Front Row At The White House,* p. 70.

EPILOGUE

480 American Society of Newspaper Editors' Annual Newsroom Census, viewed January 27, 2016, at http://asne.org/content. asp?pl=140&sl=129&contentid=129.

481 Jodi Enda, Katerina Eva Matsa and Jan Lauren Boyles, "America's Shifting State House Press," Pew Research Center, July 10, 2014, at http://www.journalism.org/2014/07/10/ americas-shifting-statehouse-press/.

482 Pew Research Center, "Today's Washington Press Corps More Digital, Specialized," December 3, 2015, at http://www.journal-ism.org/files/2015/12/PJ_2015-12-03_Washington-Press-Corps_FINAL.pdf.

483 Pew Research Center, "State of the News Media 2015," April 29, 2015, at http://www.journalism.org/2015/04/29/newspapers-fact-sheet/.

INDEX